Tallulah

my autobiography

Tallulah Bankhead

UNIVERSITY PRESS OF MISSISSIPPI

JACKSON

www.upress.state.ms.us

The University Press of Mississippi is a member of the
Association of American University Presses.

Library of Congress Cataloging-in-Publication Data

Bankhead, Tallulah, 1902–1968.
Tallulah : my autobiography / Tallulah Bankhead
    p. cm. — (Southern icons series)
Originally published New York : Harper and Brothers, 1952.
ISBN 1-57806-635-2 (pbk. : alk. paper)
    1. Bankhead, Tallulah, 1902–1968. 2. Actors—United States—
Biography. I. Title. II. Series.
PN2287.B17A3 2004
792.02'8'092—DC22

2004041907

British Library Cataloging-in-Publication Data available

For Daddy

Contents

A CITATION
to Richard Maney
For Conduct Above and Beyond the Call of Duty

Tallulah

I.

Exercise on the Trapeze

Despite all you may have heard to the contrary, I have never had a ride in a patrol wagon.

I have milked a mammoth, and I travel with adjustable window screens. I have been up in a balloon with Sir Nigel Playfair, and down in a submarine with Gary Cooper. I have scaled an elephant in a St. Louis zoo, and christened an electric rabbit with a jeroboam of Lanson 1912. I have clerked behind a counter with Margot Asquith, and sung duets with Margaret Truman. Charged with two double-daiquiris I have churned with the conviction that I can do the Indian rope trick.

My voice has been likened to the mating call of the caribou, and to the haunting note of a Strad. Apostates have hinted that I'm the ill-begotten daughter of Medusa and the Marquis de Sade. As against these slanders there are the hymns of my champions, equally inaccurate, that I'm a fusion of Annie Laurie, Bopeep, Florence Nightingale and whichever waif Lillian Gish played in *The Orphans of the Storm*. Somewhere in between these contrary verdicts lies the truth. With Montaigne "I speak truth, not so much as I would, but as much as I dare; and I dare a little the more, as I grow older."

I've had tea with Lloyd George, tiffin with Ramsay MacDonald, and I've aced Greta Garbo on Clifton Webb's court. Forced to vote for a Davis, I'll take Jefferson and give you Bette. To the consternation of the world of science my endorsement once glowed on the jacket of a book by Sir James Hapwood Jeans, great English astronomer. In it he was speculating on the age of stars—in the heavens rather than on the stage. To please the Maharanee of Cooch Behar I once togged myself out in a sari, and I won five pounds from Lord Birkenhead when he bet that Cleopatra was a brunette. Later I sued Birkenhead's daughter, Lady Eleanor Smith, for libel. She wrote in Lord Rothermere's London *Dispatch* that I was an Anglophobe. What's more, I collected.

I slept fitfully in Kimbolton, the haunted castle in which Henry VIII locked up Catherine of Aragon, and I suffer from chronic anemia. (Just a minute while I take a look at the ticker! I want to get the last quotation on Billy Rose, common. Here it is. Nothing asked and nothing bid.) I've played Newcastle-on-Tyne and Terre Haute, Indiana, and when the London *News Chronicle* sought to rouse the parish with "Do Brainy People Play Bridge?" I took the affirmative along with H. G. Wells and Rose Macaulay, with Bernard Shaw and John Galsworthy dissenting.

Under oath I'd like to refute the canard that I'm an old chum of Winston Churchill's—a fable that constantly bobs up in print. But he did come to see me five times when I was playing in *Fallen Angels.*

I have three phobias which, could I mute them, would make my life as slick as a sonnet, but as dull as ditch water: I hate to go to bed, I hate to get up, and I hate to be alone. My inability to cope with these prejudices leads to complications, excesses and heresies frowned upon in stuffier circles, circles I avoid as I would exposure to the black pox. My caprices, born of my fears, frequently find a vent in the romantic pursuits, enthusiasms and experiments at odds with the code affirmed by Elsie Dinsmore.

Over-stimulated, more than once I have breached the peace, curdled the night with monologues, war cries and filibusters. These violations of established order might well land a less artful dodger in the clink, but in these crises my acting skill (isn't it a little early to start bragging?) stands me in good stead. Jug Tallulah, the toast of the Yangtze and the Yukon? What constable would wax so bold?

Testifying for the defense may I add that I've only been married once, a humdrum record in a profession where husbands come and go like express trains between New York and Philadelphia. By way of compensation my sister Eugenia has been hitched seven times, three times to the same victim. The Bankhead girls strike a high average, even by the standards of Peggy Joyce.

Are you haunted by those adjustable window screens cited in my first sentence? On tour I carry them that my parakeet, Gaylord, may have *Lebensraum*. He sulks when caged, and I sulk in a room without ventilation. You'll hear more about Gaylord. He was named in good faith for that gambler in *Show Boat*, but whoever speculated on his sex was mad as an adagio dancer. He's a she.

I loathe acting. Unless the sheriff barges in to drag out my piano I'll never act on a stage again. Above the members of any other profession actors are slaves to the clock. Who cares if a politician, a policeman or a college professor comes to work late? He can plead a hangover or other occupational wound and get away with it. At most he'll get a slight reprimand, the frown of a superior. But in theaters curtains go up at eight-thirty, or thereabouts, and come down around eleven. Woe betide the star who flouts this time bracket. She is looked upon as a traitor to her class, a jade who through whim or amnesia, has let both the audience and the management down, a cross between Lucrezia Borgia and Mata Hari. I once played a performance in *Clash by Night* when a jump ahead of an oxygen tent—temperature 105 degrees. The slogan "the show must go on" is one of the daffiest, one of the most illogical, ever coined.

I detest acting because it is sheer drudgery. In the thirty-three years that I've been on the stage I have appeared in thirty-five plays—only three of which had any merit. I've been a star since I played in *Conchita* in London in 1924, and a star enjoys privileges and rewards beyond those given less fortunate players. No aspirant for fame and its alloys was ever more stage-struck than I when I tore up from the South to joust with the Broadway windmills. But once I achieved stardom, the whole apparatus of the theater palled on me.

The humiliation of being in a poor play, of playing a shabby role, of appearing before disgruntled audiences, if any, of being curdled by hostile reviews, can outrage all human dignity. Being caught in a long-run success is almost as bad. The fearful monotony, the boredom of saying the same words every night, at the same minute, has unhinged the mind of more than one actress.

The author writes a play, then is through with it, aside from collecting royalties. Four weeks of rehearsing and the director's work is done. Theirs are creative jobs. But how would the author feel if he had to write the same play over each night for a year? Or the director restage it before each performance? They'd be as balmy as Nijinsky in a week. Even the ushers traffic with different people every night. But the actress? She's a caged parrot.

Though I say it who shouldn't, I was born an actress. I never had any formal instruction, never cased a drama school. Acting is an astonishingly easy profession. I've given no more thought to my best roles than I have to my worst. Asked about my technique, I grow evasive. I'm not aware I have any. I'm violating no confidences, least of all my own, when I say my performances have saved many a frowzy charade, prolonged their runs long beyond their deserts. I have a dark suspicion that only ersatz actors can explain the thing called technique. I could list a hundred right here, but there is little to be gained by starting a riot so early. I have enough feuds on my hands.

Between you and me, the critics don't know a great deal about acting, either. The more experienced and scholarly can detect feeble plays without a Geiger counter, even though occasionally they hail as masterpieces items which offend the nose of the property man.

Well-met fellows, they, and hale, if I may plagiarize the style of the Henry Luce periodicals. I'm talking about those powerful and capricious gentlemen who sit in judgment on New York's stage entertainment. I've had considerable traffic with these magistrates, professional and otherwise. With them I've broken bread, slaked a common thirst, plumbed Gordon Craig, debated the architecture of an ingénue, palavered over the lunatic whims of my employers. On the whole I find them a stimulating, if erratic crew. Gordon Craig? He is the son of Ellen Terry. He renounced acting to bring new magic to scene designing.

Though all of them ooze integrity, they have chinks in their armor through which you could drive a Greyhound bus. Some have high standards, approach a play their heads ringing with the Greek unities. Some have low standards, think in terms of Minsky-*cum*-marten. Some have standards that would embarrass the readers of *The Police Gazette*. One or two are hell-bent on a revival of *Sherlock Holmes*, even if they have to dig up William Gillette to play his original role. In varying degrees they love the theater, though their passion is not always reciprocated. Scorn for the opinions of fellow critics is their common bond.

A visitor reading all the reviews the day after a New York opening would arrive at the conclusion that these men had not all seen the same play, so conflicting are their judgments. Rarely does a drama, a comedy or a musical get a unanimous verdict. Louis Kronenberger, one of the best equipped of the critics, turned in a sour report on *South Pacific*. Wolcott Gibbs is allergic to Shakespeare. In general they know what they like, express their opinions in words that reflect their background, taste and experience. The charge that they're biased and prejudiced is of no consequence. Criticism is the distillation of bias and prejudice. One man's meat is another man's poison. Most of them can distinguish between a hawk and a handsaw, but they're easily swindled by a showy performance. Frequently they confuse a role and its player, fail to observe that the last named has not realized on the potential of the first. A great part is no less great because it's indifferently played.

Proof? When Maurice Evans appeared in New York in Shakespeare's *Richard II*, the reviewers hosannaed him as the finest actor of our time. Now Mr. Evans is a competent and articulate player, but that verdict was sheer rubbish. Up to the time of Evans' performance there had been only a half-dozen professional showings of *Richard II* in New York in its stage history. Most of the critics, and most of the audience, were hearing the play's magnificent poetry for the first time. It was like a Shakespearean first night. The words that came from Mr. Evans' mouth were so memorable, so magical, that critics and audience alike cheered him as if he were a double Barrymore. In their rapture, they did not distinguish between the Bard and his instrument. There is a distinction. Every actor in the land, including Lou Holtz, wants to play Hamlet. The urge is understandable. The Dane is sure-fire, but the actor who plays him may have rents in his doublet.

Playing Hamlet or another of Shakespeare's classic heroes is no guarantee of immortality. You have this on the authority of an actress who risked his Cleopatra only to escape by a hair the fate

6.

EXERCISE ON THE TRAPEZE

of Custer. Alec Guinness, one of the most brilliant actors of our time, in 1951 set himself up as Hamlet in London. Mr. Guinness is a thinker as well as an actor—a fusion encountered as seldom as Halley's comet. After much consideration, he decided to play the Dane with a beard. He won't do it again. The hue and cry was deafening. It couldn't have been more indignant had he tried to snatch Prince Charley. You can't play ducks and drakes with tradition in England. Had David Garrick or Sir Henry Irving or Beerbohm Tree profaned Hamlet with whiskers? No! Then let's have no more of such hanky-panky!

Where was I before I got tangled up with Shakespeare? Oh, yes! The theater! And the critics! I should be the last woman to thumb my nose at the gentlemen whose judgments make or break a play in New York. They have treated me handsomely. But two or three of them write with a chisel. Trying to fathom their verdicts I sometimes get the impression they're writing in code, that the editor has failed to supply the key to same.

There are a lot of things about the theater that bore me stiff: trying on costumes, being photographed, going to hairdressers, dieting that I may not overlap the costumes, the wretched dressing rooms, the overheated theaters, the grim mutes who make up benefit audiences who, for all their concern with charity, can't be thawed out with an acetylene torch.

And there's still another reason why the theater is not the glamorous, exciting and mysterious profession it's been branded ever since the Hallams started their impersonations down in John Street, Manhattan, in the 1700's. Acting is the most insecure of all the trades, the most risky. In their professional lifetime most actors rehearse longer than they play, spend more time traipsing from office to office in search of jobs than they rehearse and play combined.

In a survey for the year ending June 1, 1951, Actors' Equity Association revealed that over that span a sixth of the membership found no employment in the theater. Those who worked averaged a ten-week season. Their average income was $790. Of these fortunates only one in eight made as much as $5,000. The survey ended with this official warning: "Anyone primarily concerned with earning a living by his profession should try elsewhere than the theater."

It's one of the tragic ironies of the theater that only one man in it can count on steady work—the night watchman. Insurance companies insist on his year-round employment. A bank teller or a bus driver has more security than anyone in my business. Assured of continuous work at a fixed wage, they can adjust their scale of living to their incomes.

The star? One season I'm in a New York hit, making what's left of four or five thousand a week after the Collector of Internal Revenue is through hacking at it. I begin to feel my oats, start to toss money about as though the play was to run forever. My expenses skyrocket. A victim of self-hypnosis, I get a rude awakening the following season when trapped in a stinker which opens and closes like a camera shutter after four weeks' rehearsal and rancid tryouts in New Haven or Wilmington or Boston. Plummeting from four thousand a week to nothing a week is quite a plummet, calls for adjustments that send the adjuster scurrying to the pawnshop.

Since mid-April of 1947 I have played only one role in the theater—Amanda Prynne in Noel Coward's *Private Lives*. I played it for an entire summer in Chicago, while wracked with neuritis; for an entire season in New York. I played it in summer theaters, in Shrine mosques, in school auditoriums, in a blizzard in Minneapolis, in a coma in Westport. I played it in Passaic, in Flatbush, in Pueblo, in Cedar Rapids, in Peoria, in the Bronx, in Joplin, in

8.

"thunder, lightning and in rain" (*Macbeth*), in towns known but to God and Rand-McNally. Unless my abacus is out of order I impersonated Amanda—a Riviera doxy of a bigamous turn—for over two hundred weeks, hither and yon, as well as in Montgomery, Alabama, flying the Confederate flag.

Does my squawk seem ungracious, in view of the steady and profitable employment given me by play and part? Hear me out before you condemn me. I played Amanda out of necessity, because I couldn't get any other part to play. I played her to escape debtor's prison. *Private Lives* was first produced in America in 1931—with Noel Coward and Gertrude Lawrence in the leading roles. Noel is a man of courage and independence. He and Gertie played it for six months, withdrew when it was still a sellout at the Times Square Theatre because they were bored to death.

Now actresses, modern playwrights being either delinquent, sterile or frying fish in Hollywood, often add to their prestige, bolster up their budgets, by enlisting in a revival—something out of Ibsen, Sheridan or that rake from Stratford. This feigned interest in the classics adds a cachet to their reputations. But no actress in her right mind, least of all Tallulah, elects to toil in the renewal of so feathery a trifle as *Private Lives* from choice. Creating a role is an actress's most rewarding experience. To duplicate, with such variations as suggest themselves, a role created by another, is not my idea of Paradise.

So, darlings, when you read that a stage star has fled the reservation, bolted to Hollywood or taken a stance before a microphone or the TV cameras, don't judge her hastily. It isn't a case of infidelity, it's a case of survival. Percy Hammond, in my judgment the most amusing critic, the greatest stylist in his field, once observed: "The theater is the shell game of the arts." Bravo, Percy!

In view of my scorn for the theater, its practices and delin-

9.

quencies, why have I continued to act in it for thirty years? I have no alternate profession. Lobster-trapping? Placer-mining? Smuggling? I haven't the muscles, the equipment or the nerve. How many actors could make fifty dollars a week were all forms of amusement barred by edict? Harpo Marx? He could strum his lyre on a ferry boat and pass the hat. Alfred Lunt might make out as a chef. He's skilled at *soufflés* and similar ambrosia. Leo Genn, one of the prosecutors of the fiends who ran the infamous concentration camp at Belsen, could practice law. Billy Gaxton prospers from a perfume sideline. Barry Fitzgerald might return to the Dublin desk at which he sat during his seventeen years in civil service, and Charles Laughton resume greeting behind a hotel desk. But these boys are exceptions. What screen cowboy could qualify for the mounted police? I'll lay you three to one Hopalong What's-His-Name would flunk the simplest test.

Should I later repudiate any part of this sermon on the theater, its agues and its agonies, remember I'm supposed to be mercurial! Honey-haired, cello-voiced, mercurial Tallulah, that's me! There is evidence to support the argument that some of my decisions and judgments are open to suspicion. An example: Back in February of 1928 I was impersonating Daphne Manning, daughter of an antique dealer, in *Blackmail*. Miffed because her intended had given her a brushoff, Daphne sought solace with a young artist in his studio. This was a tactical error. The juvenile Rembrandt, inflamed by her aromas and contours, sought to despoil her. Dismayed at his animal action, Daphne snatched up a breadknife and cut the culprit's throat from ear to ear.

The London critics took a dim view of these shenanigans but my disciples in the gallery carried on as though I had kicked a field goal to beat Princeton. In the midst of this delirium I was approached by Max Beaverbrook—Lord Beaverbrook to you—waving sheaves of pound notes. Would I write my confessions for his Sunday *Express?* Though I had little to confess, though my prose had not aroused the envy of Rebecca West or Victoria May Sackville-West, I agreed. The sight of so much folding money scuttled my scruples. My "Confessions" will never occupy a shelf with those of Jean Jacques Rousseau or Thomas de Quincey, but they are notable for the final sentence of the last installment:

"I shall never write another life story, even if I live a hundred years. So you, like me, are about to enjoy a holiday, as I cannot be a hundred until after A.D. 2000."

Here it's only 1952 and again I'm doing a duet with the perpendicular pronoun.

I would be an ingrate and a liar did I give the impression that I've never had any thrills in the theater. There's a large dash of show-off in me, as there is in every actor worth his salt. I'm intoxicated by applause. It's my nectar. For all my griping, nothing has so tingled my spine as stepping down to the foots after the fall of a first-night curtain to be greeted by the acclaim of my peers, or an approximation thereof. Let's have no beating about the bush. Not every yahoo in a first-night seat is my peer.

For all its flaws and demands, for all its stupidities, the theater will outlive all the mechanical contraptions schemed to ape it. It has survived the bicycle, the Stutz Bearcat, the double feature, Mr. Marconi's trinket and the tabloid newspapers. Will TV kill the theater? If the programs I have seen, save for "Kukla, Fran and Ollie," the ball games and fights, are any criterion, the theater need not wake up in a cold sweat. The theater will be kayoed by the vocal mirrors on the day its champions vote to interrupt the duel between Laertes and Hamlet that they may pick up a quick buck through a tribute to a deodorant, repeat the offense every ten minutes throughout the Dane's ordeal. I've prowled on my hands and knees clear back through Aeschylus and Aristophanes and in twenty-five hundred years no theater man has tolerated such vandalism. Television could perform a great service in mass education, but there's no indication its sponsors have anything like this on their minds. When some historian gets around to talking about its origin and growth he cannot but hint that in its pioneer phase television's chief service was as a soporific. TV, if you ask me, has a suicide complex.

Some paragraphs back I was muttering about an alternate profession. I'm not daft enough to think, after thirty-three years in the theater, I can master another profession, even become moderately proficient in one. There's more to it than turning on a tap. I could have been a great dancer and I propose to prove it. As I was born with acting talent, so I was born with a sense of rhythm. My body is lithe and flexible. I have considerable feline grace. (I wish I could think of another word for "feline"; it leaves me open to counterattack.)

I was seventeen when hired to understudy Constance Binney in Rachel Crothers' 39 East. "Can you dance?" Miss Crothers asked me. "Of course," I replied, "otherwise I wouldn't have applied for the job." I had seen Miss Binney in the comedy, thus knew she had to spin on her toes in the second act. Though the thought of speaking lines terrified me, I was unruffled by the ballet demands. It was a triumph of mind over matter. I gave the impression of a budding Pavlova because I felt I was one. Why? I had recently seen sub-deb service in Washington. Though pudgy and pimpled, I was the toast of the stag line at such parties as I stimulated.

Facing my first London audience in The Dancers, on the curtain's rise I was dancing for my supper in a British Columbia saloon, on its fall the toast of Paris, a ballerina! Actor-manager Sir Gerald du Maurier was a perfectionist. Feeling the demands of the part might be beyond my dancing range, he sent me to a ballet teacher. Reluctantly I went to the studio—a bleak, dark and empty room. There I was greeted by a rapt young man.

The rapt young man was Léonide Massine, whose jetés and tournées and what-have-yous are discussed in hushed tones wherever balletomanes engage in their rituals. He told Sir Gerald, who in turn told me, I was a natural-born dancer, that I could have won international fame on my toes. He had discovered me fifteen years too late. Ballerinas start their spins and leaps at five. I was twenty.

Ballet dancers, out of their stylized routines, are fish out of water. On a ballroom floor they're as awkward as other clods, musclebound, rhythmless. At parties I've danced with the likes of Lifar, Massine and Anton Dolin. All of them would have profited by a course under Arthur Murray. No rug-cutters, they!

My Charleston in *The Gold Diggers*, London, '26, was hot stuff! Adele Astaire (she and Fred were then the toast of Piccadilly) said she had never seen a better dance. She was ecstatic about the cartwheel I flipped at the finish. She was going to take up dramatic acting by way of reprisal, she said. Was Adele having me on? I think so. When a dramatic actress breaks into a dance, surprise has considerable to do with the resulting applause. Remember how Alfred Lunt was cheered for his tap dance in *Idiot's Delight*? The unexpected always creates a commotion in the theater. Think of the sensation Katharine Cornell would cause did she do bird calls or a turn on the trapeze!

Acting is the laziest of the professions. A ballet dancer must limber up two or three hours a day, working or idle. The great musicians practice three or four hours a day, willy-nilly. Opera singers must go easy on cigarettes, learn half a dozen languages. The demands on an actress consist in learning the role, interpreting

to the best of her ability the intent of the author as outlined by
the director. When not on stage? She sits around chewing her
nails, waiting for the telephone to ring. She toils not, neither does
she spin. She may fume. She may even read. But she doesn't
practice.

What would I do were platforms, microphones and screens
denied me? That's easy. I'd go to the races, I'd sit up all night
gambling in the most convenient casino, I'd enjoy an emotional
jag while suffering with the New York Giants. I might glut myself
with bridge could I find players agreeable to my wayward strategies.
Cooking? Writing? These require powers of concentration and
industry which I don't possess. The theater has spoiled me for the
more demanding arts.

My first performance had two distinguished spectators: Orville
and Wilbur Wright. Kitty Hawk was history when Aunt Marie
gave them a party at her country home near Montgomery, Alabama.
This was quite a shindig. The Governor was there and a great press
of judges, lawyers, Congressmen and local celebrities. It was a stunt
party. The guests were called upon to entertain. A Montgomery
doctor fouled up "Casey at the Bat," made immortal by DeWolfe
Hopper. Ballad singers had their hour, and impromptu quartets. I
won the prize for the top performance, with an imitation of my
kindergarten teacher. The judges? Orville and Wilbur Wright.
I'd like to believe they detected in me an obscure talent, but I'm
afraid I won because I was the niece of the hostess. Another
thing worked in my favor. I was the youngest and smallest of the
contestants.

Envious of my elders, thirsty for recognition, I plotted many a
ruse when Daddy, Sister and I were living at grandfather's house
in Jasper. To get me out of her hair, grandmother would bribe me

to take my primers out on the lawn. This irked me. I scorned the games and assignments of children of my age. Poring over a primer was not my notion of maturity. Even then a direct actionist, I found a way out of this humiliation. Lifting two law journals from Daddy's room, I tottered to the lawn. Flat on the grass I pored over these, unaware they were upside down. I placed myself so that I could observe passersby, note their reactions to my profundity.

As long as I can remember I dramatized everything I did. I wasn't the only Bankhead to follow this formula. My mother, Daddy, my aunts and uncles, even my grandparents, carried out the simplest chore with a style and dash at odds with its demands. In the theater there are players who can make a production out of eating an apple, out of opening a letter. That's the Bankheads!

My doom was sealed when I saw a girl turn cartwheels at a circus in Birmingham. A contortionist, she could bend backwards until her head was between her feet, highlight the trick by picking up a handkerchief with her teeth. This demonstration addled my mind. Within a week I mastered cartwheel and backbend, added a third stunt to my repertory, standing on my head.

Shortly I made my first parachute jump. Unthinkingly one of my relatives took me to a country fair. As a climax to the carnival a young girl in tights jumped from a balloon, her descent checked as her chute opened. My hair was on fire! Back home, I sneaked into Grandmother's closet and snatched up her parasol. I raced to the barn, scaled to the hayloft. Clambering through the mow window, the catch on the parasol released, I took off. What followed confirmed an earlier observation of Sir Isaac Newton. I wound up flattened, my coccyx splintered. Dismayed? No whit!

Later my cartwheels were to draw official fire. Aunt Marie's house in Montgomery stood on a corner. The street sloped sharply down within our block. This block was my arena. Engaged in a chain of cartwheels one afternoon, halfway through the block I was hailed by an elderly gentleman: "Stop that, little girl! Stop that! Come back here! Come back here!" I ignored the summons, continued my revolutions to the block's end. When I scampered back my tormenter was waiting. "Didn't you hear me when I told you to stop?" "Yes, sir. I did." "Why didn't you stop?" "Because my grandfather told me never to start anything I couldn't finish." "Oh, is that so?" said my challenger. "And who is your grandfather?"

"Senator John Hollis Bankhead," I said proudly.

"Well, I'm Braxton Comer, the Governor of Alabama."

So he was. This was my first defiance of constituted power.

My dramatic urge preceded the Wright brothers, the cartwheel lady and the parachutist. Our social hub was the drugstore. Of a late afternoon the town's bloods and belles gathered there for Cokes and sodas and gossip. Grandmother would be driven down in her four-seater surrey, wait outside while Sister and I tossed off a Coke.

On our exit, one afternoon, Grandmother was chatting with Miss Clara Novel, of the Novels of Virginia, suh! Miss Novel dressed in purple, carried a purple parasol. Later she was Daddy's secretary in Congress. As we drove off, Miss Novel said to Grandmother: "That child has the most gracious smile."

That did it. Home, I scuttled up to my bedroom, anchored myself before the mirror, then smiled and smiled and smiled. For a week I was beside myself until everyone got out of the house, that I might resume my experiments. That's my first recollection of acting without an audience—save myself.

I was all of five when Daddy took me to Birmingham to have my tonsils removed—the start of my mezzo-basso voice. As a reward for my courage under the knife he took me to a vaudeville show. A woman single, to use a trade term, sang slightly risqué songs as she played the piano. A born mimic, I mastered her routine over-night. I still remember the final line of one song: "And when he took his hat I wondered when he'd come again." Naughty? It had implications. At least Daddy thought so. He was fascinated by my impersonation. Sometimes he'd come home a little high from *vin du pays*—bourbon, that is—wake me up, bring me downstairs in my nightgown, stand me up on the table in the dining room, ask me to give my impression of the Birmingham lark. Then he'd roar with laughter.

I reacted violently to applause, to recognition from my elders. The dining room was only used for large family dinners. Usually we ate in the breakfast room. Atop that rarely used table, I felt exalted. Here was a rostrum! One night Daddy came home with most of the University of Alabama Glee Club. Again I was sum-moned. I've often tingled to applause but never did I have such tingles as I experienced when those collegians cheered me at mid-night.

Thanks to my acrobatics, my impersonations, that "gracious smile" cue from Miss Novel, I was acting all over the place. But I had yet to mount a platform in front of a paid audience. When the opportunity came I was not napping. One night in Jasper—it had three thousand people then, perhaps five thousand now—Sister and I attended a show put on at the schoolhouse with local talent. We sat in the front row, goggle-eyed. Suddenly a man stepped before the curtain to say there would be a delay as the scenery was fouled up. Would someone in the audience volunteer a turn? I raced to the stage like a bat out of hell, dragging Sister behind me, and launched into "Old Ironsides."

Oliver Wendell Holmes must have spun in his grave. My recita-tion caused a storm of applause and laughter. The cheering did things to my spine, to my mind. I felt consecrated. I felt I was fated for the purple, that neither fire, nor flood nor pestilence could stay me.

The mirror was to fascinate me again and again. When I was ten Daddy packed Sister and me off to the Academy of the Sacred Heart in New York. The black-robed nuns, quiet and calm, made a vivid impression on me. When we returned to Jasper I holed up in my bedroom, rooted myself before the glass. I set lighted candles on either side of it, tied a white handkerchief over my brow, draped myself in a black shawl, and spent hours practicing the rituals and devotions of those devout women. It was at a Jasper kindergarten that I had my first role. The teacher rigged us out in paper costumes and drilled us in a charade which smacked of Maurice Maeterlinck. Sister played the rainbow, her costume ablaze with color. Me? I had the role of the moon because my face was so round. I have never been so jealous.

Here, if the Chair will recognize me, I'd like to smother the myth that the Prince of Wales and I were thick as thieves. This canard pops up in almost every piece that has been written about me. Victimized by fame, you cease to be a free agent, in time grow to accept tall tales of your exploits as part of your due. The Tallulah-and-the-Prince-of-Wales fraud once reached the delirium that he had given me a house in Berkeley Square in London.

I was fourteen when I met the Prince for the first and only time, at some function to which Grandmother had dragged me and Sister, along with my stepmother and Daddy. The Prince's arm was in a sling—too much handshaking. Washington's flower and chivalry queued up to be formally presented to the young man. I was furious. Thanks to this ceremonial I missed an episode in *The Exploits of Elaine*. Few of the guests were up on protocol, thus were confused by conflicting advice on how to conduct themselves. Grandmother, enslaved by the Cinderella story, made a curtsy that brought her nose to the rug. She wasn't groveling to royalty. Since nothing in the world was good enough for her Tallulah she felt fate had brought her my Prince Charming. Grandmother was only five feet tall. At the bottom of her curtsy she seemed to be submitting her head to the ax. Her overlong salute blocked traffic for three minutes.

My stepmother, a woman of charm and honesty, had no illusions about either me or the Prince. Tall and willowy, she was directly behind Grandmother in the reception line. Turning to Daddy, she whispered: "Billy, I am not going to curtsy to that little boy. I'd just feel a fool, and what's more, I'd look a fool." And she didn't. I hope that clears up the fable about me and the Duke of Windsor. I've been tangled up with more than one prince in my time but Edward and I never conspired at anything.

Though I remain serene when confronted with royalty, I get downright hysterical when looking at a champion in action. About to fly to England to start my radio season in "The Big Show" in the fall of '51, my enthusiasm was chilled because I would miss the "Sugar Ray" Robinson–Randy Turpin fight, would be out of touch with the Giants, panting, when I left, on the heels of the Dodgers.

Attending a Giant game, say my cronies, is an experience comparable to shooting the Snake River rapids in a canoe. When they lose I taste wormwood. When they win I want to do a tarantella on top of the dugout. A Giant rally brings out the roman candle in me. The garments of adjoining box-holders start to smolder.

I once lured the young Viennese actor, Helmut Dantine, to a set-to between the Giants and the Pirates. Mr. Dantine had never seen a game before. My airy explanations confused the *émigré*. Rapt in his attention to my free translation of the sacrifice hit, Helmut was almost decapitated by a foul ball. Mr. Dantine looked upon the *faux pas* as a hostile act. He felt I had tricked him into a false sense of security that the hitter might have an unsuspecting target. He left before the ninth, a grayer if not a wiser man.

It's true I run a temperature when watching the Giants trying to come from behind in the late innings, either at the Polo Grounds or on my TV screen. I was hysterical for hours after Bobby Thomson belted Ralph Branca for that ninth inning homer in the final game of the Dodger-Giant playoff in '51. The Giants had to score four runs in the ninth to win. Remember? There was blood on the moon that night in Bedford Village. But I don't know nearly as much about baseball as Ethel Barrymore. Ethel is a real fan, can give you batting averages, the text of the infield fly rule and comment on an umpire's vision.

Someone has said that Ethel Barrymore has the reticence born of assurance whereas my monologues indicate my insecurity. The point is moot. It's unlikely I'll ever submit to a psychiatrist's couch. I don't want some stranger prowling around through my psyche, monkeying with my id. I don't need an analyst to tell me that I have never had any sense of security. Who has?

My devotion to the Giants, dating back to 1939, has drawn the fire of renegades, eager to deflate me. One of these wrote that on my first visit to Ebbets Field in Brooklyn I rooted all afternoon for Dolph Camilli, the Dodger first baseman. I had been tricked into this treason, swore my enemy, because I wasn't aware that the Giants wore gray uniforms when traveling, the residents white. Though I invaded Flatbush to cheer Mel Ott, Giant right fielder, I wound up in hysterics over Camilli, because both had the numeral "4" on the back of their uniform. Stuff, balderdash and rot, not to use a few other words too hot to handle in a memoir.

A daughter of the deep South, I have little time for the "Yankees." They're bleak perfectionists, insolent in their confidence, the snobs of the diamond. The Yankees are all technique, no color or juice. But they keep on winning pennants year after year. Not the Giants! They've won one flag in the last fourteen years.

I blew my first fuse over the Giants in the summer of '51, when introduced to Harry Danning and Mel Ott. Ott was so good-looking, so shy, so gentlemanly—and from Louisiana. For two weeks I got up in the middle of the night—around noon by the actor's clock— to charge up to the Polo Grounds.

I worked myself up into such a fever that I invited the team to see a performance of *The Little Foxes*. After the play I served them a buffet supper, and drinks compatible with their training rules, on the promenade which fringed the rear of the balcony. The Giants, following this soiree, dropped eight games in a row. Had I hexed them? The suspicion chilled me. I denied myself the Polo Grounds and they started to win again.

I have proved a hoodoo to more than one champion. I first got inflamed over sports in London. The tennis championships were being held at Wimbledon and Bill Tilden dropped into my house in Farm Street. Most Americans dropped in there, after visiting Madame Tussaud's Waxworks and the Tower, in line of duty. Tilden was temperamental, brilliant. He dramatized every lob, every serve. I was seething in the grandstand when he played the singles' final with Henri Cochet. To insure Bill's victory, I gave him a four-leaf clover to carry in his shirt pocket. Cochet was dull and methodical, completely lacking in color. Tilden won the first two sets, was at point, set, match in the third set when Cochet broke his service and went on to take the set and the next two as well.

I also carried an emotional banner for Joe Louis. When he fought Max Schmeling, the scowling Nazi, the first time, I sent him Daddy's bull's-eye, a charm of spectacular potency. I urged Joe to carry it in his robe the night of the battle. He did carry it, and was knocked stiff in the twelfth round.

When Joe and Schmeling met the second time I was there with my husband, John Emery, carrying a rug, a pair of field glasses, and a flask—just in case of snake bite. When Joe knocked the Uhlan cold in the first round, I leaped to my feet before seventy thousand people and screamed: "I told you so, you sons-of-bitches." I was addressing four bundsmen sitting directly behind us. An hour and three drinks later, Edie Smith, my secretary, phoned me at "21": "Oh, *Die Donner*, all that money you spent and it only lasted two minutes." "Edie," I said, "had it lasted a minute longer I would have died in the Stadium."

Looking back on my fiascos with wishbones and four-leaf clovers reminds me that I once put the whammy on Daddy. I went to a ball game between a team of Congressmen and the Washington's firemen's nine, played in behalf of charity. Daddy had been a great athlete at the University of Alabama. I was sure that he would distinguish himself. To my horror he fanned three times. I was crushed for days.

My heroes are not necessarily headliners. I swooned over Burgess Whitehead, Giant second baseman, because he moved like a ballet dancer. He was a Phi Beta Kappa, a brilliant fielder, but he couldn't hit his way out of a paper bag. Then there was Lou Chiozza. One of his traducers said that he weighed 170 and hit the same figure. Pursuing an outfield fly Lou collided so violently with Jo-Jo Moore that he broke his ankle. When he was carted off to the hospital, I banked his bed with flowers. Two visiting teammates were paralyzed with fright, on walking into his dimly lit room. They found their white-clad comrade asleep in a profusion of lilies and came to the conclusion he was dead. Why was I fascinated with Chiozza? He was born in Tallulah, Louisiana.

Speaking of Tallulah, it has been argued that had I been christened Jane or Julia it is unlikely I would ever have gotten out of Huntsville, Alabama, place of my birth. Of one thing I'm certain. "Tallulah" has been no handicap to me. It once moved one of my fans to this flourish:

"Mellifluous, liquid, Tallulah is a name to inflame the flank of a Pullman car, to blow on a bugle. It's a name to rally the tribesmen in battle, to summon the faithful to prayer. Because of its phonetic potential it is a challenging name, one to inspire its bearer to adventures above and beyond the call of duty—or contract. It's sole owner in the ranks of Equity, only player in the theater immediately identifiable to the remotest Eskimo by her given name, has never let down the clergyman who christened her."

Humorist Bugs Baer said the minister who christened me must have been chewing bubble gum. When first I met Ethel Barrymore she said: "You should change your name. No one will be able to pronounce it." She suggested Barbara or Mary as a substitute. She loathed "Ethel."

As a child my name embarrassed me. Ragged by normally named playmates, I'd bawl. In one school I changed to Elizabeth. This alias was annulled once Daddy heard of it.

Etymologists have worked themselves up into a tizzy trying to find the source of Tallulah. I was named for my paternal grandmother. She, in turn, was named for Tallulah Falls, Georgia, one of the scenic wonders of the South. After that the going gets rougher. One faction holds that Tallulah is an Indian word, meaning love-maiden. Another cult, partial to another tribe, holds that Tallulah means terrible or "Goddess of Vengeance." None of these analysts ever get around to identifying the Indians. Perhaps they hesitate to implicate innocent red men. When I was playing Regina Giddens in *The Little Foxes*—Regina was a bitch of the

first water—I received a letter from an Irish poet. He said Tallulah
was derived from the name of a sixth-century Irish saint. He swore
that fugitive Hibernians fled to Georgia long before Button Gwin-
nett signed the Declaration. My Irish bard said Tallulah was Gaelic
for colleen, and had charts to prove it.

Aunt Marie heads a cult which insists Tallulah means the tone
of a bell, adds that it should be spelled belle. Two visitors from
the new state of Israel say that in Hebrew my given name means
precipice or rock.

In the spring of '49 my ears were poisoned with this jingle:

> I'm Tallulah, the tube of Prell,
> And I've got a little something to tell,
> Your hair can be radiant, oh so easy,
> All you've got to do is take me home
> and squeeze me.

Another verse had this line:

> For radiant hair get a-hold of me
> Tallulah, the tube of Prell Shampoo.

This attempt to capitalize on my name stiffened my hackles.
In my thirty years in the theater I had spurned offers adding up to
a maharajah's ransom to endorse this gadget, that cure-all. Quicker
than a Prell-user could dry her mane, I slapped a suit for a million
dollars' damages on the two radio companies over whose networks
the verses were broadcast, on Procter and Gamble, sponsors for
the lather, and on the advertising agency which schemed the
outrage.

My protest created a front-page commotion. Queried by the Associated Press, I barked: "I've yet to endorse a floor wax, a flea
powder or a wart-remover, a cigar or a hookah pipe. I'll unjingle

both Mr. Procter and Mr. Gamble, their aides, their allies and their echoes."

Henry Luce, publisher of *Life, Time* and *Fortune,* and husband of an ex-Congresswoman, muscled into the act. *Life* devoted two pages to the fracas, revealed to its 5,200,000 readers that in 1941 a Metro-Goldwyn-Mayer picture called *Ship Ahoy* had a song: "I'll Take Tallulah," with this line: "No one doing the hula can do what Tallulah does to me." The analogy was as flat as a frozen fiddle. The rinse hucksters smeared me. Metro flattered me. I could have helped Mr. Luce in his research. While I was touring in *Antony and Cleopatra,* the musical comedy hit, *I'd Rather Be Right,* erupted in New York. In it George M. Cohan gaily satirized Franklin Roosevelt. One of its songs, "Off the Record," amused Republicans and Democrats alike.

> My messages to Congress
> Are a lot of boola-boola,
> I'm not so fond of Bankhead
> But I'd love to meet Tallulah—
> But that's off the record!

This spoofing pleased me, even if librettist Larry Hart, America's answer to Sir William Schwenck Gilbert, had taken a few liberties. President Roosevelt and Daddy were old friends.

Threatened with a damage suit, Prell took to the hills. The offensive stanzas were snuffed off the air, and I received considerable fiscal balm, not to say pages of publicity.

When a star's integrity starts to come apart at the seams, he or she can pick up handsome sums for testimonials. I know actors whose consuming ambition is to be tapped for one of those "Men of Distinction" portraits. They look upon them as the equivalent of Hollywood "Oscars," sulk because they can't qualify for this alcoholic laurel.

Jeanne Eagles was at her peak when baited with an offer of $10,000 to endorse a cigarette. Perhaps her budget was blistered. Perhaps the winter looked bleak. In any event Jeanne accepted the loot. The late Fannie Brice was discussing this coup with her cronies. "Isn't it shocking," asked one, "that a woman of Jeanne Eagles' stature should so far forget her position as to endorse a cigarette?" "How much did you say she got?" asked Fannie. "$10,000." "For $10,000," said Miss Brice, "I'd endorse an opium pipe." Me? I'd starve first.

> Who steals my purse steals trash; 'tis something, nothing;
> 'Twas mine, 'tis his, and has been slave to thousands;
> But he that filches from me my good name
> Robs me of that which not enriches him,
> And makes me poor indeed.

A very sound observation!

Tallulah has connotations which soothe or shrivel half the population. Its cachet is the product of too much suffering, too many revolts and accusations, too many attacks and counterattacks, to be bandied about by clods.

2.

Echoes of My Childhood

I never knew my mother. She survived my birth by but three weeks. Her death was brought about by complications arising from my birth, but I never had feelings of guilt, even when old enough to be aware of the association of the two events. From the start I was too pampered by Daddy, by Aunt Marie and Aunt Louise, by my grandmother and grandfather, to brood over the loss of a mother I could not remember. Until her death, Grandmother was Mama to me.

My mother, Adelaide Eugenia Sledge, was a Southern belle, and by all evidence written, oral and photographic, an astonishing beauty. Stark Young, critic and Southern novelist, wrote "she was a creature out of *The Arabian Nights.*" " 'As beautiful as Ada Sledge,' for two generations, was the highest tribute that could be paid a woman in the South," he said. He first saw her at a ball in a private home. Surrounded by eager young men, she was weaving patterns with her fan in the manner of Madame du Barry. Mother was thirteen. Mr. Young was seven and peeking from a stairway.

Mother's grandfather was very wealthy. He had a racetrack on his plantation, was president of the Cotton Exchange and thought nothing of betting $10,000 on one of his fighting cocks, of losing thousands when cotton prices ran counter to his judgment. My knowledge of Mother's family is sketchy. Daddy used to say he had to slave for two years to pay for our baby clothes—Sister's and mine. It was a reflection of Mother's upbringing that these were heavy with lace.

But Mother was more than a great beauty. She was high-spirited, gay and a born actress. When I was playing in *The Skin of Our Teeth* a distinguished-looking woman came to my dressing room after a performance. She had gone to school with Mother. What this stranger was to say warmed me:

"Your mother was the most beautiful thing that ever lived. Many people have said you get your acting talent from your father, but I disagree. I was at school with Ada Eugenia and I knew Will well. I have followed his career. You inherited your talent from your mother. Did you know that she could faint on cue?

"Once she had a crush on a young doctor. Whenever she saw him approaching she would feign a swoon, bring him galloping across the campus. She had golden hair, dark brown eyes and pearl-white skin. Told that she looked wonderful in black, she appeared in chapel in widow's weeds, prayer book under her arm, the following Sunday."

Mother attended Salem College in Winston-Salem, North Carolina. Returning home for summer vacation she soon had all the girls in town arranged in Grecian friezes, or loping across lawns in classic dances.

I treasure another memory of her, set down in a letter from a stranger. She wrote: "I used to know your mother. I'll never forget her riding sidesaddle in a brown habit lined with red taffeta, a black tricorn hat atop her head. At a ball we'd all wait in the cloak-room until your mother arrived, just to admire her. Though we were all her age, none of us was jealous of her beauty."

Here's a tribute from another who knew her: "If Tallulah's

28 .

as mad as a hatter, she came by it honestly. So was her mother." Before her marriage to Daddy, he said, Mother had gone to Paris, rejoiced in its luxuries, then returned to Como, Mississippi, with trunks full of Worth clothes. Como was a whistle-stop. Was she dismayed because she had no arena worthy of her wardrobe? Not a bit. Radiant in a low-cut gown, she would take off down a dirt road, a basket on her arm, shopping.

With Daddy and Mother it was a case of love at first sight. Mother was engaged to a rich Virginia planter. Following the protocol of that day, she went to visit one of her prospective brides-maids in Huntsville, Alabama. There she met Daddy, then a young lawyer. With that she was through with the rich young planter. She broke off the engagement to the great annoyance of her family. Three months later she married Daddy.

At my home in Bedford Hills I have two priceless possessions: My Augustus John portrait and my father's journal. Daddy's reflections and observations are sporadic. Frequently he skips a year or more. Here is an entry dated January 31, 1904:

Six years have flown, and have flown almost with fury since last I wrote herein. The scene then was New York City, the writer a young struggler in the malls of a stupendous city, and his years were far fewer than now. Today, I write again in Huntsville, placid, tender old town in the shadow of the hills, and I am older far than they, and sadder.

This is my wedding anniversary. Four years ago I took to my heart and to my name, the tenderest and the most beautiful girl the golden sunlight of Heaven ever curtsied to in caressing. Today out at Maple Hill cemetery, sleeping beneath a white shaft of marble, not as purely white as her soul but meant to typify it, sleeps that blessed dust "dearer to me than the ruddy drops that visit this sad heart," my blessed Gene.

I have often since that greatest tragedy of my life had a purpose to write of her, of our courtship, our joyful married life, of my struggles and her sacrifices, of the coming of the babies, and of the coming of the gray angel to my home, my grief, and all the bitter-sweet days that came and went; but I have not been able to find the spirit, or the vein in which to set it down.

I am aware that my children will soon begin to make inquiries about their mother, of how she lived and loved and died, as they should and as I want them to. But I know how my heart and my speech shall fail me when the time comes, how my eyes will brine with ever-too-ready tears and my throat throb with a choking pain that ever is attendant upon that cruel retrospection. They will be able to know how beautiful she was by the pictures I have of her, and yet which are so impotent to give an idea of her glorious coloring, the tenderness and yet the spirit of her brown eyes, the beauty of her curls, the fair and rosy skin, her expression when animated or in conversation.

I met her very casually one night at the McGee Hotel in Huntsville, while she was here on a shopping expedition from Courtland. She afterwards told me she had come to buy her apparel in which to marry another man. Jessie Gilchrist and Nanette DuBose were her companions, I believe. Alas, poor Nanette, she, too, has gone in the same heroic way as my little girl.

It was truly a case of love at first sight. I continued my attentions after she went back to Aunt Alice's at Courtland, and often went down there on Sundays to see her—in fact, on the old front porch at "Summerwood" I made my first declaration of love—of a true love that still lives beyond the tomb and beyond the stars.

I have preserved for our babies our love letters—mine to her, and hers to me. If they should ever read them I hope and believe that they will feel and believe ours was a love of tenderest trust and consuming affection. Those letters tell the story of our courtship with a tenderer diction than I now can write—for then joy and beautiful anticipations ran my pen, while now I write in the shadow of the loss while choked with the anguish of absence.

The wedding took place in Memphis, on Jefferson Street. It was beautiful, the flowers, the dazzling lights, the joyous guests, the dreamful and soulful music, and far and above the beauty of the environments was the matchless beauty of my bride. I have her wedding gown. She wore it only once. I have never had the courage to look upon its silken folds since she went away to God.

Ornate, you say? Flowery? Wordy? Echo of a more leisurely age? True! But the first time I read it, it broke my heart. It still does.

I was christened beside my mother's casket, immediately thereafter packed off with Sister to Aunt Marie's home in Montgomery. For the next fifteen years we led a gypsy existence. When Congress was adjourned Daddy, Sister and I lived with Grandfather and Grandmother at their home in Jasper. Daddy lived there from the time of Mother's death until he was elected to the House of Representatives in 1916.

This cues me into an anecdote pointing up the long arm of coincidence. Shortly after the end of the Spanish-American War, Granddaddy was opposed for the Democratic nomination for Congressman from his district by Richmond Pearson Hobson. Hobson was the young naval lieutenant who volunteered to sink the collier *Merrimac* across the channel of the harbor at Santiago de Cuba, thus preclude the escape of Cervera's fleet. He did sink it, but was taken prisoner. His coup caught the imagination of the entire country even though the strategy failed. The Spanish fleet steamed out to be annihilated. But Hobson returned a hero. He added to his popularity by kissing every woman and baby he met. Grandfather was the victim of these dramatics. But he did not pine in defeat. The following year he was elected to a seat in the United States Senate, remained there until his death. Here's the payoff. Daddy was defeated in his first campaign for Congressman, but on his second try—the Bankheads had plotted a new Congressional district in the meantime—was elected. Whom did he beat? Richmond Pearson Hobson.

I can't work myself up into a lather about family trees and similar genuflections to yesterday. If you prowl back far enough you're sure to run into something unpleasant. But experts swear that John

Hollis Bankhead—that's Grandfather—was a direct descendant of Lt. John Hollis, aide to George Washington. The son of one of Grandfather's ancestors married Thomas Jefferson's granddaughter. I've been told that the name Bankhead pops up on at least one tombstone at Monticello.

Neither Sister nor I had any silver-spoon handicaps. Daddy never made much money, either as lawyer or government servant. He had no instinct for business. Granddaddy, too, was inept in money matters. He once had the controlling interest in Coca-Cola. He sold out to invest in Cherry Cola. The less said about that maneuver, the better. He had once owned the Bankhead and Caledonia coal mines of Bankhead, Alabama, had sold them for a cool million. There was little of this loot lying around on my first entrance.

Granddaddy loathed anything ostentatious. Paradoxically, I was his favorite granddaughter. When he was in the Senate, Grandmother drove about in her own car with a liveried chauffeur. Granddaddy scorned such nonsense. He rode to the Capitol in a streetcar. He never rose in the Senate to speak unless the subject was close to his heart. He was the father of Federal Good Roads. There's a monument in Washington testifying to this. It bears a sundial. On one side is engraved the name of Lincoln, on the other that of John Hollis Bankhead. The Bankhead Highway runs from Washington through the deep South and out to the Far West.

Granddaddy was the last Confederate veteran in the Senate. In the War between the States he recruited his own regiment. He was wounded eight times, was a Captain at eighteen.

A measure came up in the Senate in 1916 for an appropriation for a bust of General Robert E. Lee. There was no great enthusiasm for the proposal. Debate on the subject dawdled. Granddaddy sat through this silently. Then he thought of a way to focus attention on his resentment. He rose one morning, put on his Confederate uniform, donned his sword, then proceeded to the Capitol by street-car. Taking his seat on the floor, he remained silent, mute accuser of those lacking in respect to his hero.

During his wordless accusation Marshal Joffre and René Viviani of France, here to seek American support in their struggle with the Germans, addressed the joint Houses of Congress. Sister and I were in the gallery. We were able to understand something of Viviani's speech because of our French studies in the convents.

Viviani's address over, the Congressmen, the ambassadors, the Supreme Court Justices, filed by to greet the distinguished visitors. When Granddaddy reached out his hand to Viviani everyone in the gallery, everyone on the floor, rose to their feet and cheered, many with tears streaming down their cheeks. A week later the newspapers carried the story that Senator Bankhead of Alabama had shamed the Senate into voting the appropriation through his silent protest.

It was Granddaddy who broke the voting deadlock at the 1916 Democratic National Convention in St. Louis by casting Alabama's twenty-four votes for Woodrow Wilson. At that same convention Daddy had made the speech nominating Oscar Underwood, junior Senator from Alabama, for the Presidency.

Granddaddy was an imposing figure, six feet three inches. Because of a facial likeness he was often mistaken for William Jennings Bryan. He was opinionated, stubborn. When General Pershing led a parade down Pennsylvania Avenue before World War I, Granddaddy wouldn't get up from his chair to look out the window. Pershing, he said, was a show-off.

I'd better scramble back to my childhood. I might get in trouble talking about show-offs.

Daddy couldn't cope with Sister and me when my grandparents were in Washington. We would live with Aunt Marie in Montgomery so long as Congress was in session—usually from September to June. Aunt Marie pampered us, humored us. She sent us to Miss Gussie Woodruff's School for Girls, to still another school run by Miss Margaret Booth. And I went to public school in Jasper for two terms.

Aunt Marie is the most durable as well as the most delightful of the Bankheads. Now eighty-two and weighing 220 pounds, she was spry as a cricket when she spent last Thanksgiving at my home in a reunion that embraced Uncle Henry. She succeeded her deceased husband, Thomas M. Owen, LL.D., as archivist of the state of Alabama. To prove she was qualified for the job, Aunt Marie tossed off an eight-volume history of the state. She has written three novels and as recently as 1945 submitted a three-act play to the Theatre Guild.

The marble Memorial building in Montgomery is a tribute to her determination. Jokingly, she told me she demanded the new Memorial building that she might have a toilet in her office. In her old quarters at the Capitol she had to walk thirty feet down a hall. The Memorial required a Federal appropriation of a million dollars. Aunt Marie badgered Governor Graves into going to Washington and demanding this sum from Harry Hopkins. Hopkins demurred. He said he couldn't humor every old lady who wanted a million dollars. The Governor reminded him that Aunt Marie's brother was Speaker of the House, another brother one of the ranking members of the Senate's Appropriation Committee. Hopkins saw the light. Aunt Marie got her million.

So busy was Aunt Marie with official duties she didn't have a chance to see me act until I impersonated Cleopatra in Shakespeare's salute to that minx. When the critics flayed me, she gave me a pep talk: "Those jackasses! Those jackasses! Don't pay any attention to what they say. You go down to that theater tonight and give the best performance of your life. Remember how your grandfather acted when Hobson defeated him for Congress?"

When I was luxuriating in *The Little Foxes* in '39, Aunt Marie saw me act for the second time. I was riding high and Aunt Marie rejoiced. I showed her the town. Headed back to Jasper two weeks later, she said, "I've seen Tallulah in *The Little Foxes*, I've seen the World's Fair, and I've seen a fight at the Stork Club. Now I can go home and tell them I've seen everything."

Aunt Marie has lived for more than fifty years in that house in Montgomery where I spent so many happy days. Only four years ago she paid off the mortgage. Up to a few years ago she commuted to her little farm at Wetumka in a rattletrap car, held together with paper clips and rubber bands. One day she was rammed by a truck, went to the hospital with a split tongue and a broken kneecap. Muted by the accident, she motioned to an attendant for pencil and paper. "To hell with the kneecap, Doctor," she wrote, "but a Bankhead without a tongue is no good to the State of Alabama."

It was from Aunt Marie that I learned of the early education of her brothers, Daddy, Uncle John and Uncle Henry. Their tutor was Old Jenkins. Old Jenkins had quite a history. The legend ran that he was a Carolina blueblood who had fled Charleston after drilling a neighbor with his pistol. In his wanderings this well-heeled fugitive met and married an Indian squaw. He found life in a blanket satisfying, didn't return to Charleston until word reached him that his father had died. If he wanted to share in the loot left by his old man he'd better come home.

Telling his squaw he'd be back in three moons, he canoed away to collect. The law's delay upended him. It was six months before he got back to the reservation. The chief told him his wife had died of a broken heart. Whereupon our homicidal brave went back to

35 ·

Charleston to brood. He was still brooding, when he read an advertisement Granddaddy had inserted in the newspaper. Granddaddy sought an engineer to operate his sawmill at Fayette. The morose widower took the job, but upset Granddaddy because he refused to eat at the same table with the family. When addressed, he grunted in Indian fashion.

Taciturn, sullen, Old Jenkins had one bent which distinguished him from everyone else in Alabama. He was a subscriber to the London *Times*. He read each of the three-week-old issues to Granddaddy's sons on its arrival. That's why they knew more about Disraeli and Victoria than they did about James G. Blaine and James Garfield back in the early eighties. Old Jenkins must have been the forerunner of those boys who have been making such a good thing of reading Shaw and Dickens to our peasants at $4.80 a seat. He was born too soon.

It's reasonable to think Aunt Marie welcomed adjournments of Congress. She lost no time in getting us back to Jasper, once Granddaddy returned from Washington. There we'd be clapped in Miss Bessie Hawes' Kindergarten. When it collapsed for lack of customers, Daddy persuaded Miss Hawes to live with us. She became my Aunt Bessie.

I was ten, Sister eleven, before we ever got out of Alabama. In 1912 Aunt Louise was living in New York so Sister and I were entered at the Academy of the Sacred Heart up near City College. Now that I've conceded the year of my birth, I'll confirm it with the date: January 31, two years to the day after Mother and Daddy were married. Teddy Roosevelt was in the White House and Leo XIII in the Vatican. It was the year that Mt. Pelée erupted and wiped out the town of Saint-Pierre, Martinique. I cite this calamity that I may add this extension: On seeing me in *Private Lives*, critic John Mason Brown wrote I was "the only volcano ever dressed by Mainbocher."

36.

January 31? That makes me an Aquarian. I've never dug very deep in astrology. I know more about Harz Mountains' canaries than I do about horoscopes even if I did part with fifty dollars to have Evangeline Adams survey my future. According to Evangeline —you'll find it in her book, *Astrology, Your Place in the Sun*— Aquarians are calm, serene, temperate. They're careful of their money. I could have saved Evangeline a lot of embarrassment had I been born three months earlier. That would have made me a Scorpion. As a Scorpion I would have fitted into her astral calculations. Here's what Miss Adams had to say about those rowdies:

Ibsen drew a perfect picture of the Scorpio woman in "Hedda Gabler." The suddenness, violences and exaggerations of her frenzies are totally incomprehensible, not only to her easy-going husband—Hi, there, John— but to the clever man of the world who thinks he has outgeneraled and mastered her. In speech Scorpions are fluent, frank and vehement. They are good conversationalists, insist on being the center of attraction in whatever gatherings they find themselves. In love Scorpio produces the most intensely passionate people of any sign in the zodiac. They are admired and feared. People are violently attracted to them, violently repelled by them.

Isn't that like me? An Aquarian in the skin of a Scorpion. For years critics have been prodding me to play Hedda. Quite a rip, that Norwegian! Just between us, I think Hedda would be my cup of tea.

After a year at Sacred Heart, Sister and I were sent to Mary Baldwin Academy in Staunton, Virginia, where my grandparents could keep an eye on us. Our cousin Marion, Uncle John's eldest daughter, was there, as was the daughter of Senator Carter Glass of Virginia. Weekends we were permitted to visit the home of neighbor Cordell Hull, even ride his Shetland ponies. After a half term at Mary Baldwin, we were transferred to the Convent of the Visitation in Washington, present site of the Mayflower

Hotel. After a term and a half there we were enrolled at the Convent of the Holy Cross. A year later I would be making my last academic stand at Fairmont Seminary, Washington. In all these schools I scuffled with the violin and the piano. I read screen magazines to the exclusion of almost everything else—the sultry lives, the shady pasts of the pantomimists fascinated me. They were my heroines.

Daddy, graduate of two colleges, used to say: "If you know your Bible, Shakespeare, and can shoot craps, you have a liberal education." To me he was a fusion of Santa Claus, Galahad, D'Artagnan and Demosthenes. He was the gallant, the romantic, the poet, above all the actor.

I can still quote yards of verse just from hearing him recite: "Hiawatha," "Little Orphan Annie," "The Spell of the Yukon," Cardinal Wolsey crying out: "had I but served my God with half the zeal I served my King, he would not in my age have left me naked to mine enemies." When he launched into "For God's sake, let us sit upon the ground and tell sad stories of the death of kings" he was Shakespeare's Richard II. His stories of Samson and Delilah, of Desdemona and Othello, were as exciting as *The Perils of Pauline*. He never read the Bible to us. He would tell us Biblical tales in his own words. He believed the whale swallowed Jonah, never wavered in his faith.

It's strange that I can remember so much of the poetry he quoted, the plots he highlighted, when I can't remember a date, a telephone number, an address. I have no sense of direction. I can't tell left from right except politically. Things and places have to be pointed out to me. No blueprint will aid me. When I bought my first car, in London, I had to hire a cab to precede me to my destination. Alone, though littered with instructions, I was helpless.

I learned most of what I know from Daddy. In oral examinations

I could talk my way into the clear, hoodwink the teacher. In written tests I was a washout. My tongue worked faster than my pen. Other solutions have been offered which I will not go into here. No use giving aid and comfort to the enemy.

No Sunday passed in Jasper that Daddy didn't tell us a story from the Bible. He'd reduce us to tears with the ordeal of Lot and his wife, then calm us by promising the story of Job a week hence. When we were at Sacred Heart, one of the nuns derailed us with Dickens' *Tale of Two Cities*. She told it beautifully. When she got to Sidney Carton's " 'Tis a far, far better thing I do," we were sobbing. She had told us the story in installments, and built up such suspense Sister and I could hardly sleep between chapters.

Of the eight schools I attended in ten years I liked Sacred Heart best. Although Sister and I were there but a year, I became fairly fluent in French. I even learned to sew. That's the gospel truth.

That year at Sacred Heart was memorable for another reason. At Christmas Daddy came up to visit us. He brought us presents— little gold watches hitched to elastic wrist bands. But he had a greater treat for us. He took us to see *The Whip*, at the Manhattan Opera House.

The Whip was a blood-and-thunder melodrama in four acts and fourteen scenes imported from London's Drury Lane Theatre. It boiled with villainy and violence. Its plot embraced a twelve-horse race on a treadmill (for the Gold Cup at Newmarket), a Hunt Breakfast embellished by fifteen dogs, an auto smash-up, the Chamber of Horrors at Madame Tussaud's Waxworks, and a train wreck with a locomotive hissing real steam. It boasted a dissolute earl and a wicked marquis, and a heroine whose hand was sought by both knave and hero. It was a tremendous emotional dose for anyone as impressionable and as stage-struck as our heroine.

The curtain hadn't been up five minutes before Sister and I

were on the verge of hysterics. By the end of the first act both of us had wet our pants. Daddy's suggestion that we retire to the ladies' room for treatment was scorned. When the careening car smashed into the bridge at the start of the second act, we became so overwrought Daddy had to hang onto our collars to keep us from tumbling out of the box. At the final curtain I was a wreck, frantic, red-eyed and disheveled. I didn't sleep for two nights running. When I did nod, the treacherous marquis intruded on my dreams. Nothing I had ever seen or heard or read had made such an impact on me.

I've often wondered why Daddy elected *The Whip*. There were politer and gentler plays in New York at the time. Laurette Taylor was playing in *Peg o' My Heart*, and Jane Cowl in *Within the Law*. On the lighter side Elsie Janis and Montgomery and Stone were in a musical show; George Cohan, his father, Jerry, and mother Helen, in *Broadway Jones*. As holiday bait for children, Maude Adams was playing in *Peter Pan* at the Empire.

Why did Daddy scorn Sir James Barrie's whimsy? I suspect *he* wanted to see *The Whip*, revel in its spectacular furies, its scenic wonders, its mob scenes. He may have felt that since I was stage-struck he might as well give me the full dramatic treatment. I was exposed to *The Whip* just short of forty years ago. I've never recovered. Where can you see twelve thoroughbreds racing neck-and-neck on a treadmill? Remember, this was the first play I had ever seen, anywhere!

Later that winter Aunt Louise wangled a special dispensation from the nuns. She took us to a matinee of *The Good Little Devil*. This was a gentle fairy tale, staged and produced by the sainted David Belasco, he of the clerical collar and the hypnotic manner. *The Good Little Devil* lacked the emotional fevers of *The Whip* but it, too, left its mark on me. Although five years would elapse before I would face a New York audience I felt dedicated. Over that span I fretted and fumed. I might survive my martyrdom, but I'd never condone it.

Just for the record, there were two young ladies in the cast of *The Good Little Devil* who later would create quite a commotion on our screens—Mary Pickford and Lillian Gish. They may have been stage-struck, too.

Daddy used to call me Dutch because I was fat. He called Sister Kildee. The bird watchers in the audience will know why. The kildee is a small plover, so named for its plaintive cry. Sister was skinny and sickly. She was the favorite of Daddy and Aunt Marie. I was sickly, too, but got little sympathy because I was so plump. Into six years I crowded whooping cough, measles, pneumonia, the mumps, erysipelas, croup, tonsillitis, even smallpox. All of these focused in my throat and chest. That's one of the reasons for my deep voice. Though Sister's ills couldn't match mine, one of them took a more serious turn. When two she had measles and whooping cough at the same time. Left in a sun-flooded room she became blind. She had to play at night and sleep in the daytime. Finally she was taken off on a pillow to Washington to see Dr. Wilmer, the specialist who later operated on the King of Siam. Dr. Wilmer saved Sister's sight. Sensitive to the dramatic, I envied her that pillow exit.

To deny me anything only inflames my desire. One of my first recollections is of my rage and shame when Daddy took Sister off on a picnic, left me behind. I flung myself on the floor, got purple in the face and screamed blue murder. Grandmother had a solution. She threw a bucket of water in my face. This cooled me off but I was never to forget being left behind. Psychiatrists will now surge to their feet and shout that from this incident flowered my notion that I was unwanted. I deny this, and in terms you'd best be spared. But there's no denying I smoldered for years over this snub.

Daddy didn't always leave me behind. Let me cite my passport to London in 1923. In the blank following "Distinguishing Marks" I wrote "Snakebite." This was the product of a picnic I did go on, along with Sister and a lot of other youngsters. We were looking for dogwood when a whirring noise in the grass fascinated me.

"Look, Daddy, look!" I cried, as I leaned over to find out the cause of the disturbance. Then the rattler fanged me in the thigh. Quick as a flash Daddy snatched off my panties, and sucked the blood from the wound. Subsequently he was quite ill. He had an abrasion in his gums and the poison infected them.

If Sister was the favorite of Daddy and Aunt Marie because of her smallness, her beauty and her illnesses, I was the pet of Grand-daddy and Grandmother. They lavished affection on me, humored me beyond reason, were tolerant of my tantrums. Grandmother, once she had discovered the antidote, was not above sloshing me down when I went berserk. She was no woman to shrink from a remedy once its potency was established.

I've mentioned Sister's beauty. There's no denying that I was the ugly duckling, thanks to my fat and my pimples. Sister was the top Bankhead girl until I got into the theater. She liked to dance and swim and ride. She was an excellent student, I was an indifferent one. Sister was the party girl. I was the homebody. She liked to be up at the crack of dawn. I liked to lie in bed and meditate on the future. I would grow furious when awakened to pin up Sister's hair. I loathed parties. I had a preference for the mirror.

It was Sister who won the *Très Biens* at the Sacred Heart convent, reward for consistent good conduct and good marks which entitled the recipient to wear a blue sash for a month. I could never win a *Très Bien*. My conduct was off-key. When thwarted I re-

sorted to biting, a form of mayhem not encouraged by the nuns.
Sister was mouselike. She copped three *Très Biens* in a row. When
denied a fourth, I was so outraged I picked up an inkwell and
hurled it against the wall.

My best friend at Sacred Heart was Linda Lee Wallace, great
granddaughter of Robert E. Lee. She's the niece of Cole Porter's
wife, if that theatrical interruption doesn't seem too contrived. At
the exercises at the end of the term the more well-behaved girls
wore white veils and carried white lillies. I was an outlaw in the
procession, in a short black veil, and without a lily, the penalty
for misconduct. I felt like an untouchable. We paraded down a
long corridor into the chapel. When I looked up and saw Daddy
and Aunt Louise I broke down and bawled. Daddy went to the
Mother Superior and said, "Sister, I'm sorry. I'm afraid my girls
are a little too young for the Convent."

Though Sister excelled me in school and got along better with
our teachers, I wasn't jealous although we fought constantly. When
I entered Holy Cross Convent, Sister was ill. For the first time I
was on my own. Because of her early blindness we had started
school together, always had been in the same classes.

Daddy accompanied me on my first day at Holy Cross. As he
was about to leave I started to bawl. "Daddy, don't leave me! Don't
leave me, Daddy!" On his departure, I kept right on wailing.

One of the required studies at Holy Cross was Latin. My tears
kept me from concentrating on this baffling tongue. This led to a
lot of confusion. The nuns got the impression that the gerunds
and gerundives caused my tears. My tears were due to separation
from Sister. My squalls had lasted a month when Daddy withdrew
me. He arranged for me to stay with friends until Sister recovered.
I put on ten pounds, thanks to my capacity for popovers, and was
permitted to go to the movies. Then, accompanied by Sister, I went

back to Holy Cross. For the rest of my stay there I shed not a tear, save those born of rage or frustration.

At the University of Alabama Daddy had been president of his class, '93, had won his Phi Beta Kappa key. Once he had his law degree from Georgetown University, he briefly practiced in Huntsville. Then, with two fellow Alabamans, he challenged New York. The trio set up a brokerage office called, oddly enough, The Atlantic Charter. An entry in his Journal, dated January 3, 1898, reads:

My life in New York has been more of a struggle than I have heretofore known. We have had some hard cuffs. We have stood on powder mines, and squeezed through tight places by the score. There have been times in our business when the end of the rope seemed at hand, when the camel's back seemed about to pop . . . and yet, by the grace of God, we have withstood the tempest, still look men fair in the face.

A day later the entry started: "I expect to attend the Wednesday Cotillion tonight at Sherry's," ended with "I doubt whether I shall go to this affair or not. I have no gloves anyhow." After a five-day lapse he resumed his comment with: "After all, I went to the ball. I borrowed $1.50 from my good friend Baer, the cigar man, purchased a pair of gloves . . . , donned my best togs and pranced up to Sherrys."

The Atlantic Charter was in trouble from the jump. The three partners lived in East Fifteenth Street where their shelter cost $3.50 a week, but they had trouble meeting that. Once, desperate and hungry, they hit upon a rewarding ruse. Either Rick or Mose, as Daddy identified his business allies, brought up from Alabama an eighty-year-old Negro, bent and toothless. After rehearsal, they anchored him on a Fifth Avenue corner. Pointing him out to scurrying passersby they'd cry: "Look what those frightful Confederates have done to this sweet old man." Their charge was all the more grotesque since they spoke with sirupy Southern accents. The object of their grief, hat in hand, rarely failed to bag enough coins to enable the quartet to resume eating. In those days Daddy was a frequent visitor to Simpson's, a pawnbroker I later honored with my trade.

As vital to Daddy as food and drink was a forum, a stage, a pulpit. A skilled conversationalist, a born story-teller, a gentleman who rejoiced in rolling sentences and rococo rhetoric, he could have been another Edwin Booth (his profile was not unlike Booth's), another Billy Sunday, another William Jennings Bryan. He might even have been a dramatic critic. His journal has many pithy comments on plays he saw in New York.

After seeing Paul Potter's *The Conquerors* at the Empire in '98 he wrote: "The play will make money because of its advertised risquéness. It will not live in the annals of the Drama." And he had sound notions about acting, and overacting. Of Charles Coqueland, whom he saw in *The Royal Box* he said: "He acted his lines with virility, ease and discretion. He was natural when he should have been, and ranted his heroics decently. A toast to the play-actor who has that art. A plague on your leather-lunger spouters who order a bottle of wine with the same gusto with which they anathematize the villain." A sage observation, that last.

Since Daddy needed a rostrum, he joined Tammany Hall. He was an active campaigner for Robert Van Wyck, candidate for mayor of New York. From cart tails in Chinatown and the Bowery he spoke for Van Wyck, lashed his opponent with Southern scorn.

Then another forum beckoned. An advertisement in a theatrical weekly stated young actors might find employment in a Boston stock company. Daddy applied forthwith, inventing a considerable professional past. To his joy and astonishment, he was told to report for rehearsal. Report he did, first writing Grandmother of his change of base and profession. He had just started to rehearse when he received a letter from Jasper in Grandmother's familiar hand. He knew its contents. He went through what was to be his last stage drill, then crept away to a bench on the Common. He was to tell me years afterward that had it been a warmer day he might have flouted authority, stuck it out. But the chill of winter was in the air, he was broke, and his clothes were thin. He opened Grandmother's letter. As he suspected, she vetoed his theatrical career. "And so I decided 'this little country boy had better go home,'" he told me years later.

He told me, too, that as I had been deranged by *The Whip*, so he had given himself up for lost on seeing *The Count of Monte Cristo* when he came to Washington in 1889 to see the inauguration of Benjamin Harrison. Years later when I was in Washington with a play and Daddy was Speaker of the House, he drove me to the stage door one night. As we parted he said, "Oh, Tallulah, if I had only had one whack at it!"

Do you see why Daddy was my hero? My beau ideal?

Daddy loved to tell of returning to Jasper after succeeding Joseph W. Byrns as Speaker of the House in 1936. The day was made a holiday. The school closed. Everyone was at the station to meet him. An old friend greeted him: "Will, you've always wanted to be met by a brass band. Well, here it is." But it was a conversation between two hillsmen that impressed Daddy most. Said one: "What's going on down here? 'Tain't the Fourth of July! What are all the flags out for? Why all the popcorn and buntin'?" "Ain't you heard?" said the other. "Will Bankhead's come home." "Home?" said the first. "Where the hell's Willie been?"

With Aunt Marie or Aunt Louise clucking over us, with Daddy hustling us from one school to another, Sister and I slithered

46 .

through three convents and Mary Baldwin Seminary, before I entered my last school, Fairmont Seminary in Washington.

My education? Thanks to Daddy's thirst for drama, his devotion to the classics, his preoccupation with poetry and his gifts as a storyteller, he instilled in me a desire to ape him. I developed an itch to read, if not to study. The first book to make an impression on me was Grimm's *Fairy Tales*. I was a sponge for Shakespeare's poetry. It wasn't long before I was spouting "Romeo, Romeo! wherefore art thou, Romeo? . . . Thou knowest the mask of night is on my face; else would a maiden blush" and "Friends, Romans, Countrymen! Lend me your ears. I come to bury Caesar, not to praise him . . ."

I'd like to interrupt this monologue to say I've never had the urge to impersonate Juliet. I'm as fascinated as the next woman with the romance that jarred the Montagues and the Capulets, but I've always thought it a little sacrilegious for a forty-year-old actress to try to carry on like a sixteen-year-old girl. Juliet is a contradiction. In Shakespeare's romantic tragedy she's just a chit of a child. But what chit, what child, knows enough about Shakespeare or his verse, or about acting, to attempt the role at sixteen? Or at twenty-six? Granted great acting skill, long experience, familiarity with the Bard's poetry and meaning, by the time an actress is capable of trying Juliet she's disqualified by the mirror.

I've always felt, familiar as I am with the lusts of my sisters, that they undertake Juliet, once their sun is over the yardarm, because they like to mount that balcony, upstage Romeo, look down on the unfortunate youth from an advantageous height. It's a strategy implicit in Shakespeare's stage directions.

I had my Ernest Dowson moments, too. And my *Madame Bovary* phase. I was a sucker for Rupert Brooke. I ran a temperature over Beaudelaire. Was it André Maurois or one of the Zweigs who so vividly wrote the scene in which John Knox and the aroused Scots at Holyrood screamed up to Mary Stuart's castle window: "Harlot! Harlot! Harlot!"? Her reply still electrifies me: "Pupil of Roussain! Queen of France! Queen of Scotland! Queen of England!"

Daddy not only quoted poetry at the drop of a hat, he wrote it. He recited "Little Breeches" so often I thought he was its author. I could rattle it off in my sleep.

Back in the thirties I had a great crush on Jock Whitney. I was boasting to him of Daddy's poetry, cited among his accomplishments "Little Breeches." "Are you sure your father wrote it?" said Jock. "Positive!" "Want to bet?" "I certainly will bet." "Come with me," said Jock, "I want to show you something." We drove to his boathouse at Manhasset, Long Island. There he took down a book and pointed out "Little Breeches." Alas and alack! The author was John Hay. Was I embarrassed? John Hay had been Abraham Lincoln's secretary. He was the grandfather of John Hay Whitney. John Hay Whitney was Jock. Jock had caught me with my quotes down.

Why, someone may ask, were Sister and I sent to Catholic convents? None of the Bankheads were Catholics. Daddy was a Methodist and a regular churchgoer. He said grace before each meal, frowned when Sister and I giggled. Grandmother was a devout Presbyterian. But every Sunday Sister and I attended services at the little Episcopal chapel set up in a loft over a seed store. We had to climb up rickety stairs, masked in with faded cheesecloth in the interests of dignity. This was on Daddy's insistence. Mother had been an Episcopalian, and in tribute to her memory and wishes he felt we should be raised in her faith.

When it became necessary to send us away to school, Daddy, my aunts and Grandmother, despite their conflicting faiths, agreed that we'd fare best under the care and instructions of the nuns. There were few schools in the South prepared to care for children so young as we were. I suspect, too, that Daddy felt the teaching in the convents would most closely approximate what Mother would have schemed for us, that he was aware of the long affinity of the two faiths.

Daddy had no talent for imposing discipline. That was a woman's work. He bribed us to go to bed with promises of crackerjack and candy. I knew when I incurred his displeasure. Then he would address me as Tallulah rather than Dutch or Sugar.

Even as a child I had a throaty laugh, vibrant and penetrating. On that tonsil trip to Birmingham Daddy took me to the Tutweiler Hotel for lunch. He told me an amusing story, whereupon I let loose a hoarse guffaw. Every head came up, every eye was on me. "Don't laugh so loud, baby," he warned. "Never make yourself conspicuous. It's bad form, bad manners."

Three years ago I had an echo of that warning. In the mail came a letter which read: "Dear Miss Bankhead: In the name of Southern womanhood, can't you do something about that God-awful laugh of yours?"

Daddy loathed profanity. I never heard him curse. His notion of an epithet was jackass. "Never take the name of the Lord in vain," he would say when I would rip out a goddam. I might reply, "I'm sorry, Daddy, but goddam it—" Then he'd laugh.

In my living room there rests my mother's Bible. When he gave it to me, Daddy wrote on the flyleaf: "As a spiritual source at the end of each exacting day may I recommend to you your little mother's favorite, the 103rd Psalm."

While I have never gone to church since I could avoid it without penalty, I have found consolation in: "He will not always chide: neither will he keep *his anger* for ever. He hath not dealt with us after our sins; nor rewarded us according to our iniquities. . . . For he knoweth our frame; he remembereth that we *are dust.*"

49 ·

I saw little of Daddy in the last twenty years of his life. We rarely corresponded. A letter from me is a collector's item. My secretary answers my urgent mail, but a telegram is about the limit of my correspondence. My telephone bills are hair-raising.

Politics and its by-products spiced my childhood. Daddy, Granddaddy and Uncle John were always running for public office. This led to considerable anxiety in election years. A lot of political talk swirled about my ears. I couldn't have been more than six when I started to develop my "Vote for Daddy" smile. There were no treacherous Dixiecrats in those days. The Democratic nomination, no matter how petty the office, was assurance of election. But there was a passel of underprivileged Democrats seeking the nomination for every office on the ticket, state or national. Hadn't Hobson unhorsed Granddaddy? Getting the nomination often necessitated long and bitter campaigning.

Daddy won his first office in 1900 when elected to the State Legislature. From 1901 to 1905 he was city attorney for Huntsville, from 1910 to 1917 served as Solicitor General for the 14th Judicial District. When he sought the Congressional nomination the first time the opposition charged that a man who saw fit to educate his daughters outside the state, and in Catholic convents to boot, could hardly expect rewards. There was still another reason why Daddy was thwarted. It was claimed he was too devoted to the bottle. Although it may dismay some of the Bankheads I must admit the charge, to a degree, was true. It was a lapse he was quick to correct. Through the last twenty-five years of his life Daddy drank sparingly, but he never became a teetotaler.

I loved to charge about with Daddy when he was campaigning. It made me feel important. I would clamber into a buggy with him and drive off to a picnic, a barbecue, a church social or a rally in a schoolhouse. Here he would harangue the voters, point out flaws in his opponents. Daddy pulled out all the stops. He brought into play his oratorical tricks, his fund of funny stories, his sonorous quotations. The campaigns were theatrical, before an ever-changing audience, in ever-changing locales.

Once Daddy went to a small schoolhouse to address fifty farmers. To his dismay only five showed up. "I'll speak to you for only a few minutes, since I have a long schedule . . ." he started. Quickly he realized that to dismiss them so casually would be unprofessional. So he spoke for three hours. Later he told me this had been one of his finest efforts. "Those five men could have elected me," he used to say. "When I left they were my champions, campaigners for Will Bankhead."

Electioneering for Uncle John, a candidate for the nomination for the U.S. Senate, Daddy once got so excited he skidded across the border into Tennessee, there made an hour speech to friendly, if non-voting, aliens.

I'm pleased to think I soaked up Daddy's campaigning integrity. I try to give as good a performance to an empty house as to a first-night throng. Unlike my sire, I've never tossed off a performance in a theater other than the one for which I was scheduled. I've given unscheduled performances, but not in a theater.

For all my involvements with politics and politicians I've never thought of seeking office. Once in London, on the brink of marrying the Count de Bosardi, I told a newspaperman: "My ambition is to reverse the performance of Lady Astor. She is an American woman who got elected to the House of Commons. I will shortly become an Englishwoman through my marriage to Count de Bosardi. Then I will try to capture a seat in the American Congress. This will be possible because I will retain my American citizenship rights." It must have been something I et.

3.

Nibbling at Fame

The Russian Revolution erupted in 1917, thanks to the activities of Mr. Lenin. Daddy took his seat in the House of Representatives. Your author was ransomed from school, intransitive verbs and other befuddlements, and resumed her relationship with the theater, smoldering since *The Whip*.

My reading was to pay off in unsuspected fashion. Moving picture mad, I pored over fan magazines, quivered over the lives of the screen stars. Scouring *Pictureplay* one evening, I was numbed on reading that the magazine was conducting a beauty contest for youngsters. The ten winners were to get screen contracts in New York, at fifty dollars a week. One hasty look in the mirror convinced me I was eligible. Juveniles of both sexes were to be considered from photographs. I didn't have many pictures but that didn't block me. I came up with a chromo which showed me in a high collar, a shovel-shaped hat which concealed my best feature, my hair, a cloak draped about my shoulders. Off it went, special delivery. In my frenzy I forgot to identify myself. Hastily I dispatched a letter, explaining the omission. I kept my strategy to myself, sat back to await my inauguration.

The contest dragged out endlessly. *Pictureplay* was a monthly, and its editors resorted to the ruse of printing pictures of also-rans, to build up suspense. I pounced on each new issue for months. An impetuous type, the delay first annoyed, then angered me. Then my indignation ebbed. I dismissed the whole affair as a hoax, resumed my stewing at Fairmont Seminary.

We were living in an apartment house on Connecticut Avenue. Daddy had one floor, Granddaddy the one above it. One afternoon I capered down to the drugstore for a Coke, found myself facing the new issue of *Pictureplay*. Riffling its pages, I grew taut when I saw the winners were named. Not until I reached the last page did I see my profile. Over it was the caption:

"WHO IS SHE?"

An unidentified candidate, address unknown, was one of the fortunates. Could she properly identify herself she would be certified as one of the elite. I damned near fainted. But I had great recuperative powers. I dashed out of the drugstore, magazine in hand, screaming: "I've won it! I've won it! I'm going on the stage!"

Ricocheting along the street, like a witch who had lost her broom, I streaked for home. Daddy and Grandmother thought I had gone crazy. Once I cooled off to the point of coherency, they were, I think, pleased. At least Daddy was. Daddy, the frustrated actor. Immediately he addressed a letter to the editors, assuring them that the unknown was his daughter.

Their reply further confused an already confused affair. The editors had received fifty letters from parents, swearing the anonymous belle was their daughter. To validate my claim he must submit a duplicate of the controversial picture. The house was ransacked. Shortly my claim was conceded. I never had doubts of the verdict, once Daddy undertook management of the negotiations. My hour had struck.

The Bankheads hadn't loitered while the editors fiddled. The night of the drugstore riot Daddy, Granddaddy and Grandmother met in solemn session. Familiar with my fevers, they conceded that only in the theater might I find an outlet for my savage desires. Daddy was sympathetic. Grandmother, like most Southern women of that day, took a dim view of a girl going off to work. No Southern woman worked unless from necessity.

Daddy's words still ring in my ears. "On a Congressman's salary, I can't afford to send this girl to New York with a chaperone."

Granddaddy was my rescuer. "Stand back, Will. I'm underwriting this child. Let her go on the stage. She's not worth a damn for anything but acting. If she isn't permitted to go she'll brood all her life. If she has talent, perhaps she'll achieve success. If she hasn't, it's best to find out now."

In retrospect, I'm sure they felt that I was without talent. Aside from my tantrums, my moderate skill as a mimic, there was little to inspire the belief that I was fated for the marquees. Daddy was on my side because he did not want me to suffer the disappointment that haunted him.

I arrived in New York under the wing of Aunt Louise. She had been married to Congressman Perry of South Carolina, son of that Governor Perry who foresaw the tragedy of secession, opposed it, but went with Carolina once the war started. He died when her two children were quite young. For a time she operated a girls' seminary at Sans Souci, the governor's mansion in Greenville, which belonged to the Perry family rather than to the state. On its failure she came to live with Granddaddy at Jasper, along with her son, William, and daughter, Louise. Bill died when but eighteen. He had been in love with a beautiful girl, Ola Davis. When Bill died Aunt Louise was grief-torn. She and the family had thought Bill and Ola too young for marriage. Conscience-stricken, Aunt Louise brought Ola to New York with us. She was very attractive and had a lovely singing voice.

Aunt Louise rented a small apartment in West Forty-fifth Street. Almost every evening she dragged us to spiritualist meetings. Although a brilliant woman—she had been a star scholar at what is now Ward Belmont School in Nashville—she was obsessed with the desire to communicate with her son and to get Ola on the stage. She had slight concern with me—thought I was a little tetched in the head.

After a few months Ola went back to Alabama. She had no interest in a career. She only agreed to come to New York on Aunt Louise's insistence. With her departure Aunt Louise felt the apartment was too large for us. She started to look around for a small hotel. By a rare stroke of fortune, she elected the Algonquin.

Neither of us knew that the Algonquin was the most famous theatrical hotel in New York. Operated by Frank Case, it had long been the favored inn of actors, critics, producers and literary folk. The Algonquin Round Table was the informal meeting place of the wits and cynics of the day—Alexander Woollcott, F.P.A., the columnist, Dorothy Parker, Deems Taylor, Marc Connelly, Robert Benchley, Robert E. Sherwood, Laurence Stallings, Harold Ross, late editor of *The New Yorker*, Heywood Broun, Edna Ferber, Peggy Wood, Ruth Hale, Neysa McMein and George S. Kaufman.

It has been said that Aunt Louise elected the Algonquin on learning it was the New York headquarters of Commander Evangeline Booth of the Salvation Army. Whatever the reason her choice was providential. At once I was rubbing elbows with the theater's great and notorious. I'll never forget the first night we walked into the dining room. At various tables were seated Texas

Guinan, the Talmadge Sisters, Laurette Taylor, Douglas Fairbanks. My one fear was that Aunt Louise would move out, once she learned the identity of the guests. She might think the Algonquin a jot disorderly. Proximity to these sophisticates was a challenge. With such old-world boredom as I could muster, I whipped out a cigarette and lit it. Then I cringed. A great voice had barked: "Take that cigarette out of your mouth, you infant." Its owner was the six-foot Jobyna Howland, later one of my closest friends.

My fears about Aunt Louise were groundless. The floor show at the Algonquin at dinner time, when the parade of notables reached its peak, fascinated her as much as it did me. Haven't I said that all the Bankheads leaned to the dramatic? If they couldn't participate in a rodeo they did the next best thing—rejoiced as spectators.

As a winner in *Pictureplay*'s contest I awaited my screen baptism. Agog with excitement through attendance at Broadway plays and observance of the theater's pets at the Algonquin, I was not disturbed by the delay. My one fear was that Aunt Louise might think the venture a waste of time, take me back to Daddy, Washington and oblivion. Her concern with the mediums, with the headliners in the Algonquin, was my salvation. But she did make a token gesture in my behalf.

One day, after I had been properly groomed and ribboned, she took me to the studio of David Belasco, then serving the theater as director, producer and playwright. It was an awesome experience. With his white mane, his clerical collar, his mystic manner, his sense of the theatrical, Belasco was one of the demigods of the day.

I don't know by what ruse Aunt Louise wangled the appointment. The interview was short. In the manner of a priest giving absolution Belasco said: "Let me see your hands." I was a fingernail chewer. When he saw my nails he said, "Ah, temperament!" He was gracious and charming and careful—careful not to say anything that I might interpret as promise of employment.

No sooner were we outside than Aunt Louise said, "Tallulah, wait here a minute. I want to speak to Mr. Belasco alone."

Later an eye witness told me she blackjacked me. "This child has no talent. The family is only humoring her for the moment. There's no need to encourage her," she told Belasco.

Christmas of 1917 brought no change in my status. The screen still seemed remote. Since I boiled with excitement and ambition, I desperately attempted to plot a ruse, create a sensation, that might enable me to cross the line that separated the hopefuls from the professionals. Time was my enemy. Convinced that Mary Pickford's success on the screen was due to her curls, I tried to outcurl her. The strategy was sour. I did manage invitations to a few theater parties. At these, on the slightest cue, I'd toss off one of my imitations, limited in number. Even I couldn't caricature actresses I hadn't seen.

When Aunt Louise had to return to Alabama I felt I was doomed. Daddy came up from Washington. I feared he'd say I'd had my chance, that there was no point in staying longer. But he didn't. He huddled with Frank Case. That gallant gentleman agreed to keep an eye on me. So did Jobyna Howland. Later Mr. Case was to tell his daughter, Margaret, that running the Algonquin and keeping an eye on me was a tough assignment.

In Margaret Case Harriman's *The Vicious Circle*, a gay book about the fey folk who fed and frolicked under her father's roof, she introduced your heroine in this fashion:

"Tallulah was crowding seventeen when she arrived from Alabama, stage-struck, sultry-voiced, and brimming with a roseleaf beauty which she determinedly hid under the then-fashionable mask of white powder, blue eye-shadow, and bee-colored lipstick.

She fondly believed that this made her look like Ethel Barrymore,
who was her idol." (Just for the record, Maggie, it was sixteen I
was crowding.)

I'm glad Maggie Harriman said it first. I was consumed by a
fever to be famous, even infamous. At such parties as I could be
smuggled into by Jobyna Howland or Estelle Winwood—I managed
to create a stir. I was a vivid type, oozing vitality. Though liquor
was yet to scorch my lips, I gave the impression of being high as a
kite, so charged was I with excitement and desire for approval. I
would have jumped off a cliff to gain the praise of the quality folk
I met on these midnight parties.

Estelle Winwood was one of the first actresses I met at the Algonquin. She introduced me to the Barrymores, John and Lionel and
Ethel, to any number of the famous folk then on the New York
stage. Not all of them were devoted to decorum and sobriety but
their heresies made them all the more attractive to me. It was at a
theater party that I met Frank Crowninshield, a gentleman who
never failed to solace and encourage me when the vapors were
upon me.

Mr. Crowninshield was one of the last of the aristocrats. He was
editor of *Vanity Fair*, a monthly dedicated to the pleasure of those
ankle-deep in art, *belles lettres*, music, the ballet, the French im-
pressionists and modernists. He was president of the Coffee House
Club, haven for the elite among the editors, writers, painters and
stage folk deemed to have contributed something to culture and
civilization.

Crownie liked me from the first. He used to rhapsodize over my
ebullience (not a word I toss about in everyday conversation), my
coloring, my slightly tipsy air, my gift for mimicry, my throaty
voice, my scorching eagerness to be a somebody. With him as a
patron I managed more and more parties, thus more and more

meals. I must admit a slight flaw in my appearance. I was a dash pudgy, a touch rolypoly. And my wardrobe was scant.

The first fault was solved without effort on my part. On Aunt Louise's return to Alabama I was given an allowance of fifty dollars a week by Granddaddy. Immediately I proved I would not grow up to be another Beardsley Ruml, or a distaff Keynes. The rent for my room at the Algonquin was twenty-one dollars a week. Completely incapable of doing anything for myself, I engaged a French maid. That splurge nicked me for twenty-five dollars, created a crisis that would have curdled a saner citizen. I was left with four dollars for food, clothes and entertainment. Under an obligatory diet, shortly I was as slender as a sylph, though ravaged by hunger.

I solved this pinch through low animal cunning. With the instinct we all share for survival, I started to forage. At lunch or dinner I'd saunter into the Algonquin dining room with the bravado of a bullfighter, weasel my way around the tables as if looking for a tardy squire. Invariably someone would ask me to sit down for a minute. Just as invariably I'd be sampling the food. Airily I'd say: "That looks good. Let me taste it. I may have some for lunch—or dinner." In an hour I would repeat this deceit three or four times, depart fuller but shameless. The wits of the Round Table christened me "The Great Maw." The habit clings to me, if for different reasons. I still find the food on other people's plates more interesting than my own.

Recently playwright Zoe Akins, whose *Footloose* was to give me my first speaking part in New York, saluted me in *Town and Country* in a piece titled "Happy Birthday, Dear Tallulah." Were I as brazen as when I patrolled the Algonquin I'd quote Zoe's whole article. She says things about me that I, slave to modesty, could never voice.

Wrote Miss Akins:

She was a no good, beautiful, put-upon creature deserving the fair awards. Hers was to be no Cinderella fairy tale. She had neither the patience nor the intention of waiting for opportunity. She was driven by forces of her own stronger than chance. When Tallulah, who looked exactly like a child's dream of a Christmas doll, talked of the theater one noticed an intensity greatly at variance with the cover-girl face. One realized nothing existed for her except the stage. She was obsessed.

Asked to Washington for Christmas with Daddy and Grand-daddy, Grandmother and Sister, I evaded the issue by saying I was about to sign a contract for a new play. This was sheer invention. Back in Washington, I was afraid I'd be trapped into admission of failure.

Two months later I got my toe in the theater, thanks to a letter from Daddy to some nabob in the Shubert office. J. C. Huffman, a director for the Shuberts, needed four young girls—walk-ons—to dress up the stage in *The Squab Farm*. I applied and was named one of the squabs. *The Squab Farm* was a crude attempt to satirize the lunacies of Hollywood, "a garish travesty on life in the movies, all in bad taste," to quote the *New York Times*.

Although programmed, only one critic—the gentleman on the *World*—noticed us. If history is to be served you must read my first, if somewhat oblique citation: "There are three or four young girls in the company who might better be back in the care of their mothers."

A mute child in a flop. That was my beginning.

I was too jumpy to have any notion of the merit of *The Squab Farm*, or its lack of it. From the first rehearsal I was eager to please everyone—the actors, Mr. Huffman, even J. J. Shubert. I was scared stiff. Heretofore I'd always had someone to lean on in an emergency. On my own, I was horribly lonely. The rehearsals were a nightmare. The other girls had experience. The four of us dressed together. When I whistled in the dressing room—a violation of one of the theater's oldest taboos—they damned near lynched me.

I was horribly hurt, cried my heart out. Julie Bruns, one of the featured players, took pity on me, and let me share her dressing room. This further alienated the girls in my class. I must have looked like a gargoyle. So hell-bent was I on looking sophisticated that I made up like Theda Bara, the screen vamp. *The Squab Farm* played three days in New Haven before opening in New York. I still associate the Elms and old Eli with that ordeal.

Shortly I was branded a pariah. On the day the comedy opened in New York one of the newspapers ran a story inspired by the political note of Grandfather, Daddy and Uncle. It was headed: SOCIETY GIRL GOES ON STAGE.

This libel said I had the featured role in *The Squab Farm*, then added that I had shelved the luxuries of society to gamble on a career in the theater.

This was a lot of bilge. I wasn't a society girl and my role in *The Squab Farm* was obscure and wordless. Though none of my doing, the story irked the other members of the company, particularly Alma Tell, the leading lady. Later I was to understand why people of substance and position in the theater are so jealous of their reputations, why they resent the pretenses of upstarts.

Immediately I was aware they thought me guilty of the unpardonable sin—seeking billing far beyond my deserts or experience. Humiliated, I handed in my notice. I felt more lonely than ever. To climax my embarrassment Aunt Louise bounced into town two days after the opening. Illogically she reasoned that her niece had hit the jackpot—at sixteen had scaled the heights. I may have inspired her optimism. In my enthusiasm at getting even so tiny a role I'm afraid I overemphasized the nature of my contribution.

Terrified, I approached one of the girls who had a single line. I pleaded with her to let me speak her line on the night Aunt Louise would be bubbling in the audience. Graciously she consented. When my cue came I was so shriveled with fear I couldn't open my mouth. A nasty little stage wait ensued. The girl who had befriended me was bawled out by the stage manager who thought she had dried up. It's a good thing *The Squab Farm* only lasted four weeks. In the company I was rapidly achieving the status of Typhoid Mary. The closing of *The Squab Farm* meant taps for me, of that I was certain. Even as a pantomimist I was a washout. Shattered, I waited the tolling of the knell.

But, to maim a metaphor, I misread my tea leaves. Though *The Squab Farm* was rated an odious mishap, and my doings in it something less than noteworthy, it had only been shuttered a week when a Mr. Ivan Abramson paged me at the Algonquin. His words were electrifying. He had seen me in the play and thought I had beauty and poise. How would I like to appear in a picture he was about to direct?

Thus did I learn the reactions of a condemned man saved by the Governor's reprieve. A minor, and without an agent, I had to get Daddy's permission. This was forthcoming at once. The picture was *When Men Betray*. It was made in June, within a month of the closing of *The Squab Farm*. For the first time I felt I was on my way. *When Men Betray* was as trifling as it was silent, but employment in it meant I was self-sustaining, in no immediate danger of recall. I don't remember how much I got for the picture. I judged it in terms of satisfaction rather than salary.

When Men Betray enabled me to boast that I had both my stage and my screen christening within a year. Theater bigwigs look more favorably on employed actors than on idle ones. I had just finished *When Men Betray*, when Samuel Goldfish baited me with an offer to appear opposite Tom Moore in *Thirty-a-Week*. Under the name of Samuel Goldwyn, Mr. Goldfish has since scaled the motion picture peaks and, thanks to his scorn for syntax, has dethroned Mrs. Malaprop.

Thirty-a-Week was completed in November of 1918. Identified as one of the screen's leading ladies by you know who, I returned to Washington for the holidays with the assurance of a woman who has swum the channel against a rip tide. I looked upon relatives and friends and other skeptics with genial tolerance.

Sister was cutting quite a swath in Washington. She was about to have her coming-out party. Sister was one of the first girls to wear an Annette Kellerman bathing suit. This green one-piece garment showed her off to great advantage. Alice Roosevelt called Sister "Froggie." Arching off a diving board she was a provocative minx. If I was to participate in Sister's social certification I felt I must have a low-cut evening gown. This hint was not received with applause, so I resorted to a tantrum. No hose being handy, my ruse succeeded.

The first time I wore the gown I was squired by Bobby Carrére, one of the most eligible of Washington beaux. He took me to see Helen Hayes in Barrie's *Dear Brutus*. I was thrilled by Helen's performance—she is about two years older than I—envied her because her mother had permitted her to go on the stage when she was six. She had appeared in one of the Weber and Fields extravaganzas in New York when only eight. A fine example of parental co-operation.

Once in my evening dress I was filled with alarm. By present-day standards it wasn't very daring—cut down only to my wishbone— but I felt absolutely naked. When Bobby urged me to take off my wrap I declined. There was a chill in the theater, I pleaded. I wouldn't even remove my cloak when we went dancing after the theater. This was a scruple I was to overcome.

That evening dress cues me into my first fur coat. In my year at Fairmont I was briefly sidelined by a virus. Daddy sent me off with Aunt Louise to Atlantic City to sniff a little sea air. Aunt Louise bought me a sealskin coat. As I draped it about me my imagination ran riot. I had achieved maturity. At last I was a grown woman, a grown woman trapped in a silly school.

Walking across the lobby to the elevator I was reduced to aspic in brushing against Nora Bayes. Miss Bayes, one of the great entertainers of our time, was playing Atlantic City in vaudeville. I stalked her for the entire week. When she eluded me I'd sit in the lobby awaiting her return. I trailed her in a wheelchair when she took a ride on the boardwalk. I shadowed her between performances, bullied Aunt Louise into giving me money for every matinee. I had first seen Nora Bayes when she and George M. Cohan sang "Over There" at a Liberty Bond drive in Washington. I was so moved I wanted to go out and enlist. Between me and Nora Bayes, Aunt Louise had a pretty rough week at the shore. I guess she thought I was a little mad. She may have been right. The jury is still out.

The holidays came and went, Sister came out, January ebbed, and still no word from New York that producers were clamoring for my services. Suspicion started to chew at me. Was I to be retired on the brink of a career? I started to toss on my cot. Grandmother kept the cold water tap turned on. Then came an incident that went far toward convincing me I was destiny's darling.

In late February 39 East came to Washington for a week's engagement. Written by Rachel Crothers, it was produced by Lee and J. J. Shubert in association with Mary Kirkpatrick. Miss Kirkpatrick was from Alabama. Her brother had been a classmate of Daddy's in college. The Bankheads and the Kirkpatricks were friends of long standing.

Mary called up Grandmother: "I know how stage-struck Tallulah is. Please bring her to the matinee tomorrow. I'm leaving two tickets for you at the box office." Coming home in Grandmother's limousine after the performance I started to wail like a banshee. "I can play that part as well as she can," I keened. "If I'm not permitted to return to the stage I'll kill myself."

The "she" whom I traduced was Constance Binney. My suicide threat impressed no one but because a smoldering Tallulah is far from an ideal companion, Daddy, my aunts, my grandparents, all agreed I should return to the Algonquin, job or no job. Their lives would be more peaceful. So, they hoped, would mine.

I idled through most of the summer. Through the kindness of Lyman Brown I played for two weeks in summer stock in Somerville, Mass., another two weeks in Baltimore. Two years had almost elapsed since I invaded Manhattan, and I had yet to speak a word on its stage. I dreaded every visit of the postman. Hadn't Grandmother stymied Daddy in Boston? She might do as much for me. Grandmother was no one to monkey with, once she'd made up her mind.

One day the awesome Jobyna Howland, then playing in Rachel Crothers' *The Little Journey*, tapped me in the lobby. "They're casting a second company of *39 East*, and I've spoken to Miss Crothers. She's agreed to hear you read for the Constance Binney part. There will be fifteen other girls trying for the role, but I think you might get it. And please, Tallulah, don't make up like a tart. Wear a simple little dress. Look and act your age."

Jobyna briefed me thoroughly on how to behave: "Miss Crothers is a very opinionated person who knows exactly what she wants. Should she stop you after you've read only four or five lines, don't be disappointed. She may have made up her mind that quickly.

Don't waste her time pleading for a second chance if she thumbs you down."

The reading was on a cold, badly lit stage. I was paralyzed with fright. I had never read or had sides in my hands before. Remember, I was mute in *The Squab Farm*, silent on the screen. Skip those stock engagements in Somerville and Baltimore. Just before my ordeal I was upset when a fifteen-year-old girl read for one of the minor roles. She was accompanied by her father who in his fright started off with: "Miss Carruthers . . ." "*Crothers* is the name," the author replied in chilly fashion. I wanted to bawl in sympathy.

In those days I felt stark naked unless I had my hat and gloves on. Handed the part, I was unable to get my gloves off. The sides of the part were typed on flimsy paper. I had difficulty trying to turn the sheets with my gloves half on, half off. I had read only ten or twelve lines when Miss Crothers stopped me. Despite Jobyna's briefing, I felt I had failed. I was certain my fumbling, my quivering voice, had betrayed me. Without further ado I burst into tears. To my astonishment Miss Crothers spoke up: "That's very good indeed. Come to my house Friday evening and you can go over the role with the young man who will play opposite you." Believe it or not, I had started crying at the moment the lines indi-cated emotional upset.

It developed Henry Hull and Constance Binney were to be given long week ends—from Friday night to Tuesday night—instead of vacations. I was to play Miss Binney's role for three performances weekly throughout the month of August. At Miss Crothers' I met the actor who was to play the Hull part. He was a young Southerner named Sidney Blackmer, the same Sidney Black-mer who recently gave such a terrifying performance of the crazed drunkard in *Come Back, Little Sheba*.

After rehearsals Sidney would take me for drives through Central Park in a victoria. With a lilac or a gardenia in my hand, I'd rehearse with him on these jaunts, feeling romantic as all getou⁺ Sidney told me later he had an awful crush on me. A gentleman dedicated to Carolina gallantry he went no further than poetry and kissing my hand. Ah, me!

As the night of our first performance approached, I developed a case of the fantods. There seemed no escape unless the theater burned down. To make matters worse Granddaddy popped up from Hot Springs, and presented me with a platinum wrist watch circled with diamonds. Throughout that first performance I was in a trance. I felt I was acting under water. My blood thundered in my ears. My hands shook. My knees knocked! Granddaddy didn't recognize me until the curtain had been up half an hour. "When is Tallulah coming on?" he kept thinking.

His confusion was understandable. Unconsciously I was imitating Constance Binney down to her slightest gesture, the tricks of her voice, her walk. I was parroting her, in no sense giving a performance of my own. I had completely obliterated Tallulah Bankhead, a feat contrary to my intent.

Granddaddy's wrist watch was to come in handy. When in financial straits it could get me a hundred dollars at Simpson's. When I'd pawn it I'd say defiantly: "Please give it to me in small bills. I've had a taxi waiting quite a while."

Assured of twelve performances in 39 East, and a subsequent tour, I felt I had hit the bull's-eye. Instead I was about to fall down a manhole.

I was getting over my jitters when the amusement world was rocked by the Actors' Strike. The producing managers and the actors were at each other's throats. For years the actors had submitted to all sorts of indignities. Often they were stranded in

67.

remote towns; often they were not paid. They had to undergo weeks of rehearsal without wages, play as many as twelve performances a week without additional salary. The players banded together in the Actors' Equity Association. They asked for a uniform contract for all players with a minimum salary clause.

The producers looked upon actors as silly children, vain, illogical, capricious, even slightly demented. How could artists hope to function in something so plebeian as a union, they jeered. Such a protection might be all right for stage hands, musicians and other craftsmen in the theater. But for actors? The idea was preposterous. So the producers resorted to delaying tactics, to long and fruitless palavers with our representatives. It was their conviction that the players, mercurial and emotionally unstable, could not long maintain their indignation. They could never act in concert, so torn were they with envy and other petty considerations.

The actors threatened to walk out and leave the theaters empty. The producers laughed uproariously. They'd like to see the day actors would walk out of fat-salaried jobs in long-run hits, just to establish the rights of minor players. If they laughed early, they did not laugh last. In mid-August the players walked out. Practically every theater was closed overnight. The fight that followed was bitter and spectacular. Friendships of a lifetime were shattered. Public sympathy was all with the players. The press, for the most part, was on our side.

Actors, who for years had given of their time and talent for this charity and that, now had to provide for their own. With practically the whole craft unemployed, distress was the rule. To raise funds for the needy, Equity benefits were given in which most of the stars of the theater participated.

The Actors' Strike created some astonishing paradoxes. Consider the fix in which George M. Cohan found himself. Mr. Cohan, you

68 .

may remember, was half of the producing firm of Cohan and Harris. He was also a playwright, a dancer, an actor. To which side did he owe allegiance? Mr. Cohan elected to side with the producers, even when the whole membership of the Friars' Club, of which he was Abbott, paraded to his theater to plead with him to support his fellow players. Mr. Cohan's reply was to start a second actors' union, Fidelity—its members contemptuously called "Fidos" by the strikers.

Sidney Blackmer and I had played in 39 East through two week ends when the strike unhorsed us. Being broke and unemployed was my conventional status, so I suffered less than most. I reveled in the revolt. It gave me exceptional opportunities to meet the top-notchers in the theater at benefits.

My attendance at one of these led me into a spectacular piece of folly. Halfway through the exercises there was a recess that our leaders might exhort us to never say die. They stressed the righteousness of our cause. They whaled the daylights out of our common enemy, the producers. This was climaxed by a plea for funds. One famous player after another proceeded to the platform, there pledged a sum in keeping with his bank balance and devotion. Ethel Barrymore gave one thousand dollars, as did her brother, Lionel. Though among those in need, I felt that I would be failing myself, the South and my profession, did I not make a contribution. And there was another consideration. As the martyrs proceeded to the platform they were applauded stormily.

Here was my opportunity. I bounced out of my seat, raced to the stage, certain that every eye was fixed upon me. I whispered to the chairman I was giving one hundred dollars. When this was relayed to the audience there was the customary thunder of applause. My head spun, my eyes moistened. I experienced sensations not unlike those Jeanne d'Arc must have felt when licked by the flames at Rouen. Hadn't I made the supreme sacrifice? I had given something I didn't possess.

When my fever subsided I realized the enormity of my offense. Again I had been victimized by my emotions. Did I welsh on my promise I would be branded a juvenile Judas. Where was I to get the hundred dollars?

In my plight I turned to Granddaddy. I wrote him of the Yankee actors showering out money for the needy. As a daughter of the South, I was agonized because I could not match their contributions. Then I gave the Confederate flag another flourish. I was sure that in my position he would not have done less. The hundred dollars arrived shortly. Along with it came a black-beaded evening dress. One emotionalist had succumbed to another!

The strike was in its third week when I attended my last benefit. I was selling the inevitable souvenir program, wheedling money from every man who passed. Suddenly I became nauseated. Hurriedly I handed my programs to another girl, and staggered out of the theater. The next thing I knew I was being carried down the freight elevator of the Algonquin on a mattress. Following repeated phone calls to my room, Frank Case grew alarmed. He let himself into my room, found me unconscious. When the ambulance arrived the doctor said I was too ill to move. Atop the mattress, I was placed on a stretcher. Even in my delirium my sense of the dramatic intruded. As the mattress and I were wheeled to the street an orderly covered my face with a sheet. Through the fog of pain and loneliness there flickered the thought that I was having a heroine's end. The Almighty had seen fit to take me just as I was to touch fame. In the flush of my youth I was about to pay "the last full measure of devotion."

At St. Elizabeth's it was discovered I had an acute gangrenous appendix, complicated by peritonitis. Being a minor, Daddy's con-

70.

sent was necessary before an operation. He raced up from Washington to find me in a coma, took one look at me and said, "Operate!"

My appendix had burst. I suffered from violent gas pains in my post-operative state. My feet were pulled high over my head. By way of compensation I received the attention I craved. My comrades on the picket lines scurried to my couch with reports on the strike. Granddaddy came up from Washington, only to flee my bedside in tears when I pleaded with him for water, denied by the nurses on the doctor's order. The gentle nuns made a great fuss over me as I lay, pale and interesting, on my bed of pain. I had to stay in St. Elizabeth's for six weeks. When I came out, wan and weak and charged with the conviction that I had all but given my life for a cause, the strike was over.

The actors had routed the enemy. They had proved that for all their bravado and caprice and childishness they had not failed their fellows. I was taken to Daddy's home in Washington to recuperate. There I schemed an evasion. The company of 39 *East*, in which Sidney Blackmer and I were to tour, was to set forth in October. Suddenly I decided that to tour was to court oblivion. Did I leave New York just when I had spoken my first words on its stage, my goose might be cooked. I might spend the rest of my life in Ann Arbors and Springfields and Terre Hautes.

I connived with a Washington doctor for a certificate stating that because of my recent operation it would be dangerous for me to tour. The ballet dance in the second act might lead to complications. This was a whopper. At that moment I was whipping around Washington like a dervish, from one party to another.

It was a cheap trick, shockingly unprofessional. I, who winced at the prospect of not being able to make good my hundred-dollar pledge to the Equity strike, now avoided my obligation to tour. I, who boast that my word is my bond! I, who rage with tooth and claw that my contractual right in the theater be honored! I don't go along with everything with which Polonius belabored Laertes in his blueprint for conduct. But when he said, "This above all: to thine own self be true, and it must follow, as the night the day, thou canst not then be false to any man," he wins my endorsement. What can I say in extenuation? I didn't have all my ethical marbles.

Shortly before, I had read my first critical appraisal. *When Men Betray* had its first New York showing in the spring of 1919. On viewing this curio, Harriett Underhill of The New York *Tribune* had written: "Miss Tallulah Bankhead is new to the screen and she proves the truth of the theory that brains are better than experience." This verdict thrilled and confused me. My elation at being cited by a motion picture critic was tempered by my conviction that brains were the monopoly of politicians and schoolteachers. Why hadn't she said anything about my beauty? Only by indirection did Miss Underhill hint I could act. Why hadn't she talked about my spirit, my rhythm and style and sense of mockery? I wasn't troubled too long. It was the only notice I had. I'd better make the most of it. Brainy, eh? And at seventeen? It's the consensus of both critics and congregation that I operate exclusively on emotion, rarely resort to so primitive a device as thinking. I may have some rebuttal to offer later. Just now a defense would seem a touch stuffy.

The curious may be muttering; "What about your love life, honey chile? If you were as beautiful as your partisans insist, as magnetic as you hint, as provocative and heretic as you boast, why, at seventeen, weren't you head over heels in love, with a queue of blades panting behind you?"

It's a fair question. Burning with ambition, scorched with the desire to please at whatever cost, why hadn't I capitulated to some ardent young man on his promise that surrender would validate my womanhood, endear me to such Bohemians as scorned conventional sex taboos, add both to my sophistication and my experience?

The truth is that while curious, even eager, I was scared, too. My family, without laying undue stress on penalties, had hinted that New York was booby-trapped with enticements for young girls, particularly young girls who sought advancement in so loose a profession as the theater. I had been hedged in with chaperones, with a grandmother and aunts who still looked upon me as a child—as indeed I was. One false step and I might be withdrawn from the tournament.

I am pleased, as you may be disappointed, to say that at seventeen I was a virgin. I certainly didn't look like one. The screen's sirens and seductresses, those vixens whose physical charms and brazen displays reduced strong men to putty, fascinated me. A virgin at seventeen, I was a technical virgin at twenty, when I took to the deep and London. I use the phrase "technical virgin" advisedly. I had my share of necking. More than once I trembled on the brink of compliance. More than one night I lay in my bed rejoicing in thoughts of conquests, the scandal and stir that would erupt did I bring a great warrior or a great poet whimpering to my couch, desolated because I had denied him my favors.

Don't think from this that I had been baited by any barons, that I had been challenged by any knights. I had been pawed in taxi-cabs, even found this agreeable. Faced with the great sacrifice, I retreated at the last split second. Later I was to scrap my scruples, indulge myself in my desires, think no less of myself for giving way to a primitive urge. I was a hedonist, long before I knew what a hedonist was.

Though my virtue may have been intact my flashy deportment, my seeming scorn for convention, my lust for the spotlight, led many a peasant to believe I was a latter-day version of Ninon

73·

d'Enclos or Lola Montez. I didn't help matters by boasting, if cued, that I was "pure as the driven slush."

I heard an echo of this as I lay prostrate in St. Elizabeth's. Hopeful, though horizontal, I was cheered by a visit from Jobyna Howland, my rugged actress friend. The day that I was stricken Joby had been at a cocktail party with some opulent riffraff. The host had stunned her by saying:

"Did you know that Tallulah Bankhead has been thrown out of the Algonquin for sneaking up to an actor's room on the fire escape?"

"That's a goddam lie," snapped the blunt Joby, as she got up and left. "I'll make you eat your words, you scum!"

On the chance she was defending a guilty woman she drove to the Algonquin. "Where's Tallulah?" she asked the clerk. "Haven't you heard? She was taken to the hospital this morning."

Joby would have made a great detective. She questioned everyone in the lobby, eventually came up with the seed of the accusation. A young Russian actress was enchanted by another guest, a brilliant English comedian named Kenneth Douglas. Ardent, but fearful of the wrath of proprietor Case, she had clambered up the fire escape—it was on the outside of the hotel—from her room to his. She had been nabbed just as she was about to score a touchdown.

Joby, a woman of action as well as words, called my slanderer. If he didn't call up everyone who had been at the party and tell them he had defamed me, she would horsewhip him on sight. She would have and he did. An aroused Joby could have terrified Samson, or either of the Shuberts. There was another flaw in the tale, too. I have a paralyzing fear of heights—save when enclosed in an airplane. I could no more have scaled the Algonquin's outer wall than I could have painted the steeple of St. Patrick's. I'm an acrophobe!

A veteran of six stage performances, two silent pictures and some pantomime in *The Squab Farm*, my confidence soared, for reasons that are obscure. Daddy and my grandparents knew nothing of the duplicity by which I escaped the tour in *39 East*. If they had they might have sent me scurrying back to Jasper to resume my meditations before the mirror. After a decent interval, lest friends get suspicious about my rapid recovery, I announced I must return to New York to resume my career. All hands thought it best to humor me. It would be cruel to deny Tallulah this request, Tallulah who had just been brushed by the angel of death, and was making the most of it.

Fortune, fickle wench, played into my hands. I had been loitering about the Algonquin for two weeks—at night I'd mousetrap the doorman at the Empire to exult in Ethel Barrymore in *Déclassée*—when I was tapped for the leading role in *The Hottentot*. I was to play opposite Willie Collier, one of the great comedians of his time, and with Ann Andrews, an experienced and beautiful actress. I'm not quite sure how I got the assignment. But I am not confused about how I lost it.

It was a farce about horse-racing. At its climax I was to grow hysterical as another actor described the running of an off-stage sweepstakes. I never had a chance to get hysterical. Collier, Ann Andrews and Donald Meek dawdled through their roles the first two days of rehearsal. They read seated at a table facing the director. A quick study, as we say in the trade, I was letter-perfect in my part a week before rehearsals started. An eager beaver! In view of the casual approach of the others I hesitated to cast my part aside lest they think me a show-off. Part in my hand, I read badly, suffered occupational pains and disorders. I wanted to get on my feet and root the winner home.

I stifled my impulsiveness. After all, I had the leading feminine role. And I was getting two hundred dollars a week. That was as much as Daddy was making in the House of Representatives. Immediately I had the part I called Daddy to let him in on the good news. In spite of all family doubts I'd come through. That's what *I* thought.

After two days' rehearsal I was knocked flat when the stage manager handed me my notice. It read in part:

Dear Miss Bankhead:
We are very sorry but we don't think that your voice is strong enough for the part.

It was signed by Sam H. Harris. I drained the dregs. What folly had led me to boast to Daddy! How could I explain it to him? This could be the final straw—dismissed for incompetency. In my resentment and shock I felt I must be less an actress than I thought. To cite my voice as a reason, that was the payoff. From the day I was born I could be heard out in left field, even with an unfavorable wind. "For God's sake let's bring her home," I could hear them chant. "The girl can't act anyway. We've spent enough money on her."

The next morning I steeled myself. Unless I wanted to rot in Jasper, I had to act, pronto! Togging myself out in my limited finery I tore to Sam Harris's office. I waved aside the receptionist, by-passed the only occupant of his anteroom, and swept in, unannounced. I engaged in no airy banter, lest my courage ebb.

"Look here, Mr. Harris," I spit out, "you can't do this to me. If my father learns that I've been discharged he'll take me back to Washington and I'll have to suffer through those goddam dinner

76.

parties all season. It's to escape them that I went on the stage in the first place. I insist that you write me a letter saying that you are terribly sorry that I don't think the part good enough for me, and that you hope that you will find something more to my liking. Otherwise you'll be directly responsible for ruining a great career."

Later Mr. Harris told me he was so amused by my ultimatum, so impressed by the anger in my eyes and the insistence in my chin, that he could only humor me, though he had never encountered such a demand before. He even improved on my text. He closed with: "I admire you very much as an actress."

I rifled this letter off to Daddy before he could get any hostile reports. Two days later I received this reply:

My dear child:
Beggars can't be choosers. Whatever you are given you must take. Every little bit of experience counts.

My angry cry stirred something in Sam Harris. A year later he would summon me to appear with another young actress in support of Francine Larrimore in Rachel Crothers' Nice People. The other young actress? Katharine Cornell.

It may add zest to the tale of my raid on Sam Harris, if I identify the occupant of the anteroom whose priority rights I outraged. She was Jane Cowl. I learned of her indignation from Edie Van Cleve, long one of my closest friends. Miss Van Cleve, now a skilled plotter for the Music Corporation of America, was then in Miss Cowl's company. She had accompanied the star to Mr. Harris's office, had waited below in Jane's limousine while that great lady palavered with the producer.

Miss Van Cleve had noticed my entrance to the building, my subsequent departure. Idly she speculated on what was delaying Jane. She was soon to find out.

"Did you see that girl come out?" said Miss Cowl. "Her face is like an evil flower. She has a slash of rouge for a mouth. She's so intense she vibrates. She's one of the most violently beautiful women I've ever seen, and she seems completely unconscious of it. But she's doomed. She'll come to no good! I made Sam Harris promise me to get her out of the city before something awful happens to her."

This citation from Jane Cowl, a radiant beauty in her own right, made me purr like a kitten when I heard of it fifteen years later.

Here it's February of 1920, and I'm at liberty again. To steal a line from James Thurber, I had taken a spectacular step, but in the wrong direction.

At such times as you collide with a date in this memoir, don't take it too seriously. Thanks to the theater yearbooks of the late Burns Mantle and his successor, John Chapman, I can establish the time any play of mine opened in New York. Unfortunately Mr. Mantle and Mr. Chapman have not seen fit to include in these works off-stage records of the players involved. Perhaps it's just as well. The postal authorities might grow a little nettled over the juicier escapades of me and my colleagues.

It was about this time that I met John Barrymore. His sister Ethel frequented the Algonquin. I had first encountered Ethel in the Algonquin's elevator. I had to lean against the wall of the car to keep from collapsing, so overpowered was I by her presence. Her imperious manner, the scorn in her voice, the contempt in her eyes, the great reputation in which she was cloaked, made a violent impact on me. When introduced to her by Estelle Winwood, I was struck dumb. In view of my vocal record, what higher proof can I offer of my awe, my devotion?

But to get back to John. One day, dining with sister Ethel, his eye rested on me, snacking from table to table. "Who is that beautiful girl?" he asked Estelle. Whereupon she signaled me. My insides started to do nip-ups. My temples throbbed. My brow grew clammy. To be seated at the table with two Barrymores was an emotional experience beyond my capacity.

John Barrymore had yet to immortalize himself in *Hamlet*, but even then he was something beyond the pale. Successively in *The Fortune Hunter, Kick In,* Galsworthy's *Justice, Peter Ibbetson* and *Redemption,* he had established himself as a brilliant young actor. The late Arthur Hopkins was to tell me years later that Jack could have been the greatest actor of all time had he any respect for acting. He had only contempt for it. Jack lost all interest in a play, in his role, once he had given his first performance in New York.

It wasn't for his acting skill alone that John was famous or notorious. Handsome as a Greek god, with a profile to challenge the sculptor's chisel, his effect upon women was shocking. With some notable exceptions most of them would have hurdled a twenty-foot chasm at his beck. Given to extraordinary excesses of conduct, rakish in dress and manner, breaker of all the rules, he was the contemptuous conqueror, the outrageous brigand, to whom the girls paid homage. Homage? What a euphemism!

I elected to pay my homage from afar, although as addled as the next girl when in the same room with him. His visits to the Algonquin became more frequent. "And he isn't coming here just to see Ethel," said my spy. I was flattered and terrified. Looking at him across the lobby I was stabbed with a mixture of pain and promise. Occasionally I wasted this amalgam on the wrong man. At that time the ballroom dancing team of Hyson and Dixon were almost as popular as had been the Vernon Castles. Carl Hyson lived at the Algonquin, and from the rear he looked astonishingly like Jack. More than once I was chagrined to find I had waxed oozy through proximity to the dancer.

To slash through all this emotional underbrush, Barrymore sent me a note asking me to see him in his dressing room at the Plymouth after a matinee. He was playing in *The Jest* with brother Lionel.

Outwardly calm, inwardly queasy, I mounted the steps to the dressing room, which later was to shelter me in *Dark Victory, The Skin of Our Teeth, Private Lives* and *The Eagle Has Two Heads.* Were the Barrymore intentions professional or carnal? That was the question! I tottered at his first suggestion. He was about to start on a motion picture—*Dr. Jekyll and Mr. Hyde.* It would be made in New York at such moments as he was not in *The Jest.* How would I like to be his leading lady?

Some defiant influence prompted me to a delaying tactic. I wasn't interested in the screen, I said. I wanted to make my mark on the stage. Until I had—and I was almost strangled by my words—I felt that I must decline his offer, flattered though I was. Jack took this in stride. Then he started to make little animal noises. Freely translated these indicated his desire to shred the seventh commandment! He rose and took my hands in his and started to lead me to a convenient couch. With such dignity as I could simulate under these fiery circumstances, I declined. With difficulty I withstood his pleading, shortly found myself in West Forty-fifth Street, shaken and seared. What a crowded hour! Two propositions had been made to me. But I wasn't up to continuing my pursuit of sophistication to such lengths. A great display of will power, you say? Rot! My animal instinct told me that quick surrender could only cheapen me—in my own eyes. I had no prejudices against informal alliances, provided the contenders were charged with either mutual affection or desire. But I felt no good could come of trying to blend business with pleasure.

Shortly my virtue was again put to the test, or so I hoped.

Willard Mack, author-actor, was about to appear in a play called *The Unknown Woman* under the management of A. H. Woods. Mack was rugged, romantic, swashbuckling. He was another outlaw, a heavy drinker, a scorner of the conventions. When I applied for a role I was told to return that evening to read for him privately.

My fascination with Mack can do with a little explaining. I had first seen him when he was playing with Lenore Ulric in *Tiger Rose*. I became goggle-eyed over his nonchalance, his bravado. There was another reason for my infatuation. He had been married to the tall and graceful Pauline Frederick, one of my schoolgirl idols, and to Marjorie Rambeau, one of the judges in *Pictureplay's* contest. Any man who could qualify for their favors must have gifts over and above those visible to the eye.

At the witching hour of nine I entered the Woods' studio. Mack was gallant and as masterful off-stage as on. This, I felt, was the hour of decision. I read the role through and still he had not been guilty of so much as one sexual sigh—somewhat to my disappointment. He said I had style and personality. Would I care to go out with him for a touch of supper? For all the tremors produced by Mack's presence, I was hungry as usual. Readily I agreed. As he helped me on with my coat he leaned over and touched the back of my neck with his lips. Temple bells pealed in my head. But they pealed prematurely. Mack took me to a Chinese restaurant in Columbus Circle, talked vividly about the theater and himself, then frisked me back to the Algonquin unsullied.

Have I mentioned the scantiness of my wardrobe, the durability of my one black dress? My devotion to this garment became a small scandal in the Algonquin. At the instigation of Alexander Woollcott, a collection was taken up to get me another blanket. When the move was brought to my attention I thanked such wags as were available. My more immediate concern, I said, was a penny. Added to what cash I had it would enable me to take a trolley on whatever errand I was bent.

It was through Alex Woollcott that I won my first citation as a wit. Aware of my concern with the stage, Alex asked me if I would like to attend an opening night performance. Would I? I'd have attended any performance with anyone. The opening was Maeterlinck's *The Burgomaster of Stilemonde*, one of the Belgian's minor inventions. At the end of the first act I turned to my escort to say, "There's less in this than meets the eye."

I wasn't aware I'd said anything devastating, but the next morning the comment was repeated in Woollcott's review in the *Times*. It was attributed to "the beautiful young woman who accompanied me." This item gave me considerable prestige among those jesters who took such delight in ridicule of their peers, even their betters. Shortly I received another opening night bid from George S. Kaufman, second-string cynic on the *Times*. I failed to meet the challenge. I didn't get a second. Since this is supposed to be a frank and open review of my life it is only fair to say that most of the wisecracks I have mothered have been accidental quips.

So long as I have dragged Alexander Woollcott into this saga I may as well voice my opinion of him. It isn't high. He was vindictive, shockingly petty in a feminine fashion, given to excesses when expressing his preferences or his prejudices. He probably endorsed more second-rate books than any man of his time. To him the acting nobility was confined to Minnie Maddern Fiske and Harpo Marx. In condemnation of a play or an actor he could be downright vicious. Like your historian, Mr. W. was an emotionalist who rarely succumbed to the chill demands of logic. Woollcott was less a critic than an amusing hysteric.

When I detoured to reveal the details of my phantom seductions, I had just been sacked from *The Hottentot*. My confidence was

82.

shaken. So, too, was my budget. I was two weeks in arrears at the Algonquin. I had nothing left to pawn. Promise of employment seemed remote. In my role of raffish waif I solved this crisis by taking refuge with Uncle Henry on Governor's Island, in New York harbor.

Uncle Henry was the youngest of the five Bankhead children. Today he's living in Miami Beach, bright as a button at the age of seventy-five. He was in the class of 1897 at the University of Alabama. Uncle Henry, unlike his brothers, scorned both the law and politics. In 1898 he resigned as Granddaddy's secretary in Washington to enlist in the army for the war with Spain.

Both as a niece and a memorist I have reason to be grateful to Uncle Henry. When I addressed him in the summer of 1951 to say that I would like a refresher on his background, Uncle Henry replied at length and in the third person. I can't improve on that reply. The next typewriter you'll hear will be his:

Congress authorized the raising of ten volunteer regiments in the Gulf states, in addition to the National Guard. One of these regiments, the Fifth Volunteer Infantry, was assigned to Alabama and Mississippi. These ten regiments were called Immune Regiments, because the intent was to fill them with men who had had yellow fever. Very few of them met with these requirements. The Fifth Volunteers was being organized at Columbus, Mississippi. After enlistment Uncle Henry proceeded there to offer himself for duty. He aspired to be a Captain as his father had been before him in the War between the States.

Uncle Henry being only twenty-one, the Regimental Commander had some doubts about him being qualified for a captaincy. To overcome these doubts Uncle Henry told him that he had had a lot of military experience at the University of Alabama. What he did not tell the Colonel was that the highest rank he had enjoyed there was that of Corporal, and that he had been reduced to the grade of Private for cutting the church formation and going fishing on Sunday.

The Colonel told Uncle Henry that if he could recruit seventy-two men he would be commissioned a Captain. Recruiting for this Volunteer regiment was in competition with the National Guard and men were hard to get. Uncle Henry went to Jasper, Alabama, the family home, and submitted his problem to brother John. John, being resourceful and having some political connections, suggested to the Sheriff and Probate Judge that the eight young men in the County jail be turned over to Uncle Henry for service in the Army. These officials agreed and Uncle Henry was the proud possessor of his first recruits.

Uncle Henry got about fifty men to camp, but they soon began to desert on him as they could not be sworn into service until the full complement were in camp. Uncle Henry had to cease his recruiting in the field and go back to Columbus to sit on these men to keep them from going home. Two other Captains who were having the same difficulty, went to St. Louis and Chicago, and in about ten days returned to camp with two hundred men. They filled their quotas and then sold the other candidates for five dollars a head. Uncle Henry bid in twenty of them, thus won his Captaincy.

Quite a lad, Uncle Henry! He remained in the Army until 1922 when, after twenty-four years of service, he retired. He served in Cuba, in the Philippines with the elder MacArthur as a major of scouts. In World War I he was made a colonel, assigned to the 81st Division as quartermaster. He was quartermaster with the Second Army Corps at the time of the armistice. He is the only veteran of that fracas to be decorated by Prince Albert of Monaco, the Order of St. Charles. On his return from France Uncle Henry was selected by General Robert Bullard to serve on his staff at Governor's Island. Franklin Roosevelt was to honor Uncle Henry further. In 1933 he appointed him to the Foreign Service. He sent him to the American Embassy in Ottawa, where he served for fifteen years.

With this respite from rent and its embarrassments, I had more time to investigate employment clues. Almost at once things looked

84.

up. *Footloose* was to be the frame for my official New York baptism. You can skip *The Squab Farm*, in which I was mute and inglorious. Skip, too, *39 East* in which I was a four-day fill-in for Constance Binney.

I have other reasons for by-passing *The Squab Farm* and *39 East* for *Footloose*. For the first time I could pick up the morning papers, and read a report on my performance. What did they have to say of the actress who played the tearful widow, Rose de Brissac? Burns Mantle of the *Evening Mail* warmed the cockles of my heart. "A most promising young ingénue who is Tallulah Bankhead, with only a year's stage experience, was able to inject a telling realism into a difficult role," he wrote. It was generous of Mr. Mantle to credit me with a year's experience. Six weeks was the sum of my service.

Zoe Akins, the author of *Footloose,* was riding high. Earlier that year her *Déclassée* had opened at the Empire with Ethel Barrymore as its star. It was a stunning success. I must have seen it, in its entirety or in fragments, fifteen times. I was so enthralled by Ethel that I gave an impersonation of her Lady Helen Haden at every opportunity. It was through one of these demonstrations that I had caught the attention of Miss Akins.

"It wasn't the cleverness or the real feeling of the imitation itself which interested me," Miss Akins said later. "It was her memory. Memory, the Greeks had it, was the mother of the arts, and I have always found it the invariable attribute of high talents. Tallulah had never seen the manuscript of the play; she could only have seen a few performances; yet she knew not only Miss Barrymore's long role almost word for word, but also most of the other parts. She could quote from the play endlessly, and still can."

Footloose was a four-week flop, but it added to my experience. In Emily Stevens it had one of our finest actresses. Association with her, observing her performance, her off-stage conduct, was an education beyond that I could have gained in a drama school. I've never had any truck with drama schools. I doubt they serve any useful end.

Footloose folded for the right reasons, as do most plays. Don't be taken in by the guff that critics are killing the theater. Commonly they sin on the side of enthusiasm. Too often they give their blessing to trash. Miss Akins wasn't responsible for Footloose. Her producer, George Tyler, was fascinated by the French original. He bullied Miss Akins into adapting it, placed it in rehearsal before Zoe had finished the second act.

In it Miss Stevens was the Marquise de Mohrivart, a gal with a shady past who had weaseled her way into the home of Alice Verney that she might luxuriate in respectability for a few weeks. The Marquise was doing fine until Barrato, a Corsican scum, put her to flight through threat of exposure. One hell of a plot, eh? But Emily Stevens was one of the theater's elite. She contributed to the bogus Marquise all her vocal magic, her personal charm, her smoldering personality. To what avail? It went down the drain before you could say Klaw and Erlanger.

Footloose was set up in the Greenwich Village Theater. Its locale, thanks to the state of my finances, made it necessary for me to approach it on the Elevated. This experience gave me a few qualms about life in general. En route to the Greenwich Village I could look into the third-floor living room of the tenements. What I saw was not pleasant. It upset me to know such conditions prevailed in the heart of New York.

I was queasy the first day of rehearsals. I remember thinking: "Oh, God! Will there ever come a day when I'll be able to walk in, sit down and read a part, without my nerves snarled, without being sick inside?" I got through rehearsals without collapsing. I was

86.

surprised when Emily Stevens told me not only was she physically ill at rehearsals, but on opening night, and before every performance. This admission should have cheered me up. A contrary hoyden, I felt worse than ever.

Shortly after *Footloose* opened I popped in of a Wednesday afternoon on Ann Andrews, in *The Hottentot*, the farce from which I had been fired by Sam Harris. She took one look at me, then said, "What's happened? It's only three-thirty! Why aren't you at your play?"

I was numbed. I had walked off the stage at the end of the first act, in the belief the play was over. I've done that since, removed my make-up and started to leave the theater halfway through a play. Usually this happens after months in the same role, when I've lost all sense of time, of the words I'm speaking, of the act I'm in. But it was a dash eccentric for a young squirt who professed to be ready to die to get into the theater.

Producer George Tyler had been suspicious of me from the start. He had hired me on Zoe Akins' insistence. Tyler looked upon me as a problem child and my conduct, off-stage and on, did not ease his misgivings. I was driving the stage managers crazy, he told Zoe. I was eating up the properties. In the play Miss Stevens nibbled at some confections provided by the property man. The sight of this unguarded food was too much for me. When no one was looking I'd bolt them down. Tyler even accused me of eating the tops off the second-act candles.

The knell sounded for *Footloose*. I was again a vagrant. I was not to draw another week's salary in eleven months. What did I do in that interval?

I went to Washington for the summer. I sponged on Daddy and Granddaddy. I did what I could to inflate the rumor I was on my way to stardom. What I was on my way to, by any mathematical standards known to man, was oblivion, by way of obscurity. My progress reminded me of the horses in *The Whip*. They raced at the limit of their speed directly toward the audience. But they raced on a treadmill which canceled out their progress.

Daddy, now in the third year in Congress, used to take a house in the country for the spring and summer months—in Georgetown, Arlington or Chevy Chase—"to be near my cardinals and orioles." Tolerant, understanding, sympathetic, I suspect he knew of my ordeals, the result of my nibbles at fame. If he suffered from parental astigmatism, it was because he believed anything easily won is scarce worth winning. Summoned for rehearsal in *Nice People* in April of 1921 it was over three years since first I stormed, if you'll pardon the hyperbole, New York. Over that span I had received eleven weeks' salary. Repeatedly I had been on the edge of extinction. I had dodged and cadged and bluffed my way through any number of predicaments.

My rewards? I was known in a limited set as a vivid young girl who went to great pains to outrage the conventions, a hoarse baggage who impersonated Ethel Barrymore or Emily Stevens to anyone she could tree.

Nice People was by the Rachel Crothers who had misread my tears when I was trying to wriggle into *39 East*. It was produced by Sam Harris. In it I played Hallie Livingston, "twenty-three, beautiful in a large and brilliantly blonde way, who sips her Scotch whisky with a slow and self-centered enjoyment indicative of her general psychology." Katharine Cornell was Eileen Baxter Jones, "dark and piquant, frankly impertinent and wholesomely lovable." "The girls," that would be me and Kit, continued Miss Crothers in her instructions, "are exquisite in their youth and freshness, finely bred young animals of care and health and money—dressed with daring emphasis on the prevailing fashion, startling in their delicate nakedness and sensuous charm."

Provocative, eh? Too bad she didn't graft the stage directions onto the dialogue. The critics would have been vaulting the orchestra pit. Mr. Woollcott, whom I was slurring a few parasangs back, branded the play "an arraignment of the upper classes," then relaxed to say, "there should be a special word of appreciation for the comely and competent Tallulah Bankhead, who luxuriates in a feline role." Could I have been a touch hasty in my judgment of Alex? "Comely and competent, eh?" No hysteria there!

Mr. W. was not content with assaying the play. He also commented on the Klaw Theatre—*Nice People* was its first tenant—in doing so came up with a pun that validated his training at the Algonquin. Brazenly he said that the Klaw was roomy, then added that it was also rheumy, since the cement had not yet dried. So far as I know Adolph Ochs, owner of the *Times*, never reprimanded his employee for this outrage. Men have been keel-hauled for less!

Nice People was no great shakes as a play. How many good plays do you get in a lifetime? Three, if you're one of fortune's pets. Successful plays? That's something else again. The most successful plays are commonly trashy. Merit and success are rarely mated in the theater. For all my belated scorn for *Nice People* it thrilled me. Why shouldn't I have been thrilled? As Hallie Livingston I flouted the conventions, dressed and acted daringly, revealed a considerable fraction of my person. And she was five years my elder, the model of my dreams. There was another reason I should have been grateful to *Nice People*. It gave me employment—consecutive employment—for twenty weeks, doubling all my prior service in the New York theater.

I left *Nice People* before it finished its run. Miss Crothers had written a new play for me: *Everyday*. She let me recess that I might

89.

rest a week before rehearsals. A vacation was hardly what I needed. I hadn't recovered from my recent eleven months' vacation. An imaginative elf, with this gesture I sniffed stardom. But my nose betrayed me.

The critics found *Everyday* something south of Shakespeare or Sheridan. All save Alec Woollcott. "Here is the beauteous Tallulah Bankhead quite justifying her choice for the central role," he wrote in the *Times*. Guess who played my husband? Henry Hull, the same Henry Hull to whom I would be married twenty-four years later in Philip Barry's *Foolish Notion*, one of the most enduring marriages in all theatrical history.

The demise of *Everyday* started me on a chain of vacations. When Kathlene MacDonnell came down with the croup or something I replaced her in *Danger*. Save for this pinch-hit, I was idle until the fall of 1922 when I impersonated Rufus Rand in *The Exciters*, a comedy which belied its title. It succumbed to popular disapproval after five weeks. I'll capsule the plot. Rufus was nineteen, semi-paralyzed because of a motor accident. In a fit of caprice she married a burglar. Want to hear more? I didn't think so.

Percy Hammond identified it as "a delirious charade," then caressed me. "Few actresses can portray more convincingly than Miss Bankhead the difficult part of a pretty girl. 'The Exciters' provides her with several handsome spasms of neuroses," he crooned.

Time out while I play on my abacus. It's November 1, 1922. Four years and eight months have passed since I faced New York's princes and paupers in *The Squab Farm*. I had created four roles. In all save *Nice People* I was a victim of box-office poisoning. My progress was on the snail side. Yet I am proud of that record. Starting from scratch, without experience, without any professional instruction, without friends at court, if you'll ignore Daddy's letter to the Shuberts, I fared pretty well. Frequently wracked with terror and despair, often hungry, often broke, I stuck to my rifles. I had little choice. The alternatives were Washington, Jasper or Montgomery.

I never whimpered or cried aloud. What pangs I suffered in the dark were not inflicted on my friends. I survived through feigned bravado, through the intangible called personality, through determination to conquer or perish.

At the bottom of the pit I sought solace in dramatizing my mischances. I looked about for a proverb on which to lean. Perhaps I was being cleansed by fire. My success would be all the sweeter for the ordeals I suffered in achieving it. A pretty thought, but unnourishing. More soothing, even more rewarding, was my visit to Evangeline Adams, an astrologer on whose visions the elder Pierpont Morgan was wont to bank. Miss Adams told me my future lay across the water. I was about to be paged from afar. In dismissing me she said: "Go if you have to swim." This advice set me back fifty dollars, a sum that beggared me. Once I have my sins behind me, I'll reveal the device by which I added to Evangeline's reputation.

4.

Flirtation with Sin

You've heard, I'm sure, about Tallulah the toper! Tallulah the tosspot! Tallulah, the gal who gets tight as a tick! Let's face it, my dears, I have been tight as a tick! Fried as a mink! Stiff as a goat! But I'm no toper. No tosspot, I. In all my years in the theater I've never missed a performance because of alcoholic wounds. I have never skidded into the footlights through confused vision. No curtain has been prematurely lowered on a play of mine that the litter-bearers might get an emergency workout. That's more than I can say of some of my contemporaries in the higher echelons. I shall not cite these contemporaries here. No use starting a pot-and-kettle controversy.

Before we pursue this delicate subject further it might be wise to define intoxication. If you wake up in bed with your hat on you, it's my guess you may have been addled on retirement. A friend of mine given to overindulgence was horizontal for ten hours in his derby. It was three months before the ring on his brow faded. The hat theory doesn't cover me. I haven't worn one since Daddy's funeral. Joe E. Lewis, the night club cutup, heads another school of thought. It's Joe's conviction you're sober until, lying flat on the floor, you have to hang on to avoid falling.

Frankly, I have contributed a great deal to the carousing phase of my legend. When newspapermen question me on cosmic affairs and other irrelevancies, I ooze hospitality. Knowing their thirsts I'm quick on the bottle. Since I never drink alone, I would be remiss as a hostess did I not drink with them. Consecutive toasts lead to confusion. Most of my interviews reek of vermouth, bourbon and the smoky juice of barley. Whipped into frenzies through association with me and Manhattans simultaneously, my friends compose tales that echo the shore-leave sailors in *South Pacific,* James Barton in his "Mad Dog" specialty, or one of Ernest Hemingway's heroes.

I do not wince at these gentle libels. They're the fruit of collusion. Because of my reputation for rowdiness and scorn of convention, my biographers feel they would be betraying their parishioners, false to their oath, did they paint me cuddled up before a grate fire, a cookie jar on the mantle, Louisa May Alcott's *Little Women* in my lap. And they would!

An actress who submits to interviews—one of the sweet uses of publicity—will get nowhere bellowing she's been misquoted. I've been misquoted often. I was all for suing the newspaper *PM* and one of its feature writers, Robert Rice, son of Elmer Rice, the playwright, for hinting that my consumption was running well ahead of the output of the distilleries. In the end cooler heads prevailed. I'll have at him with my dirk do I ever get him in an alley.

I have been abstemious for long stretches but even deep in self-denial I am suspect. Once a rumor raced up and down Broadway that though I had forsaken intoxicants, I had found an astonishing substitute. By dissolving two aspirin tablets in a beaker of Coca-Cola and draining same down I was stimulated, said my foes, to the extent of four juleps. Had the charge been true I would rate with Pasteur and the discoverer of penicillin in the field of chemistry.

Were such a concoction potent it would wipe out the saloons over night. Utter rubbish!

Let's not quibble! I'm the foe of moderation, the champion of excess. If I may lift a line from a die-hard whose identity is lost in the shuffle, "I'd rather be strongly wrong than weakly right." A congenital emotionalist, restive and wired for sound—I operate on either direct or alternating current—I frequently give the impression I'm awash when I haven't had so much as a snifter. On the edge of a crisis I shun the sauce. The climax behind me, I find drink stimulating. It's a worry-extinguisher that up to three in the morning makes for ease and confidence. At three-fifteen the issue may cloud up. I wouldn't think of tippling before an opening night. Once it is behind me and the decision beyond recall, I'm ready for such wassail as is available.

In any drinker's census you'll not find me in the two-cocktails-before-dinner file. After two cocktails I don't want any dinner, or any lunch. The so-called civilized drinkers who follow this tidy pattern are wrestling with desire and remorse at the same time. Food defeats the very thing for which you took the drink. It smothers the glow which the drink lets loose.

I like to drink best when I'm with challenging, exciting people. If I'm in the dumps liquor depresses me further. Circumstance rules my thirst. A thrilling knockout, a ninth-inning finish, a headline that stabs my spine—these can touch me off. I also find drinking pleasant, if not profitable, when I'm in love. It seems to give zest to my emotions, elevate the reading on my romantic thermometer. I'm not fascinated by the taste of liquor. A frozen daiquiri of a scorching afternoon is soothing. It makes living more tolerable. But, given any option, I'll by-pass Martinis and Scotch highballs, stiff-arm those pink or purple concoctions, equal parts of bilge water, anisette and rum, with which hostesses sabotage a party. Asked to name my poison, out of loyalty to the South and my stomach I'll settle for bourbon. If the auspices are favorable, my host under no fiscal strain, I'll go for champagne, the most inspiring of all the juices. Wracked with a hangover I do my muttering over a Black Velvet, a union of champagne and stout. Don't be swindled into believing there's any cure for a hangover. I've tried them all: iced tomatoes, hot clam juice, brandy punches. Like the common cold it defies solution. Time alone can stay it. The hair of the dog? That way lies folly. It's as logical as trying to put out a fire with applications of kerosene.

When overheated I have a tendency to monopolize attention and conversation. I'm not content with boiling. I boil over! Havoc often ensues. I provoke some of my companions into controversy. Others grab their duffel and, to quote J. Caesar, put safety in flight. Edged, my conversation may be spiced with invectives and profanities, condoned in Hemingway, but not in Homer.

Drink reacts on its practitioners in conflicting ways. One brave can knock off a quart of Scotch and look and act as sober as Herbert Hoover. Another, after three Martinis, makes two-cushion caroms off the chaise longue as he attempts to negotiate the bathroom. One gentleman of my acquaintance bolts upstairs to plough through Proust and James Joyce, after he's latched onto his fourth rum-and-coke. With the same handicap, another sobs his heart out when someone starts to monkey with "Mother Macree" on the piano. As a rule of thumb, liquor sharpens and inflates our natural, if hidden, bent.

Of the mots coined to fit my deportment when on a rampage of good will, the most acid and accurate dropped from the lips of Dorothy Parker. Justly famed for her critiques, her poisonous impeachments of her sex, Dotty Parker is the mistress of the verbal grenade. Miss Parker, after seeing Katharine Hepburn in *The Lake*, wrote of her performance: "She runs the gamut of emotions from A to B." And it was Miss Parker, after swooning through two columns over the imagery and style of James Branch Cabell in *The Silver Stallion,* concluded by saying: "To save my mother from the electric chair, I couldn't read three pages of it."

A party-tosser of talent, Miss Parker touched off a shindig in tribute to Edie Smith, my secretary and confessor, shortly after my escape from Hollywood in the early thirties. To her hutch in the Algonquin she invited assorted wags, cynics and idlers, among them humorists Frank Sullivan and Corey Ford, screen director George Cukor.

Elated that my friend was to be saluted I made the mistake of taking a few nips before I got to the arena. There I added to my content. I distracted the guests with backbends, cartwheels and monologues. Enough of this shillyshallying! I was noisy, tight and obstreperous!

Miss Parker and Edie were in the kitchen setting up refills, when George Cukor, gentleman and diplomat, decided that in the interests of tranquillity I should go home. Through some ruse he tricked me to the street. Shortly after our departure Miss Parker came out of the kitchen, looked about, then said sweetly: "Oh, has Whistler's mother gone?"

It's true that I once pinwheeled for a block on Piccadilly, but it was three o'clock in the morning. The street was bare and silent. I was only answering a taunt of my companion—Prince Nicholas of Roumania. You know those Roumanian princes! Not all of them are on key.

When I came up from Washington to make my mark on Broadway, I had yet to take a drink other than a sip of eggnog at Christmas. I shuttled about quite a bit in my first two years in Manhattan. I lived for a time with Bijou Martin, a young actress. She was the daughter of Ricardo Martin, the opera star. Her mother was in Europe. I was broke. I welcomed the chance to share her apartment in West Fifty-seventh Street—a five-flight walk-up with two bedrooms, living room and a bath. This shelter was an oddity in that all the doors opened into the corridor. The only way to get from one room to another was to prowl that hall.

One afternoon Biji came home with a bottle of port and suggested we sample it.

"Oh, Biji, I couldn't. I promised Daddy I wouldn't take a drink if he let me go on the stage."

"This isn't a drink," she said. "It's only wine. In Europe children drink wine as we drink water."

My resolve sagged. Eventually I'd get Daddy's permission. I must try everything once. "All right! You're my friend and you'll take care of me. I'll see how it affects me," I said.

We had no wine glasses so we used our toothbrush tumblers. Biji and I filled our mugs to the brim and tossed them off. I had no reaction. Disappointed, I said, "Let's try another." A third beaker, and the roof fell in. Both of us were so tight we couldn't walk. We had to crawl through the hall to our bedrooms on our hands and knees. I don't know which was greater, my horror or my surprise. I felt sick, and I *was* sick. The room was spinning like a top. In my agony I heard Biji moaning. I crawled back down the hall. Biji was trying to get into the bathtub. "I want to take a shower," she pleaded. I saw no flaw in this, though she was fully clothed. I put her hat on her head, she clambered into the vat, and I turned on the water. Then I crawled away to die.

We woke the next morning with devastating hangovers—me in bed, Biji on the bathroom floor. There was a note under the door from Biji's father: "I came to take you and Tallulah to dinner tonight and missed you. You must have gone out." Out indeed!

Numbed and nauseated, I was full of remorse. Serves me right for not minding Daddy, I thought. Thereafter when offered a drink at parties, I'd say, "No, thank you. I don't drink. Got any cocaine?" Thus did I start the myth that I was an addict. I talked so much, my manner was so animated, it was not hard to believe I was overstimulated.

That was the sum of my drinking until I sailed for London two years later. Then I got a reprieve. Daddy came up from Washington to wish me Godspeed. General Coleman du Pont, who had served in the Senate with Granddaddy, gave us a dinner party in his suite at the old Waldorf Astoria. I felt important because the guests included General Pershing, Commissioner of Police Enright and my beloved Frank Crowninshield. Dinner over, we were driven to the pier in General du Pont's car. On the gangplank Daddy gave me last-minute advice. "Now, Sugar, I know you're going to be seasick (I used to get sick when he'd take me out fishing on Mobile Bay). When you do, take something simple: cold chicken, tomatoes and a glass of champagne. The champagne can't hurt you! It may help you."

Thus with Daddy's benediction I started my champagne flight in London. Daddy's alarms about my drinking were born of his fear it might be hereditary.

In my first four years in New York I was constantly driven by the desire to appear daring and dashing. I used heavy make-up, slashed my mouth with crimson, touched up my brows. My talent my secret, I could cope with my betters and attract attention through heresies of deportment and conversation.

These ruses more than once defeated me. I hadn't been in New York long when Winthrop Ames announced a production of Maeterlinck's *The Betrothal*. The large cast called for six young girls of my age. When I presented my credentials to Guthrie Mc-

Clintic, Mr. Ames' casting director, I was heavily made up—aping Pauline Frederick, Olga Petrova, Theda Bara and other screen sirens. Guthrie and Mr. Ames decided I was far too mature for the gentle Belgian's play. I had my hair piled on top of my head, in the fashion of Elsie Ferguson, my momentary idol. I affected a slink and a world-weary air. The six girls elected for the play were all older than I was. They were brighter, too.

My "have you any cocaine?" gambit turned up to haunt me. Repeating the line at a party, the host took me at my word. He led me into the bathroom, handed me a paper of glistening crystals. I was shaking in my boots but, after all my boasts, I couldn't back down. I hadn't the faintest notion how to take it, so I said: "You take some first." He took some on the end of a nail file and sniffed it up either nostril. My bluff called, in terror I followed suit. I was sure I'd take off through the air like a rocket. To my surprise I experienced no sensation save that born of another achievement. For weeks I confused my friends by saying at every opportunity: "My dear, cocaine is simply divine." (I'll go into my excessive use of that debatable adjective, later, perhaps under the subhead, "To err is human, to forgive divine.")

Months later when playing in Rachel Crothers' *Nice People* I went to a penthouse party. "Like some cocaine?" said mine host. "Of course," I replied. This time the reaction was different. I didn't get exhilarated, instead had a woozy comfortable feeling. I wanted to sit quietly and smoke my cigarette—very un-Tallulah-like conduct. My escort took me home in the early morning to the apartment I shared with Bijou Martin. I became violently ill in the taxicab. Happily there were few people in the streets at that hour, thus few witnesses to my shame. I was sick all the rest of the morning. The blood vessels in my eyelids turned purple. I couldn't keep a glass of water down.

With the knowledge that I couldn't make the matinee because

of my up-chucking, I was desolated. Terrified, I phoned the theater to say I had ptomaine poisoning from eating spoiled fish. Miss Crothers sent her doctor to me immediately. To my great relief he concurred in my verdict.

My deception confirmed, I resumed my retching, missed the night performance too. Here and now I swear on Equity's constitution and bylaws that those are the only two performances I've missed because of malfeasance. By way of atonement I've played when miserably ill. I've played when every move was agonizing.

Miss Crothers told me later she sent the doctor to me because she suspected my excuse. She felt I was masking some transgression. "We know how young and excitable and spontaneous you are," she explained. "We thought perhaps you'd been out on a party and had been taunted into a drinking bout by unthinking people. I'm sorry we misjudged you."

It was rash escapades like this that later led Mrs. Pat Campbell, acid-tongued English actress, to say: "Tallulah is always skating on thin ice. Everyone wants to be there when it breaks." Now that I've introduced Mrs. Pat I may as well remind you she was the first woman to spit out "bloody" on a London stage. When she loosed it in George Bernard Shaw's *Pygmalion*, she rocked the British Empire. "Bloody" was taboo by the standards of costermonger or commoner.

Shortly I learned the reason for my illness following the penthouse party. I had been given heroin, not cocaine. Cocaine is supposed to exhilarate you, heroin to give you a feeling of ease and relaxation. I've never touched either since, except medicinally. In London, when I had one of my frequent attacks of the actor's nightmare, laryngitis, Sir Milson Reese, the King's doctor, sprayed my throat with a solution laced with cocaine. It stimulated my larynx, relieved strain on my vocal chords, reduced my chances of becoming mute during a performance. At Boots, the London chemists, where I presented the prescription, I was given a bottle of pale little lozenges, labeled "Cocaine and Menthol." Obsessed with the desire to shock people, I whipped the vial out at every opportunity. I'd hold it out to my friends: "Have some cocaine?" "Tallulah, isn't it habit-forming?" "Cocaine habit-forming? Of course not. I ought to know. I've been using it for years."

Because of these blusters it is awkward for me to complain when charged with misconduct. Who started the rumor? Those winds I sowed are still whipping up clouds of dust.

Remember Prince Florizel of Bohemia in Robert Louis Stevenson's *New Arabian Nights?* The Prince, eager for adventure, was so rash as to enroll in The Suicide Club, was damn near bumped off for his pains. There must be a dash of Florizel in me. In London I visited a charming little house in Chelsea, with a top-floor room lined with tinfoil. The habitués called it Silvertown. A quite respectable friend asked me if I'd like to smoke some opium.

Acceptance was obligatory for a *femme fatale.* I was fascinated by the preliminaries, melting the pellets, tamping them into the bowl of the pipe. My imagination running riot, I felt like the daughter of Fu Manchu, Sax Rohmer's malign Chinese. The effects were pleasant and dreamy. The world seemed uncommonly rosy, but not for long.

Fortunately it was Saturday night. Two days before I had laid out fifteen pounds to talk with Daddy on Sunday afternoon by transatlantic telephone. This, too, was an excitement. The only such call made up to that time had been a conversation between Washington and our Embassy in London.

On the way home to my service flat, my escort and I became actively ill. We were so sick that we flung ourselves on my bed and collapsed. There my maid found us in the morning, ashen and wretched. Panicky, I feared that in risking one thrill I had canceled out another—that I would not be able to talk to Daddy. Between spasms I cursed my stupidity. I hoped against hope that through some miracle the call might be delayed. But there were as few miracles then as there are now. Punctually at three the bell tingled and Daddy's voice came through as if he were in the next room.

The conversation which ensued would have given Alexander Graham Bell a turn. It ran like this:

"Hello, Daddy, darling, how are you?"

"I'm fine. How are you?"

"I'm fine. How is Florence?"

"She's fine."

"Well, how's Sister?"

"She's fine. I'll put her on."

I told Sister I was fine, and she verified Daddy's report on her own health. Then it was Florence's turn—Florence was my stepmother—and, believe it or not, she was fine, too. After that we engaged in variations on the same theme, until three minutes and fifteen pounds had been ticked off. Then I collapsed again. Opium? Never again so much as a whiff!

Since I'm in my narcotic phase I might as well let you in on my reefer binge, if a handful of reefers spread over four weeks can be so classified. I was carrying on a lopsided duel with Cleopatra when I first tested marijuana on the cue of a friend who swore reefers were the next thing to ambrosia.

They may have been ambrosia to him, but my first one only brought on a fit of giggles and an overpowering hunger. Hunger is something I can't afford to create artificially, since I'm always either dieting or about to start. At the time I was deep in theosophy, and Madame Blavatsky's *Isis Unveiled* and *Secret Doctrine*. My giggles over, unreliable witnesses report I started to spout poetry of my own coinage. Very good it was, swore those perjurers. What with Cleopatra, back income taxes, a lost love and other considerations too gruesome to set down here, I was very depressed, not to say broke. The reefer consumed, I felt that I had the key to the universe. Never more need I fret and worry. The complexities of my life became crystal clear. For a few moments so vivid seemed my comprehension of the things that conventionally haunt me I felt kinship with God. In retrospect I distrust my emotions. Perhaps it was the spell of Madame Blavatsky. Perhaps I'd fused Poe and his laudanum with me and my reefer. Thus exalted, shortly I repeated the experiment. It didn't come off. I was closer to the pawnbroker than to God.

That is the sum of my trifling. I was a noodlehead to thus flirt with fire! Fortunately my skirmishes with forbidden fumes and philters never created in me any craving, physical or mental, any desire to promote an experience to a practice.

Tippling? That's something else again. I enjoy drinking with friends, even though I know it occasionally leads me to conduct not easy to condone. If, after four snorts I'm convinced I can do the Indian rope trick, the damage is slight. You'll rarely find rope in a liquor closet. Indians? Yes! When I go on the wagon my abstinence is not due to moral scruples. The day that I find liquids jeopardizing my livelihood or my health you'll find an arid Bankhead. I'm not a compulsive drinker. I'll drink what and when I damn well please.

My most notable attack of sobriety began the day the British started to evacuate Dunkirk, while I was playing in *The Little Foxes* in Chicago. That night in my bedroom I dropped to my knees and prayed that through some miracle the British might escape annihilation.

On the theory their deliverance might be effected through the

French artillery, I came into my living room at the Ambassador Hotel, nudged Room Service, and ordered up three French 75s. This drink, served in a tall highball glass, is a blend of champagne, gin, a spot of sugar, a squirt of lemon juice, the whole topped off with a brandy float. Consumed in quantity they can flatten a longshoreman. I drained all three, then weaved to my feet and announced: "As of now I'm on the wagon! And I'm staying on the wagon until the British are back in Dunkirk!"

This provoked the customary snickers. But I meant it. Save when I contracted pneumonia making *Lifeboat* for Alfred Hitchcock in 1943, I stuck to my vow. Then I took whisky on the orders of the studio doctor. High as was my resolve it couldn't match the potency of my legend. Playing in San Francisco, I was outraged to read I had been stoking up on mint juleps in the Omar Khayyam Restaurant. This was the invention of a columnist. He saw me dining with friends, saw them drinking, presumed that I must be. I blasted him to his editor, as a dastard and a poltroon, a disgrace to the name of Winchell. But I got no apology. Column writers, I have found, have delusions of omniscience. Never do you trap one in a retraction.

Why didn't the studio doctor recommend sulfa rather than bourbon? He did. More than once sulfa saved me, but I had evil reactions. Unwittingly I did violate my oath of abstinence. When low I found a dash of spirits of ammonia picked me up. The British were back in Dunkirk before I discovered aromatic spirits of ammonia have an alcoholic content of sixty-five per cent.

The flight from Dunkirk was not my only agonizing day in World War II. Another came in the spring of 1940, when Grover Whalen was wrestling with a World's Fair on the Flushing Meadows. To stimulate a becalmed box office the Fair management dedicated certain days to certain characters—in the hope the peasants would flock to the grounds to gaze upon this hero, that masquerader. I confess I glowed when June 15, 1940, was named "Tallulah Bankhead Day." I rejoiced in the ceremonials, wound up by reviewing the Boy Scouts. That evening I was to be guest of honor at a dinner at the French Pavilion.

Going up to the dining hall the girl elevator operator was in tears. Everyone seemed depressed. I had scarcely been seated when the headwaiter approached me: *"Madame, j'ai peur . . ."* Then my heart broke. I had been honored on the day Paris fell. The world wept.

That summer Daddy died. After the funeral my friend, Dola Cavendish, said: "Tallulah, you need a drink. At a time like this you should not hold yourself to your vow. Circumstances alter all things."

But this seemed the great challenge to my determination. "I'm not going to break it, darling. Of all times, not now!"

Since I'm cataloguing my sins, I must embrace another defect I have long coddled to no profit: Gambling.

Aware the admission may win me the frown of Estes Kefauver and Senator Tobey, I'm fascinated by projects that enable me to get rid of money in a hurry. Sages have told me that gambling is a symbol of insecurity, as is drinking. In my case their theory leaks. My urge to gamble comes and goes like hot flashes. It's an outlet for excessive enthusiasm. Emotionally wrought up, I'll gamble on anything—ball games, fights, dice, *chemin de fer*, fan-tan or the sixth at Pimlico. Challenged by a cocky opponent I'll risk a few farthings to prove I can surpass him spitting at a crack, throwing playing cards into a derby.

With me gambling is a device to endorse my convictions. I'm not the cool calculating type. I never give a second thought to odds, past performances or form. A wishful thinker, I bet on the horse, the team, the fighter I'm rooting for. My bets are symbols of my devotion.

I became a fanatic horse-player in London because of my friendship for Steve Donoghue, greatest of all British jockeys. Didn't he win the Derby at Epsom three times in succession? Steve used to cue me on entering the paddock before a race. Did he think his nag was going to win, he'd hold his crop in his right hand. Convinced his mount was a beetle, in his left. My biggest killing was at Manchester. About to set off on a holiday in the South of France, after a season in *Her Cardboard Lover*, I won seven hundred pounds on a Donoghue tip, but not before I'd almost collapsed. I had backed this steed to win at 4 to 1, but he finished second. I was keening on the lawn when the winner was disqualified, my thoroughbred led into the winner's circle. Even then I didn't know the extent of my coup. It was five times as great as I thought. I didn't distinguish between pounds and dollars.

Two years earlier I had an unholy run of luck at *chemin de fer* at Deauville. I was down to my last fifty pounds when I went there with Sister and her husband, Morton Hoyt, for a week-end holiday. We stayed three weeks and on our departure I still had my fifty pounds, after picking up all the tabs. Our first night in the casino a crusty dowager nodded at me, then said to Sister, "Wouldn't you know that that rich young American in those huge pearls would make a killing?" My pearls were paste, put out by Chanel. Hoyt? He's the one Sister bagged three different times. He was the brother of Elinor Wylie, the poet and novelist.

I get just as much fun out of playing two-bit limit with the stage hands as cashing in on a long shot, and get just as excited. When playing in *The Little Foxes* at the National Theatre in New York, I wasted a lot of sleep playing the match game with newspapermen at Bleeck's saloon around the corner. One night I reduced Stanley

Walker, long famed city editor of the *Herald Tribune*, to bankruptcy with my fey playing.

Since my bets are rooted in emotion, the New York Giants have cost me a pretty penny in the past ten years. They even addled my nest egg when they nosed out the Dodgers in '51. Electrified by their last-minute victory, I bet all my friends they'd pull the rug out from under the Yankees in the World Series—at even money when I could have gotten 11 to 5 at any cigar store.

Here's a rule I recommend. Never practice two vices at once. High as a kite of an early morning in Milwaukee, I invaded a gambling house with Donald Cook. Thanks to excessive optimism I lost all my cash at the roulette table within an hour. But the management was gracious and was only too glad to cash my check for a hundred dollars. I lost that, too. At the end of the month, I was reminded of my folly. The check so rashly cashed had been tilted to a thousand dollars. What's more, my bank had cashed it. And why not? It bore my signature.

5.

Invasion of the British Isles

The *Exciters* had been moldering for six weeks when my nail-biting was interrupted by a cablegram, the first I had ever received. My knees started to buckle before I opened it. The text all but upended me. Dated London, December 10, 1922, it read:

POSSIBILITY ENGAGEMENT WITH GERALD DU MAURIER IN ABOUT EIGHT WEEKS WRITING FULLY CABLE IF FREE.

CHARLES B. COCHRAN

Sir Gerald du Maurier was one of the theater's elite, one of England's most noted actors, directors and producers. He was the son of the George du Maurier who wrote *Trilby* and *Peter Ibbetson*, the sire of the Daphne du Maurier who was to write *Rebecca*. A summons from him was a bugle call from Olympus.

Was I free? Within an hour my reply was singing under the Atlantic. I was also announcing to one and all that shortly I'd be off to London to play with Sir Gerald du Maurier. How I was going to get there was the least of my concerns.

For the next eight days I was fit to be tied. I chafed at Cochran's delay. My friends counseled patience. As well recommend I solve a problem in Euclid! Cochran's letter lies before me. It is one of the few I have ever kept. I can recite it on cue. I have often recited it without cue when three sheets in the wind and touched with nostalgia.

My dear Tallulah,
This is the position.

Sir Gerald du Maurier is producing in about eight weeks' time a new play. The part-authoress tells me that there are two good women parts in it, one an American, the other an English girl. She tells me, and Sir Gerald confirms this, that the American is the better of the two parts. She is, I understand, somewhat of a siren and in one scene has to dance. She must be a lady, and altogether sounds like you. She is, in the play, supposed to be of surpassing beauty. I have told the part-authoress and Sir Gerald that I believe you are "the goods." They are quite excited about you and I think there is little doubt that if you care to take the risk of coming over you will be engaged. In any case your expenses will be paid.

Now as to salary. You will get little more than half of what you have had in New York, if, as I understand, your last salary was $500 a week. In favor of your coming I would say that the management is the best in London for comedy actresses. It is the ambition of every young actress to be with Sir Gerald. Moreover Sir Gerald is the best stage director in this country and Miss Gladys Cooper and several other actresses owe their present positions to his help.

Against the proposition is the salary, the risk that Sir Gerald might think you too young, or in some other way not suitable for the part, or that you might not think the part good enough.

I have put all the facts before you, as I know them, and feel that I can only leave it to you to make a decision. Think it over very carefully, ask the advice of your friends and cable me when you have come to a decision, please. I have no axe to grind other than my desire to see you properly launched here and to do a good turn to my friends, Sir Gerald and the part-authoress.

With kindest regards to yourself, and all our mutual friends, believe me, yours, sincerely, Charles B. Cochran.

To this day I don't know why Cochran was so coy about naming the "part-authoress." She was Viola Tree, daughter of Sir Herbert

Beerbohm Tree, niece of Max Beerbohm, noted author, artist and critic, and a distinguished actress in her own right.

When was I to sail? When did rehearsals start? What was the name of the play? When would I get the money for my passage?

If these questions taunted me, you are probably taunted with questions of your own. Who was Cochran? How, when and where did I meet him? Why did he display such interest in me?

Well Cochran, then, and until his death a few years ago, was one of England's greatest producers and theater operators. His interests were wide and spectacular. He introduced Georges Hackenschmidt, the wrestler, Harry Houdini, the Handcuff King, Eleanora Duse and the Guitrys to London. He had converted the French to roller-skating. What more logical than that he should be fascinated by Tallulah?

It was Cochran's custom to visit New York each autumn in search of new plays, new musicals, new box-office phenomena. I did not fit into any of these categories. Then why did he make such an extravagant gesture in my direction. *Attendez, mes enfants!*

I have been muttering about my skill as a mimic. After four years in New York my repertoire had multiplied. Thanks to frequent attendance at *Déclassée*, my impersonation of Ethel Barrymore was still my *chef d'oeuvre*. I had Gilda Varesi, who played with the Barrymore brothers in *The Jest*, down pat, Italian accent and all. I could do a takeoff on Gilda Gray in her sensational shimmy. I could caricature the vaudeville headliner, Chic Sale.

I first met Cochran at one of Frank Crowninshield's parties, there experienced what cartoonist Webster has called "One of Life's Darkest Moments."

When Crownie asked me to do my impersonation of Miss Barrymore, I needed no urging. Wasn't I singing for my supper? But I wilted when he told me Miss Barrymore was among his guests. "What's more," he said, "she has asked that you do it."

"My God, Crownie, I couldn't do it in front of her," I said. "She scares me stiff. I get weak in the knees when I'm in the same room with her."

Though paralyzed by fright, I could not let Crownie down. He had often befriended me. He had wangled me into many parties. So, though licked by the flames of hell, I gritted my teeth and sailed into it. Miss Barrymore was seated directly in front of me. When I had finished, I went to her and said, "Miss Barrymore, please forgive my impertinence." With that she withered me with a glance—Ethel has no superior as a witherer—and said, "But my dear, you make me look so fat."

There are two versions of what followed. Mine is that in a burst of fear and defiance I blurted out: "But Miss Barrymore, I was imitating *you*." Whereupon she slapped my face. Ethel contradicts this flatly. She says her "you make me look so fat" was to chasten me, since she was slim as a reed, whereas I bulged in awkward places. I prefer to think that Ethel was not as sylphlike as she thinks, that it was me who was on the cornstalk side. I'm never going to take the debate into court. Miss Barrymore has been my friend for thirty-three years. She is still my nominee as the most exciting actress of our time. She still awes me. She still does things to my spine when I confront her.

But to get back to Cochran! He saw my impersonation and liked it. Later I amused him with other items in my gallery. Estelle Winwood and Blythe Daly—both friends of mine—were old friends of his. He'd known them in London. Shortly before returning to London in November, Cochran saw *Rain* at Maxine Elliott's Theatre. In it Jeanne Eagles had scored a sensational success in the role of a gaudy strumpet loose on a South Sea island. Cochran tried to buy the London rights to the play from producer Sam Harris. He thought it would prove the right play to introduce me to London. Harris turned him down. Then Cochran tried to buy the rights

to another New York success, *Seventh Heaven.* Again he was rebuffed. But on sailing he promised he'd keep an eye out for me.
He was sure London would cotton to me. Just how he convinced
Du Maurier to give me this role would have given a more rational
girl pause. All he had to support his enthusiasm was a picture which
showed me off to advantage.

Immediately I read Cochran's letter I phoned Daddy and persuaded him to let me make the trip. Since I was a minor, he had
to cable Cochran his consent. Cochran's second cablegram jellied
me. It read: TERRIBLY SORRY. DU MAURIER'S CHANGED PLANS. My
blood turned to gravy. I didn't have the courage to face my friends
and tell them of this reversal. Curdled, I ran to Estelle Winwood,
cried out my shame and agony.

"Why be upset?" said Estelle. "Go to England anyway. There
are other plays. The moment they see you you'll be offered a part
because your hair is so beautiful."

Estelle solaced me, steeled me. I cabled Cochran:

I'M COMING ANYWAY.

He replied:

DON'T COME. THERE'S A DEPRESSION HERE. IT'S VERY BAD. THERE'S
NOTHING GOING ON. IT'S TOO MUCH OF A RISK. I DON'T WANT TO BE
RESPONSIBLE FOR YOU TAKING THE CHANCE.

Determined to leave on the first boat, I was faced with a problem.
I had no money for my fare. I couldn't confess to Daddy what I
was up to. He would think the venture foolhardy. There was another reason I couldn't tell him. He knew my transportation had
been guaranteed in Cochran's letter. Daddy couldn't spare the
money to send me, even could I win him over to so crackpot a sortie.

Flat broke, I knew I must rake up a thousand dollars. Who did

I know who had a thousand dollars? Who with a thousand dollars would lend me that sum on such spooky security? Ransacking my mind, I finally settled on General Coleman du Pont. General du Pont was very wealthy. He was an old friend of Granddaddy. They had served together in the Senate for seven years.

My approach to General du Pont was awkward. I had never borrowed money before, except at a pawnbroker's. Facing him, I became self-conscious. I hemmed and hawed for fifteen minutes. I couldn't mask my anxiety. He knew at once my problem was money. General du Pont was a delightful old gentleman, devoted to the theater. When I blurted out my dilemma, my fear that Daddy would put a damper on such a rash business, he said: "How much do you want?"

Before I could reply, he added: "You write down what you're going to ask for. I'll write down what I think you should ask for."

He took my slip, read it, then showed me his own. I had written $1,000. He had written $1,500. But he didn't volunteer the difference.

Armed with a letter of credit, I was seized with a new set of fears. What if I didn't find a part in England? My humiliation would be all the greater. By this time I knew Du Maurier had engaged another girl for the role. Once my thousand dollars was gone I'd have to return, disgraced.

My concern was eased, my vapors dissipated, by a note from Frank Crowninshield:

Dear Spirit:

You have been the unseen sugar in my very black coffee, the little threads of red that run through a dull gray Persian rug, Pierrot among a lot of tragic muses. I am too old to seem to you but a figure of fun, but you are not too young to be a rare and companionable spirit.

Aboard ship I picked up amazingly. I was edging up on a role that had long fascinated me—an international adventuress. No sooner had I unpacked my other dress than I wirelessed Cochran. The next day I received his reply: I'LL MEET YOU AT PADDINGTON STATION.

The passage was stormy. Half the time the boat was standing on end, but I never ceased dancing even when the chairs and tables were piled up at one end of the salon. At Southampton my gaiety was smothered. Queued up with the rest of the passengers for customs inspection I hadn't a care in the world. I didn't have a care until a young officer said to me:

"Why are you coming to England?"

That threw me. My passport indicated my profession as "actress." When I said, "Well, I don't know," he replied: "Sit down here until you do know. Have you a contract?" No, I didn't have a contract. "Labor permit?" It was the first time I'd ever heard the term. "Have you any visible means of support?" Out of the queue, isolated from my fellow passengers, I felt every eye was on me. I was sure they thought I had been caught smuggling. But that "Any visible means of support?" snatched me from my coma. "Here's my letter of credit for $1,000," I said.

"Where are you going to stay?"

"I'm going to stay at the Ritz. It's the only hotel I know."

"Well, it's all a little strange," said the officer. "A girl of twenty, traveling alone, and about to live at the Ritz!"

With that he shrugged his shoulders, scribbled something on my manifest, and said: "You will be permitted to stay in England for two months only. Report to the Bow Street Police Station tomorrow." Obviously I was looked upon as a suspicious character, a rating that whipped up my emotions. Here I wasn't off the boat and I had caught the eye of Scotland Yard! I was elated. Another Dick Whittington, come up to conquer London.

True to his word Cochran met me at Paddington Station. That

night I checked in at the Ritz, unsung, unwept and unemployed. It hadn't taken the customs people long to rummage my luggage. I was traveling light. Friends had given me letters of introduction to many theatrical nabobs but I never got around to presenting them. Recently I discovered two of these in an old trunk, unopened. One from Lawrence Langner, dated January 5, 1923, was addressed to director-producer Basil Dean. Wrote Langner: "Miss Bankhead is one of our most talented and important young American actresses. She has made good over here, has a remarkable stage personality, and I think she will make a triumphant success in London."

Reading this note jarred my memory. Wasn't this the same Mr. Langner who sacked me after I had rehearsed two days in *Heartbreak House* in 1920? That's the time I turned atheist. On learning that the Guild was considering me for the role of Ellie Dunn in *Heartbreak House*, I decided to recruit a few allies. I went to St. Patrick's Cathedral. Day after day I burned candles, and said the Stations of the Cross. I pleaded with Captain Ian Hay, noted British writer, to put in a good word for me with Bernard Shaw. Captain Hay had no illusions about his influence with Mr. Shaw. "If I cabled him suggesting you for the role, it would damn your chances forever," he told me.

Someone in the Guild played me a nasty trick. They let me rehearse in the role for two days knowing all the time Elizabeth Risdon had been engaged. I rehearsed only because Miss Risdon was ill. In my humiliation I cried out, "There is no God," denounced all hands indiscriminately. My disbelief was born of hysteria, not conviction. Within a week I had repented, was again on the side of the angels, if not of the Guild. Isn't it ironic that the Langner who endorsed me in 1923, had ambushed me two years before? If I wrong you, Lawrence, stand up and say so. I'll apologize from a stage box.

The day after my arrival Cochran took me to lunch, then sug-

gested we see a matinee performance of *Bulldog Drummond,* which
Sir Gerald had revived at Wyndham's Theatre. We would call on
him in his dressing room after the performance.

Cochran was implicated in my deception. On tenterhooks, I sat
through the matinee, oblivious to everything that was said or done
on the stage, so worked up was I over the prospect of meeting the
gentleman who had started as my saviour, was now my nemesis.

Introduced to Sir Gerald, I said, "Well, here I am."

"But didn't you get my cable telling you not to come?"

"What cable?"

"My dear girl," he replied, "I cabled you I had engaged another
girl for the role, that she was already in rehearsal. I'm terribly sorry.
We're opening in a fortnight, you know."

My rebuttal will never make any anthology of ripostes. "I'm terribly sorry, too," I said. "But I'm happy to be in England. It's been
a great pleasure to meet you—perhaps she'll break a leg."

Cochran, thankful that his part in the hoax had not been revealed, kept me under his eye for the next day or two. He had a
feeling of guilt. He also may have felt that a girl capable of such a
deception might resort to other duplicities.

I think he admired my nerve. In any event he had me home for
dinner with Mrs. Cochran two nights later. Suddenly he said: "You
know, Tallulah, Sir Gerald has never seen you with your hat off.
I don't think he's aware of your unusual beauty. Your hat masks
your extraordinary hair."

Then and there we schemed a return visit to Sir Gerald. Cochran
was a showman with a gambling urge. He looked upon my rejection
as a personal defeat. That night we barged back to the star's dressing
room. I was decked out in my one evening gown, hatless, and, if
you'll forgive the bravado. radiant.

Sir Gerald's daughter, Daphne, was there. After we had paid our respects and departed she turned to her father and said, "Daddy, that's the most beautiful girl I ever saw in my life." So help me, Hannah, she did! I have the testimony of an eyewitness.

The next morning I received a telephone call from a Mr. Vaughn. He was Sir Gerald's business manager. Sir Gerald would like to see me in his office. I was there in a jiffy. Within a half hour I had signed for the role at a wage of thirty pounds a week. The young woman rehearsing in the part had a run-of-the-play contract, drew fifty pounds a week throughout the forty-three-week run of *The Dancers*. My predecessor wasn't too disappointed. She had a new baby, and welcomed the chance to devote all her time to it, and on full salary.

Kismet? Fifty-to-one shot? Call it what you will, my engagement for *The Dancers* convinced me that to achieve your heart's desire you must be prepared to risk all. Shrink from no challenge! Faint heart never filled an inside straight! At the risk of being penalized fifteen yards for a misquotation I'd like to insert "There's a destiny that shapes our ends, rough-hewn though they be." The author is unknown to your diarist. What seemed the most foolhardy venture of the century—born of my pride, my inability to face up to defeat—flowered into rapturous success. It touched off eight triumphant years in London. Since I seem proverb-drunk I may as well toss in another: "Where ignorance is bliss, 'tis folly to be wise."

The Dancers, by any of the standards known to Stanislavsky, Euripides, Brooks Atkinson or Beerbohm Tree, was second-rate melodrama. I played a waif trapped by circumstance in a British Columbia dance hall. There I caught the carnal eye of the proprietor, a young Englishman who had a girl pining for him in London. Informed of his inheritance he wrenched away, leaving me forlorn.

Judge of his dismay, back in Bond Street, to discover his intended was the scandal of the supper clubs, playing fast and loose with an oily gigolo.

Upbraided by him for her fickleness, in a fit of pique she killed herself. Six years later Lord Anthony Chieveley—that's young carnal eye—sought surcease in an odeon on the Champs Élysées, shed his grief on seeing a sensational young ballet dancer. Guess who she was? Tallulah! The toast of the faubourgs!

You should have seen me in the second act. I came on in a beaded buckskin dress, my head sprouting feathers, and went into an Indian dance! Alabama variation of Minnehaha!

The Dancers, for all its maize, provided me with my longest engagement in my first twenty years in the theater. It wasn't until I enrolled in The Little Foxes in 1938 that I could boast of so enduring a play.

At the end of the first act on the opening night I was convinced I was a tragic failure. My last scene was a tender one in which Tony told me he must leave. On my exit, I heard a storm of screams and roars. Terrified, I ran to my dressing room. I didn't have to return to the stage for forty minutes. In that interval I cried my heart out. I was sure that I had flopped, that I had been booed, disgraced.

After the final curtain I learned that what I thought were boos were screams of approval. I'm amused when the English are described as frigid and unemotional. They're the most sentimental people in the world. London audiences are much more demonstrative than New York's. In New York spectators either clap their approval or remain silent. In London they grow vociferous in their appreciation, as they do in their dissents. If they don't like you, or the play, they can let loose boos to freeze your marrow. I was to have proof of this in my second London play, Conchita. The boos would have rocked the walls of Jericho. The author, rather than its heroine, was the target. *Conchita* was one of the all-time clinkers! But Tallulah, darlings, in a Spanish shawl, a black wig topped with one of those two-story combs, castanets clicking, was cited for her conduct under fire.

Woe betide the London actor who gives a confidential performance. If he's inaudible to the gallery, those rugged individualists let him know it. "Speak up," they cry. And he'd better speak up. To incur their enmity is to court disaster.

The cult that was to adopt me as their beau ideal, sprouted when I was playing in *The Dancers*. Over the next six years it reached the proportions of a large and disorderly claque. My followers would queue up at the gallery thirty hours in advance of the first performance, remain there, frozen and famished, until the doors opened. Their antics annoyed the critics, and the spectators in the stalls. It annoyed them all the more because they could not establish the reason for this mass lunacy. Arnold Bennett once tried to explain it. Since his testimony should add a literary tone to these confessions, I welcome the opportunity to give him the floor. The next words you read will be those of the author of *The Old Wives' Tale*.

It begins on the previous afternoon. At 2 p.m., you see girls, girls, girls in seated queues at the pit and gallery door of the Tallulah theatre. They are a mysterious lot, these stalwarts of the cult. Without being penurious, they do not come from Grosvenor Square, nor even Dorset Square. They seem to belong to the ranks of the clerk class. But they cannot be clerks, typists, shop-assistants, *trottins:* for such people don't and can't take a day and a half off whenever their "Tallulah" opens. What manner of girls are they then?

Only a statistical individual enquiry could answer the question. All one can say is that they are bright, youthful, challenging, proud of themselves and apparently happy. It is certain that they boast afterwards to their friends about the number of hours they waited for the thrill of beholding their idol, and that those who have waited the longest become heroines to their envious acquaintances. Of course they do not sit and chatter and munch on those hired camp stools all the afternoon, all night, and all the next day. The queuing system has developed into a highly organized affair, with rules, relays, and a code of honour of its own. But at best, with all allowances made, the business of waiting must be very tedious and very exhausting, and none but the youthful or the insane-fanatical could survive it. Well, they obstinately wait for a century or so, and then the doors are unbolted and there is a rush of frocks. This is the first of the ecstatical moments.

I walk to the theatre one minute before the curtain is advertised to rise. But to get into the sacred fane is a feat. More girls, many more girls, with a few men, are trebly lined up in two groups across the pavement, and quite a number of policemen are urbanely but firmly employed in keeping the two groups apart. I have to force my way through one group and to convince policemen by a glance that I have a ticket. These girls are a little lower than the angels who by this time are already packed into the auditorium. They will not see Tallulah. The next best thing is to see the people who will see Tallulah.

The auditorium is crowded. And the price of seats has been doubled. You could buy a whole library of classics, you could go to the talkies every morning for a week, for the sum which you pay to see Tallulah on a first night. For any ordinary first night, twenty-five percent of the theatre-goers arrive either late, very late, or not at all. To be unpunctual and to disturb the rest of the audience is correct, then. To be punctual is to prove that you are of no account in the world. But for Tallulah everybody is in his seat when the band strikes up. No use pretending that you are superior, haughty, condescending! Because you aren't. You have paid, you feel excited; and you are there on time. Indeed, Tallulah makes you wait.

The play starts. Not a sound, or hardly a sound, of approving welcome. The programme, in which the names of the characters are printed in the order of their appearance, lets you know that Tallulah is not yet. And until she comes the play is reduced to a mere prologue, has no general interest. Tallulah, and nobody and nothing else, is the play. Her entrance is imminent. The next second she will appear. She appears. Ordinary stars get "hands." If Tallulah gets a "hand" it is not heard.

What is heard is a terrific, wild, passionate, hysterical roar and shriek. Only the phrase of the Psalmist can describe it: "God is gone up with a shout." The play stands still. Tallulah stands still. She is a little unnerved, and to be unnerved becomes her. The tumult dies. A number of impatient hiss for silence after there is silence. (And at frequent intervals throughout the performance these exasperating earnest ones continue to hiss for the very silence which their hissing destroys.)

The play resumes. You are startled when, on an exit, an actor gets a "hand," and a good one. Not because he has acted with great technical skill and so saved from derision a part which hovers forever on the edge of the preposterous. Not a bit. He gets a "hand" because he has uttered sentiments which appeal to the democratic heart of gold. For no other reason does a secondary actor get a "hand" at a popular performance.

I have never seen Tallulah in a good play. This play ("The Lady of the Camellias") is not bad. It is merely dead. It is one long demonstration that Dumas *fils* was not a patch on Dumas *père*. The dullness is epical. But no dullness of a play can impair the vogue of Tallulah. At every opportunity, and especially at the ends of the acts, the roars and shrieks recur in fullest volume. Hundreds and hundreds of robust young women are determined that this first night shall be a deafening success and it is. The play is the minor item of the entertainment.

What is Tallulah's secret? If she is beautiful, and she is, her beauty is not classical. How many wayfarers would look twice at her in the street? Her voice is not beautiful. It has, however, the slight seductive huskiness which lent so much enchantment to the acting of Pauline Lord. Her method of delivery is monotonous. Short rise—long fall. Short rise—long fall; endlessly. Rachel seldom understood the words she spoke; Sarah Bernhardt not always; and I doubt if Tallulah always understands hers. Anyhow, she simply threw away many points. Perhaps she could afford to be generous. For she has an exuberant, excessive vitality. She lives. True, she played Marguerite, the converted *cocotte*, with all the demeanour of a virginal soul. But she lived intensely. She never relaxed. Life radiated from her as it invariably does. I have seen Tallulah electrify the most idiotic, puerile plays into some sort of realistic coherence by individual force.

Then the end of the show. The loudest roar and shriek of all. Storms.

Thunder and lightning. Gusts. And Tallulah, still virginal, withstanding everything with a difficult smile. I looked up at the gallery. Scores of lusty girls hanging over the rail and tossing their triumphant manes and gesticulating and screeching. A strange and disturbing sight. I wondered what these girls were in private life, in the prose of the day after. And the speech of thanks. Everybody was thanked; even the limited company which put the play on was thanked. And finally Tallulah steps forward into a new storm and thanks the thanker. God save the King! The Tallulah first night is over.

But yet it is not over. One must positively go 'behind.' The stone stairs are blocked with the initiated and the inquisitive. I reach a landing and see an open door and a dressing room and a hot crowd within and Tallulah in the center. She breaks through the cordon and dashes out onto the landing.

"Are you coming to my party tonight?"

After all the terrible strain of rehearsals, of frock-fitting, of the dress rehearsal, of the first night, of the thunder and lightning and roaring of her reception, this astonishing, exhaustless creature is giving a party! Even now the hour is within a quarter of midnight, and she is still in her paint and her dying white nightgown. A difficult moment, for I am not able to go to her party; I am only able to go to bed. But she is full of tact. I love her. She returns to her worshippers. I fight my way to the stage-door. And lo! Scores and scores of girls waiting with everlasting patience to witness her departure, and Tallulah will have to face them before she goes to her party. They seem quite nice girls, too. And when Tallulah comes out they will block her passage and murmur "Tallulah." Why is Miss Bankhead always called Tallulah? Nobody, except the privileged Hannen Swaffer, speaks of Marie, Gladys, Sybil, Evelyn.

Are you curious about those girls at the tag end of Bennett's last sentence? They're Marie Tempest, Gladys Cooper, Sybil Thorndyke and Evelyn Laye, all enshrined in London stage history.

When Arnold Bennett undertook to parse and analyze my frantic fans I had seven years of London behind me. The fever of my followers had soared progressively and toward the end approached the mark tabbed "critical" by doctors. My champions went in for organized cheering. In their lofty perch they would link arms and sway from side to side, chanting strange hymns.

Psychiatry was yet to come into its own, but practitioners of that dark science would have their hands full with my mob. Surely all of them didn't have frustrated childhoods. Relaxed, they seemed normal, healthy girls. At sight of me they seemed bewitched. Why?

We're all familiar with the commotions Frank Sinatra and other crooners have created in the picture cathedrals. When Jerry Lewis and Dean Martin, two of our most violent clowns, set up show in the Paramount Theatre in New York the management couldn't get one audience out to admit the next. Unless tricked into departure, the first congregation would sit through six consecutive shows.

Remember George Jean Nathan's review of *The Vortex*, the first play in which Noel Coward revealed himself to New York? Nathan devoted most of his space to the audience. They started to cheer before the curtain rose. On Noel's first appearance they shattered the welkin with their applause. When the curtain fell on the first act, swore Nathan, so tumultuous was the cheering that the cast of *Love's Call*, playing two blocks down the street, came out and took two bows.

Would I be immodest to say the Coward clientele, the Sinatra *aficionados*, the Lewis and Martin rooters, are more easily explained than my communicants? Sinatra singing a love song is different than Tallulah coughing herself to death in *Camille*. He stirs a different set of glands or something. Noel's celebrants were white-tie and town-car and utterly utter. The riff and the raff who idolized Lewis and Martin were swept away by slapstick violence.

The delirium of my devotees touched off an epidemic of psychoanalysis among the reviewers. Their conflicting opinions added to the confusion. Hubert Griffith, in the *Evening Standard*, contended that on the stage I was what every woman wanted to be—the dream fulfillment made manifest. My daring and expensive clothes, the opulent drawings rooms and boudoirs I paraded, the dandies I attracted, stirred the frustrations of my pack. Hannen Swaffer, the seer on Beaverbrook's *Express,* jeered at Griffith's verdict. "Tallulah seldom plays a sympathetic part. She is not a stage heroine. She is the essence of sophistication. She gives electric shocks. Sex oozes from her eyes. She is daring and friendly and rude and nice, all at once."

Bravo, Hannen! At long last an expert called me sophisticated in print! A rash fellow that Swaffer. Lillian Foster, an American actress, once slapped his face in the Savoy dining room because he had turned in a sour report on one of her performances. That slap rang 'round the world.

How do I account for the fevers of my partisans. In most all my roles I scorned convention. I was rebellious, as often as not promiscuous. I twirled men about my finger. I'd as soon snub a duke as a cockney. My hoarse laugh, my American accent, the defiant tosses of my mane, the oddity of my given name, all these may have contributed to my worship.

Tantalized by the ferments of my followers, some of the London reviewers said that their frenzy was due to the fact that I was forever undressing on the stage, or smoldering in sheer negligees. The charge was as false as a smuggler's tax return. In only two plays: *The Garden of Eden* and *Her Cardboard Lover,* did I bounce about in anything approaching the buff, the better to agitate my leading man. There was another flaw in this theory. Had I been revealing my charms to excess wouldn't the gender of the crowds at the gallery door been different? The pajamas I wore in *The Gold Diggers* may have been provocative, but Ina Claire was never charged with inciting to riot when she wore their duplicates on creating the role in New York. By current standards of undress, as observed in Park

Avenue or Peekskill, I was bundled up like a temperance worker in most of my West End antics.

The customs man had told me to report to the Bow Street Police Station on my arrival in London. Remember? In the press of events I ignored his warning. In a city of seven million the police must have greater concerns than me. But I reckoned little of British thoroughness. On my third morning at the Ritz—I thought that it was the middle of the night because there was one of those pea-soup fogs —my phone rang.

"Miss Bankhead, there's a policeman downstairs to see you."

The police? Me? What had I done? Violated the Magna Charta? With low cunning I said, "Ask him to come back in half an hour." Immediately I called Cochran at his office. "Charles, there's a policeman waiting in the Ritz lobby for me. What am I going to do? What's it all about?"

Cochran came over on the double. The officer said I was wanted at the Bow Street Station. There the judge was sweet and gentle. "We're always having trouble with you Americans," he said. "What about your labor permit?" Fortunately Sir Gerald engaged me for *The Dancers* the next day. His manager and my contract eased the difficulty.

Assured of long employment in *The Dancers* I went haywire. I began to get delusions of grandeur. Since I appeared only in the first and third acts of the play, I idled for a good forty minutes in my dressing room. But not for long. My new friends, aware of this hiatus, turned my cell into a salon. We made so much noise Sir Gerald had a door built on the stairway sealing off my room. Often these friends would grab me at the end of the first act, drive me off to dinner in my make-up, get me back in time for my third-act triumph. This was very irregular, very unprofessional. I marvel Sir

Gerald tolerated such nonsense. I was ignorant, you see, of stage practice. I'd had so little of it. I should have been ironed.

Here and there in this monologue I have muttered about my hair, my crowning glory. Unbunned, unwrapped, it fell to my knees. I had hairpin trouble, particularly when circumstance or protocol called for a hat. In church, when covered, those hairpins nettled my scalp. Flushed with success, I decided my mop of hair made me top-heavy. On warm nights it suffocated me. I was cued into this discovery by the new hair cut London's smart women were affecting.

Impulsively, I summoned Monsieur Le Barbe—that was his name, believe it or not—asked him to shear me in the interval between the first and third acts. M. Le Barbe came over from Paris every other week to bob the eager and the antic. So I was shingled. On my last act entrance all a-twitter at Sir Gerald's reaction, I was let down. In conformity with stage directions, early in the act I had to let down my knee-long tresses, brush them, then put them up again while the audience gasped. Now I had nothing to let down. But Sir Gerald was oblivious to my treachery. At the end of the play I rushed to his dressing room. I swung my head about. I whipped my mane this way and that. "Look, Sir Gerald." "Well?" he said. It took him a full minute to realize the enormity of my offense. Then he broke into tears. I had ruined the play, he said.

I was to outrage Sir Gerald again. We'd been playing *The Dancers* for six weeks when he decided he needed a two-week vacation. Without ado he recessed and put on his understudy. The play was a capacity hit. His departure didn't dull the box office. But I was furious because I had to play with a lesser actor. I fumed and fussed and made a nuisance of myself.

On his return I went to him: "I'm sorry, Sir Gerald, but I can't live on thirty pounds a week." A little hysterical at my good luck,

126.

I was spending more than I made. In all my time in England I was never able to live on my salary, though it rose to five hundred pounds a week. Sir Gerald raised me to fifty pounds, masking his surprise that so young a player could be so arbitrary.

I was to annoy him further. Still rankled by his two-week desertion, I floored him with a demand that I be given a two-week holiday. This was after the play had been running six months.

My request was shocking. My contract provided for no such pause. For an actor-manager to take two weeks off was one thing. It was one of his prerogatives. For an arrogant upstart to make such a demand was heresy. I compounded my offense by upbraiding him for going off and leaving me with his understudy. What impertinence! "I'll never forgive you if you deny me this," I said. In vain he tried to placate me. He offered to tilt my wage to seventy-five pounds. I scorned mere gain.

Some of my new friends were going to Venice for a holiday. I insisted I must go with them. That was my idea of revenge. I had a recurrence of the pangs I experienced when Daddy denied me the picnic. Hadn't Sir Gerald left me behind when he went off with his golf clubs? A pretty foggy parallel, eh? No rhyme, no reason! The Bankhead gambit!

I was to be paid off in full for my cheek. In Venice we shared a small *palazzo*. I was agog. I'd never set foot on continental Europe—Paris, the Riviera, Rome and Venice were colored postcards to me. On our first day I went out sailing with Sir Francis Laking, a witty young man of cloudy gender of whom I'll have more to say later. As always, I overdid the thing. Though Francis urged a quick return, I insisted on a prolonged ride. The red and orange sails of the distant ships fascinated me. When we did turn back an adverse tide delayed us.

As I stepped out of the boat I collapsed on the sand. Viola Tree and Olga Lynn carried me to a cabana, then summoned a doctor. I had a temperature of 106, and a shocking case of sunburn. That was my first and last day in the sun on my holiday. When not buried under cold compresses I pegged around in the shade on crutches. My flesh sizzled. Every bone in my body ached. Belatedly it dawned on me that this was the fruit of my rebellion.

Chic and I were strangers on my arrival in London. My wardrobe was scant. I sought fame rather than furbelows. Viola Tree was to write later:

When first I saw Tallulah at a rehearsal of "The Dancers" she was a pretty American, a rather raw and somewhat buxom girl. Now she's a slim, thoughtful, almost too vital woman. She had green dowdy clothes and wore a rat's-tail fur when she landed here. But she must stay at the Ritz. She has Ritzed it ever since.

This is typical of her. She earns a larger and larger salary and spends it all. She lives well, gives much to friends and servants. In appearance Tallulah is like a Greek fragment—or, rather, an Egyptian head put on a Greek torso. Her head is a little large for her body, and for this reason she cuts off her immense chevelure of fair waving hair. She now scrapes it back, Garbo-like, from her high forehead.

Her eyes are hieroglyphics, and her eyelashes are as long in reality as Greta Garbo's are artificially. When nervous, she blinks them, which is foolish, but she has no other mannerism—except, perhaps, her voice. Like a cricket, she chirps all day and half the night, and gets hoarse in the process. She has made enormous advances in her art. She is one of the few actresses or (I am sorry to say) actors who read. She is one of the few who praise without qualification a fellow "trier," and she is a great conversationalist, especially when discussing politics.

The inanities and sex-appealing affectations which have been set down as hers have nothing in common with her at all. She is direct to a degree, and, according to herself, "as full of faults as any woman." If I may throw a stone, albeit through a glass window, I would say she gets through life too quickly (she has lived about four lives already in her short one), talks overtime, and was once a bit of a rebel—but maybe "consideration like an angel came."

The sentiments expressed by Viola are her own. She's entitled to them under the democratic process. They do not necessarily reflect the convictions of the author of this journal. I'd been in London six years before Viola parsed me. (She erred in saying Garbo's eyelashes were fake. They're as genuine as Chevalier's lower lip.)

Viola's right! My clothes were on the seedy side when I charged into Paddington Station. I've never been clothes conscious, although I go on clothes-buying binges. In the last ten years I've been content to prowl about in slacks, under a mink coat. Once I'd had my London bearings I had to accept the challenge of the well-dressed women in the after-theater restaurants and the supper clubs. I splurged, well beyond my means you may be sure.

Since a thirty-pound salary was incompatible with the Ritz, and its manager not such a softy as Frank Case, I set myself up in a service flat. Even there I felt I must have a personal maid, in addition to the charwoman who kept the place in some semblance of order. To further complicate matters I bought a pearl necklace to prove to the toffs and my fellow players that I knew the score. What I proved was that I didn't know the score. Eager to drive my own car, I hocked the pearls to buy a Talbot coupé, sold it after six months that I might redeem the pearls. Five years later I would go completely off my rocker, lay out twenty-four hundred pounds for a Bentley, dark green and cream, hood, fenders and body sheathed in leather.

My financial sense was at such a low ebb I didn't distinguish between dollars and pounds. The pound hadn't shriveled then. I was paying about five times as much as I thought I was. I was in England four years before I learned I was supposed to pay income tax.

A month after *The Dancers* closed, I had to borrow fifty pounds from Golding Bright, a playbroker. He was a sweet old man who seemed to have a cigarette sewed to his lip. It was months before I was able to repay him. When I did I wrapped my check about a bottle of smelling salts and sent it to him by messenger. My prankish side!

The closing of *The Dancers* not only caught me with my fiscal bloomers down, it brought the sharp realization there was no demand for young American accents. I was on the edge of disaster when paged for *Conchita. Conchita* was a stinker despite the fact it was plotted by Edward Knoblock, the gentleman who had written *Milestones.*

But *Conchita* was to give me one of the thrills of my life. We rehearsed it at the Queen's Theatre in Shaftsbury Avenue, where we were to play later. In London it was common for a new play to rehearse three or four weeks, then open without out-of-town tryout. Returning from luncheon one afternoon my hair stood up like a porcupine's quills when I saw the electric letters over the theater's marquee:

TALLULAH BANKHEAD

in

"CONCHITA"

Such billing is the payoff in the theater. It means stardom. It implies your name has more box-office pull than the play or its author. I reacted in characteristic fashion. I had hit the jackpot—at the ripe old age of twenty-one. For the remaining week of rehearsals I repeatedly circled the block that I might read the magic announcement. I dragooned acquaintances into this grand tour. I almost wore the shoes off Audrey Carten. Audrey had played the English girl in *The Dancers* brilliantly. Only one thing about the display disturbed me. The bulbs in the framed letters were tinted a dark blue. For reasons too complex to go into here I looked upon this as an evil omen.

The locale of *Conchita* was Cuba. Its heroine was at the end of her rope. The proprietor of the joint in which she danced had sold her to the Governor in the first act. Out of her wits, she was about to bolt for the Caribbean on foot, when a young American sailor loitering in the port came to her aid. In the second act, for reasons known only to Knoblock, I came on carrying a monkey. This prefaced a scene in which the eager grandee was to attack my virtue, an attack interrupted in the nick of time by the wandering gob.

On opening night the monkey went berserk. He had taken a violent dislike to me during rehearsals. About to speak my first line to the feverish Spaniard he, the monkey, not the grandee, snatched my black wig from my head, leaped from my arms and scampered down to the footlights. There he paused, peered out at the audience, then waved my wig over his head like a drunken Indian who had scalped a paleface. De-wigged I presented a grotesque appearance. Swarthy from my wig line down, I was a blonde up north.

The audience had been giggling at the absurd plot even before this simian had at me. Now it became hysterical. What did Tallulah do in this crisis? I turned a cartwheel! The audience roared. For all my apparent bravado, at the end of the play I hesitated to exercise the privilege of the star, to step before the curtain and receive the plaudits of her slaves, uncluttered with other actors. After the monkey business I was afraid they might boo me. Instead I received an ovation. The audience felt a girl who could survive Knoblock's plot, the monkey rebellion and other mishaps with which the evening was charged, should be saluted.

After that reception I was in high spirits, even though I knew the melodrama was doomed. I charged off to Ciro's for champagne and dancing. A reckless biographer has written that on this night I sloshed Miss Gladys Cooper with beer. Miss Cooper was one of England's fine actresses and a great beauty. A frothier fable has never been spread on the record. It was Francis Laking who doused her, inadvertently, at another party ten tables away. Later I shared a house in Catherine Street with Gladys, Olga Lynn, and Lady Idina Gordon. With them I also shared droves of servants and other tokens of affluence beyond my purse. Easy come, easy go, as many a noodlehead has echoed.

Association with that trio was tonic. Olga Lynn was possessed of great musical talent. She had studied under Jean de Reszke, was constantly tossing parties for charity. She had sung Musette in *Louise* at Covent Garden.

Oggie Lynn gave me my first singing lesson. Those who have heard me chant "I'll Be Seeing You" over the air probably think this is a cowardly attempt to brand her as the author of my lyric delinquency. False! About to toss up a musical charade at the home of Sir Philip Sassoon, Oggie was hell-bent on singing "Water Boy," aided and abetted by Artur Rubinstein. Now "Water Boy" has to be sung with a Southern drawl to retain its original flavor. Singing it in her clipped English accent, Oggie prostrated me. A ready volunteer for any cause, I gave "Water Boy" the full Alabaman treatment:

> Watah boy, whah yuh hidin'?
> If yuh don' come gwine tell yo' mammy!

An expert mimic, Oggie learned "Water Boy" phonetically, created a great to-do when she sang it at Sir Philip's soiree.

Out of gratitude or caprice Oggie reciprocated by giving me a lyric lesson. While my singing voice had the quality of a smothered Chaliapin, she drilled me in something classical that went:

> Do not go, my love, without asking my leave.
> I have watched all night, and now my eyes are heavy with sleep. . . .
> Do not go, my love, without asking my leave.
>
> I start up and stretch my hands to touch you.
> I ask myself, "Is it a dream?". . .
> Do not go, my love, without asking my leave.

So help me I was sure I had hit "dream" on high C. If so, it was the first time I tickled high C, and the last. Even before London I'd skirmished in lyric surroundings. More than once I'd gone to the house of wealthy Robert Chandler—then, earlier or later, married to Lina Cavalieri, the opera star—with Paul Draper, the muralist, father of the dancer of the same name. There I'd sit rapt, as Jascha Heifetz and Artur Rubinstein would merge on "The Liebestod" from *Tristan und Isolde.* If my breast was savage, those boys charmed it.

I was quite an opera fan when first I came to New York. I could get as dizzy over Geraldine Farrar as the next flapper. Both Caruso and Scotti mowed me down emotionally. I'm a quick crier. I couldn't finish Budd Schulberg's *The Disenchanted.* When his drunken hero went haywire at the winter carnival and was jeered by the nitwit students, I was desolated. It isn't because my emotions are on the surface. That oversimplifies the proposition. I'm all emotion. A year ago I went to see Charlie Chaplin in a revival of *City Lights.* I laughed and cried so hard people sitting next to me moved to quieter areas. Remember the scene in *Harvey* when Frank Fay sat alone on the stage and talked about himself? It tore me to pieces. So did Cedric Hardwicke in Shaw's *Applecart.* So, too, did Daddy when he would do John of Gaunt's speech in *Richard II*—"This sceptred isle . . . this precious stone set in the silver sea . . . this England." The beauty and brilliance of the verse reduced me to rubble.

Conchita buried, almost at once I was rehearsing in *This Marriage.* In this mistake, I reversed my role in *Conchita.* In it, you'll recall, I was pursued by a wicked grandee. In *This Marriage* I was the seductress, rather than the seductee. Herbert Marshall was my prey. I was trying to steal him from Cathleen Nesbitt, these last forty years one of the ablest actresses in the theater. Cathleen had just had a baby and I insisted that she have the star dressing room.

My motives in giving it up were not as noble as you might guess. I was fascinated by babies, on matinee day spent most of the time I was off-stage in Cathleen's dressing room playing with her youngster. The baby was much more interesting, much more amusing, than anything we did or said on the stage.

Although *This Marriage* was a failure I no longer was afraid of becoming a public charge. Now I had a following, its loyalty in nowise abated because I was the victim of two duds. My nonchalance in adversity increased their devotion. I can't recall that I ever encouraged these fanatics. I did employ one device that may have endeared me to them. When I took the final curtain call I raised my eyes to the gallery, then gradually lowered them until I was finally facing the stalls. A calculated ruse? Nothing of the sort! To me the attendance of the galleryites was a greater tribute, since it involved a greater sacrifice, than the presence of the loafers in the lower regions.

In England eighteen months, I had one hit and two failures behind me when I started to rehearse in *The Creaking Chair*, in June, 1924. I was on the *qui vive*. I didn't lack for young men to take me dancing at the Embassy Club, the Kit Kat, Ciro's, the Café de Paris, even Victor's, which flourished through connivance after hours. Many of these young bloods were of the theater, some from the Almanach de Gotha. I had feverish love affairs with more than one of them but was too concerned with advancing myself to think in terms of orange blossoms and *Lohengrin*. I had many proposals, not all of them involving matrimony. One brilliant young actor and author, after he had worked me up to a romantic pitch puzzled me for a moment: "Tallulah, it's the great regret of my life you were not born a boy." Solve that anagram!

I first met Napier, Lord Alington, when I was living with Bijou Martin, through Geoffrey Homsdale, now the Earl of Amherst, then roughing it in New York, writing a daily theatrical column in the *Morning World*. Lord Alington was being Bohemian in Greenwich Village. Over here to master the banking business, he had been the house guest of Mrs. Cornelius Vanderbilt, had fled to the Village when he found life among New York's upper crust stuffy.

Geoff Homsdale had told him about me in what must have been glowing terms. One night Geoff called Napier from our apartment and he came flying up in a taxicab in his pajamas, a bottle of gin in his overcoat pocket.

Napier had had a lot of experience with women of high degree and low. He was astonished that at nineteen I had not succumbed to any man. With eloquence and enthusiasm he undertook to remedy this omission on our first meeting. I declined, though it gave me a wrench. But Napier was impetuous. Within a week he asked me to marry him. With a lesser wrench, I waved him aside. He was pursuing a practiced tactic, I was sure. I was determined to make my mark in the theater before hitching up with anyone.

Then, and for years thereafter, Napier touched off conflicting emotions in me. With him, I was irked by his nonchalance, his cynicism, his flashes of cruelty. Away from him, I found these flaws attracted me. We were together constantly in the winter of '21–'22. Though thirty years have elapsed I vividly recall breakfasts—eggs benedict—at the Brevoort on early Sunday afternoons, dancing with him in the early hours of the morning at Reisenweber's, a gay place which flourished in Columbus Circle. Here we'd be accompanied by a frustrated young Englishman, then living on herbs and wild berries—Noel Coward.

My notions about Napier almost caused me to be dismissed from *Everyday*, the Rachel Crothers play. In it I played a nineteen-year-old who, on returning from a two-year tour of Europe, finds life in Missouri flat and vulgar. Early in the comedy, a townsman asked

me what had been my most exciting experience abroad. Was it true
I had met kings and queens? In the script I was to reply: "Oh, well,
kings and queens are really kind of a joke. The most interesting
person I met was a prostitute."

Out of loyalty to Napier, I omitted this reply at every performance. Since he was a British subject, a Lord no less, I thought the
line would offend him. He had great respect and affection for the
Royal Family. The management gave me an ultimatum. If I skipped
the reply once more, an understudy would replace me at the next
performance. I reassured them. I'd say it that night. But when the
time came I had the awful feeling Napier might be in the audience.
I couldn't and didn't say it. Before I could be court-martialed the
play closed. Ten years later in London when playing in her *Let Us
Be Gay*, I explained to Miss Crothers the reason for my mutiny.
"Why didn't you tell me? I would have understood," she said. I
couldn't have told her. I was too self-conscious about my feeling
for Napier.

When Napier returned to England I was devastated. Memories
of our hours together haunted me. It's awkward to explain his effect
on me. He wasn't good-looking, he had an almost repulsive mouth,
but he lived recklessly. He scorned the conventions, loved to
gamble, and, when it pleased him, had great charm and wit.

Napier was born Napier Stuart, direct descendant of those
Stuarts who ruled so recklessly in England and Scotland in the
seventeenth century. His elder brother had succumbed to wounds
received in World War I. Napier then succeeded to the title. He
owned thousands of acres but was land poor. Sporadically, I was in
love with him for years. But my love was mixed with resentment.
He was a riddle I couldn't solve, which made him all the more attractive, all the more desirable. He was unpredictable, irresponsible.
He rarely kept appointments, always had the most disarming
excuses.

Napier was my secret reason for being so hell-bent on going to London after I had been flagged down by both Cochran and Gerald du Maurier. I hadn't had so much as a line from him in the year since he'd sailed home. I didn't alert him on my approach, nor did I seek him out once I had set myself up at the Ritz. But I experienced tremors when, the second morning, the operator called to say: "Lord Alington's downstairs to see Miss Bankhead."

Anticipating this possibility, I had plotted my reaction in advance. I'd practice cool detachment, take my time, give him a half-hour to cool his heels. Told of his arrival, my resolve went up in smoke. I had schemed to be casual, as though meeting a chance acquaintance on the street. "Why hello, Napier, how are you, how do you do?" Instead I was in the lobby in a split second, I charged at him with complete abandon, crying out: "Napier, darling!"

When he was in London I was with him constantly, fascinated by his rakishness, his pranks, his indifference to fame and fortune. Then he'd disappear for months and I'd not hear a word from him. When he bobbed up without warning, again I'd be hypnotized, though inwardly ravaged by my inability to break off a relationship that was part ecstasy, part torture. His cruel insistence on doing only such things as pleased or interested him, his contempt for the desires of others, both fascinated and repelled me. Invariably I got furiously angry, only to melt into submission when he turned on his charm and bravado.

Torn by tuberculosis, Napier went to Switzerland to take the Sparlinger Cure. Ordered to follow a Spartan diet, he violated every rule, stayed up all night drinking and gambling. He would flee the sanatorium, disappear for weeks, then blithely return as if he'd been out to post a letter.

I recall an afternoon I stumbled into him in Paris, where I had gone to be rigged out by Molyneux for costumes in a new play. We went to Le Bœuf sur le Toit for dinner. Napier said he had to take the midnight train for Geneva. Charged with both anxiety and affection I was my gayest. Napier managed to miss the train. On five successive midnights he missed the same train. The sixth night he caught the train, but as it was pulling out threw off his bags and jumped to the platform. The seventh night we again went to the train. As it pulled out he turned to me and said, "Lulas, this train goes to Genoa." We drove to Bricktop's famous all-night carnival in Montmartre, and he took me back to the Chambord on the Champs Élysées at dawn.

Three days later I was to learn that on leaving me he had engaged a taxi to drive him to Venice—a three-day trip.

Before he left, Napier had made me promise I'd spend two weeks with him at Evian-les-Bains, on Lake Geneva, where he was taking the cure, before I went into rehearsal. I was to wire him the time of my arrival, once I was through with Molyneux. To facilitate travel in a strange land I borrowed Sister's French maid. On my arrival at the hotel I went at once to my suite, after telling the clerk: "Let Lord Alington know Miss Bankhead is here."

Miss Bankhead was there, sure enough, but Napier wasn't. He was registered but not in. Where was he? Perhaps in Montreux, across the lake. I was blazing with indignation. For forty-eight hours I never left my rooms. My insistent phone calls had no result. I would stand on my terrace for hours, awaiting the arrival of the small boats from Montreux—forty-five minutes away—in the hope that Napier might step from one of them.

Then a Belgian, whom I remember only as The Fox, called on me to say he had been sent by Napier. He offered a lot of fantastic excuses which added up to the suspicion the fugitive was on a monumental spree. My Lord would be back tomorrow, he said. Glad to escape from my rooms, I accepted this emissary's invitation to go to the casino. Crushed and humiliated, I gave no sign. We went to the *chemin de fer* table and as I sat down I looked across the green board and there sat Napier, calmly saying, "Banco! Banco!" When our eyes met, he casually said, "Hello, Lulas" and calmly continued riffling his chips.

I decided to blast him then and there, but when he approached my rage vanished. In a few minutes we were laughing and drinking together. I spent two magic weeks with him. Memories of the gin fizzes I drank with him at the Sporting Bar in Geneva still linger. My holiday over, we caught a night train for Paris, leaving Napier behind for God knows what adventure. The French maid and I went on an emotional binge. She sobbed for her lover killed in World War I, while I cried my eyes out over Napier the whole night long. I knew he was doomed. I had a feeling he welcomed that doom.

When Napier would have married me, my only concern was a career. My goal achieved, stardom in London, Napier was off on other tangents. He didn't have any overpowering sexual attraction for me. It was just that I was happiest with him, even when his conduct was outrageous. That happiness, once we were apart, was tinged with a desire to do something cruel to him, thus avenge his cruel slights. I could never bring myself to it. I think my confusion about Napier was partly due to pity—and pity is the least of the emotions.

Drinking was never a problem in my years in London. For one thing it was not looked upon as a symbol of experience and worldliness. All of us drank wine. Did I get exhilarated I soon danced off the effects. The clubs closed at one in the morning, another brake on excess. Once I started to rehearse, I denied myself all intoxicants. I even gave up cigarettes when doctors said they contributed to my chronic throatiness. At play, or after hours, the English are ruled by decorum. They'd feel disgraced did they do something scandalous while under the influence. A rare people, those English.

"The Englishman, like the Arab, has a great respect and liking for the eccentric, for the 'queer one.' The heretic, the grouser or the crank is allowed full play in club or pub. And the sabbatical orator in Hyde Park, who is generally regarded as the supreme test of British tolerance and political balance, might be more properly considered as the recipient of the tribute which, in England, is customarily paid by conformity to non-conformity." That's the verdict of Robert Law.

Could it be the English took me to their hearts because I was the nonconformist, the rebel, the invader who flouted their canons of conduct? I was not as free of inhibitions as the casual observer might believe. On the surface all confidence, all swagger and strut, inside I churned with doubt. Any minute the clock might strike twelve and I'd be back in a hall bedroom at the Algonquin, or, worse yet, in Grandfather's yard at Jasper.

In that summer of 1924 I didn't have much to worry about, and little time to do it. *The Creaking Chair* had a long and prosperous run. Thanks to Aubrey Smith, who on his death at ninety was as much a symbol of Empire as the British lion, I saved money for the first time in my life. I was paid fifty pounds a week in this spooky melodrama. Aubrey persuaded me to let him hold out ten pounds each week. It was a most satisfactory arrangement, even though I cheated occasionally by drawing advances. Aubrey also undertook to explain cricket to me, but gave up after three weeks laughing hysterically.

Although it ran for thirty weeks, *The Creaking Chair* was nothing to disturb G.B.S. or Barrie. On the opening night the author was booed. The reviews, while saluting Aubrey Smith, Nigel Bruce and your far-from-humble servant, said the melodrama was reminiscent of something that had been fished from under the East India docks in Limehouse.

Since audiences laughed at what were supposed to be its excitements, we decided to give them something to laugh about. We "hoked it up" in scandalous fashion. The author didn't protest, nor did the producer. This farcical treatment proved popular. It turned an out-and-out failure into a long-run success. Prince George, later the Duke of Kent, used to drop in to see me caper in the second act at least once a week.

Somewhere in this encyclopedia I have said that actors frequently save a silly play by their performances. No one in his right mind could stomach the plot of *The Creaking Chair*. By caricaturing the play we made a hit of it. Author and producer prospered beyond their deserts. We didn't make a good play of *The Creaking Chair*, but our improvisations provided an enjoyable evening for the customers. For reasons I will shortly disclose I lived to regret its popularity. But when it did close I was richer than I had ever been. Thanks to Aubrey Smith, I had saved three hundred pounds. No wonder a grateful Empire would later knight him.

6.

Ambushed by Somerset Maugham

My darkest hour?

I must vote for that awful afternoon when I read that Olga Lindo had been named to play the role of Sadie Thompson in *Rain*. The roof fell in and I was buried in the debris.

Rain, as all of you must know, was an adaptation of Somerset Maugham's short story, "Miss Thompson," which had first appeared in *The Smart Set*, a magazine edited by H. L. Mencken and George Jean Nathan. Dramatized by John Colton and Clemence Randolph, it had been produced in New York in 1922, shortly before my invasion of the British Isles. It was an immediate and enduring hit and Jeanne Eagles electrified the critics with her brilliant performance of the South Seas' slut.

I had been in London for eighteen months when Basil Dean approached me with an offer to play Sadie. I was beside myself. Though trapped in *The Creaking Chair*, I assured him that, once free, I would forego all other bids for Sadie. I felt my hour had struck. At last I could get my teeth into a role that had guts and swagger and shock. I was delirious when Dean wrote me:

My contracts for "Rain" were signed in New York last week. It will probably be best for us to wait until Mr. Maugham's return to England before doing the play. This would give you sufficient time after the run of "The Creaking Chair" to go to New York as you promised, and to return in time for rehearsals. Please let me know when you would propose to do this.

Earlier Dean had suggested it might be wise to see Miss Eagles in the play.

Two days later, at his instigation, I wrote Dean:

I agree to play the part of Sadie Thompson at a salary of forty pounds per week. I note that the management is to commence the production of the play not later than 30th June, 1925. I agree that if Mr. Somerset Maugham should definitely disapprove of my engagement, I will cancel it and your company will not be under liability to me in respect to it.

The stubbornness of *The Creaking Chair* agonized me. Would it never close? When it finally shuttered in mid-February I was off, hell-for-leather, for Southampton. I arrived in New York on the *Berengaria* on February 25, only to learn Miss Eagles was appearing in the play in Pittsburgh.

On my return from Pittsburgh, fate jostled me again. I had booked return passage on the *Aquitania* but Dean disapproved. He and Maugham were sailing on that boat. On the theory that familiarity breeds contempt, Dean felt I should avoid the author until rehearsals. This strategy curdled me. But I was in no position to quibble—so desperately did I want Sadie Thompson. I returned on a cattle-boat, a hulk that consumed ten days in crossing. Among the passengers was a corpse, and the two daughters of the Governor General of Canada.

Frustrated and miserable, I locked myself in my cabin. I did not leave it in the entire crossing. I had the jazz records Sadie Thompson played in the second act of *Rain*, and I spun them interminably as I acted out my part. This brought half the passengers to my door. Many of them were convinced that the tub, not content with a corpse, also boasted a lunatic.

Dedicated to solitude I had stocked up on magazines. When Sadie exhausted me, I browsed through them. In one I came across a short story: "The Man Who Wouldn't Hurt A Fly" by, guess who? Somerset Maugham! Under the sway of Algernon Charles Swinburne, I radioed Dean that the man who wouldn't hurt a fly was crucifying me.

Back in London, shaken but unchastened, I awaited rehearsals. All my eggs were in the *Rain* basket. While in *The Creaking Chair* I had turned down two promising plays. I could have played either the wife or the prostitute in Lonsdale's *Spring Cleaning*, or the wife or the tart in *Tarnish*. I wanted Sadie to be my first all-out hussy.

Maugham sat in the dark auditorium throughout the first rehearsal. Sure of every line in my role, thanks to weeks of study, I gave what I'm sure was a brilliant imitation of Jeanne Eagles. I've harped on my skill at mimicry. I felt my impersonation would electrify Maugham. If Maugham was electrified, he didn't show it. He avoided me after the rehearsal. This frightened me. Usually, an author exchanges some pleasantries with his star, no matter what he may think of her first rough reading.

At the second rehearsal, Maugham remained mute and inscrutable. Alarm started to gnaw at me. Audaciously I glided up to Dean. "Basil, who the hell's going to play this part?" His answer chilled me: "An angel from Heaven. God only knows!"

I felt my number was up. This suspicion was confirmed like a thunderclap when I read two days later that Olga Lindo had been tapped for Sadie. I wanted to drain the hemlock cup. There had been a great deal in the London papers about me playing the notorious Sadie. How could I explain?

That same evening I received a note from Dean. Would I come to see him in his office? He was horribly embarrassed, he said, that I had read of my dismissal before he had a chance to tell me. He couldn't understand how the story leaked out. As if there are any secrets in the theater!

Steeling myself, I climbed the stairs to Dean's studio in St. Martin's Theatre. Shattered! Scorched with anger!

Dean offered me a cigarette.

"No, thank you, I have a cigarette."

Then he offered me a light.

"I have my own light."

These amenities over, he told me Maugham didn't want me to play the part. He was in no position to defy so majestic a force in the theater. He couldn't challenge the goose who laid such golden eggs.

"How would you like to play Olga Lindo's part in *Tarnish*?" he asked. Now, this, if I may steal a line from Gladys Unger, was adding incest to injury. *Tarnish* was one of the plays I had turned down to play Sadie.

"No, thank you," I said. "I don't think any more of *Tarnish* than I did three months ago."

With that I turned and left. I had hysterics and fled down the stairs, sobbing as I had not sobbed since foiled as a child. On the street I bumped into Mary Claire, a fine character actress with whom I had played in *Conchita*. She took me to Lyons'—London version of Child's—and tried to cheer me up. I was inconsolable.

That night, I gave one of my phoniest performances. Returning to my service flat, I put on Sadie's Pago-Pago costume, gulped down twenty aspirin tablets, turned on Sadie's record. Then I stretched out on my bed to await the end—but not before scribbling this note: "It ain't goin' to rain no moh."

This flippant farewell had added significance. It had been raining for a solid month in London. Every day the papers carried page-one stories about the endless deluge.

I went to sleep dramatizing every detail of my suicide. London's shock! The curious and muted crowds at my door! The stern calm of the bobbies and the coroner! The headlines in the newspapers! Maugham stoned in the streets! The cables aquiver with news of the death of the American beauty who had conquered England.

I was awakened the next morning by the telephone. I felt marvelous. It was Noel Coward.

"Tallulah, can you learn one hundred sides in four days?"

To those unfamiliar with such lingo as "sides," may I say that a hundred sides make up an extravagantly long part. Whoever plays such a role rarely can leave the stage during a performance. Conventionally players sit about reading their parts for the first three or four days. But I sensed a reprieve.

"Four days. I can get up in it in four hours. Why?"

"Come up and see me at once."

Leaping from my bier, I dressed in a jiffy, shortly was facing Noel. It developed the actress, who had been rehearsing in *Fallen Angels* for three weeks, had seceded when convinced Edna Best had the better role. Coward was on the spot.

Although I didn't know a thing about *Fallen Angels*, I agreed to play the part.

"What's your salary?" asked Noel.

"One hundred pounds a week."

"But you were only getting forty pounds in *Rain*."

"That's true. But I wanted to play Sadie Thompson. I don't give a good goddam if I play this or not."

146.

"Agreed," said Noel, "if you can open Tuesday."

"I'll open in it on Tuesday, or I'll fix it so no one else will ever be able to open in it," I said.

The next day I received a chit from Somerset Maugham. From it fluttered his check for one hundred pounds. With customary skill and grace he wrote he had always found, when upset or disappointed, that a week or two abroad, a change of scene, helped him. Would I please accept the enclosure?

What with the demands of *Fallen Angels'* rehearsals, trying on new costumes, it took me four days to compose my reply. With it he got his check. Naturally, I said, I was disappointed. But I did not propose to make a career of that disappointment. I was disappointed because I had been dismissed hastily, after only two days' rehearsal. Actors were commonly given four weeks to learn a role. I was disappointed, too, because I had not had a word of advice from the author, so invaluable from so distinguished a dramatist as himself. In returning his check, I hoped he wouldn't be any more offended than was I, on receiving it. I suggested that he turn it over to his favorite charity, an identification with which I did not care to be confused.

Olga Lindo opened in *Rain*. It was an immediate failure.

In *Fallen Angels* I had a line: "Oh, dear, rain!" I couldn't resist the temptation to alter that line on opening night. On reaching it I mustered up my Sadiest Thompson voice and said: "My God, RAIN!" The audience roared!

Three or four days later Mr. Maugham parachuted down from his ivory tower and invited me to lunch. He told me my performance in *Fallen Angels* was the most brilliant comedy performance he had ever seen. I received this accolade as I had his hundred pounds.

Some years later, my friend, Rowland Leigh, playwright and

director, met Somerset Maugham in Southern France. During an evening's conversation he asked him: "What was your biggest professional mistake?" The great novelist answered: "Not letting Tallulah Bankhead play *Rain*." I wonder if Rowland invented that?

Despite my success in *Fallen Angels* I was haunted for months by my dismissal from *Rain*. I was sure there was more to it than Maugham's belief that I was not right. Searching my memory, I found a clue.

When in *The Dancers*, people used to storm back to my dressing room after the performance. One night Hugo Rumbold—he later married playwright Zoe Akins—came back. Mr. Rumbold stuttered. One of the curses of my gift for mimicry is that unconsciously I will blink if my opponent blinks, lisp if he lisps. Consciously, I wouldn't think of making fun of anyone's infirmity or affliction. I was shocked to discover that when Rumbold stuttered, I stuttered. Shortly after his departure, Somerset Maugham came in. Mr. Maugham stuttered, too. You recall his club-footed hero in *Of Human Bondage?* The clubfoot was Maugham's substitute for his stutter. I have a suspicion that I may have imitated Maugham's stutter at that backstage meeting. If I did he may have thought I was rude or cruel, or both. This suspicion is my own. It has no corroboration from any source. Perhaps I'm only seeking a means to counteract the Maugham verdict that I was an inadequate Sadie. I don't swallow such implications easily. When I apply myself to something I want to do—and I was certainly hell-bent on playing Sadie Thompson—I can play a role as well as any squaw alive. If that be ego, make the most of it!

It is theatrical irony—my profession boils with it—that ten years later I was to play Sadie Thompson in the revival of *Rain* at the Music Box in New York. Ten years, however, had slaked my thirst for the part. Most of the first-night audience had seen Jeanne

Eagles in the role. So had all the critics. Most of us like best the player we first see in a role. His interpretation leaves impressions not easily blotted out by a successor. Why did I risk the inevitable comparison? I had just crawled out of the wreckage of *Dark Victory*. There was also another consideration. I needed the money.

The *New York Times*' Brooks Atkinson, an observant and knowing critic, wrote: "It took great courage for Miss Bankhead to step into such celebrated shoes—and walk up to such an inevitable comparison. She plunged into the part with the raffish gusto of a gaudy strumpet."

Critic Gilbert Gabriel scorned caution: "Miss Bankhead is the best of all possible Sadies," wrote that Solomon.

A dubious footnote might be added about this revival of *Rain* in which I caught up with the Rev. Davidson ten years too late. It opened at the Music Box on Lincoln's birthday. Don't draw the conclusion that this date was rigged to point up my martyrdom.

One more word, and I'm through with *Rain*, if not with Somerset Maugham. Shortly after it opened, Daddy had a second heart attack and was taken to Johns Hopkins Hospital. My stepmother was at his bedside day and night. I called her on the telephone, urged her to leave Daddy for a day. "Why not come up and see me in *Rain*. Come up to a matinee. You can return to Baltimore after the performance. It will do you good."

Florence agreed. She bounced into my hotel at ten o'clock the following Wednesday morning. Belatedly I began to worry. Neither she nor Daddy ever used violent or profane language. In *Rain* I wheeled on the Rev. Davidson and screamed: "You goddam son-of-a-bitch! You'd tear the wings off a butterfly. To hell with you! And be damned to you!"

Florence would be shocked at such language. She might think my invitation a schemed affront. I arranged with an usher to bring her backstage after the second act. No use delaying her verdict. I expected her to denounce me: "Tallulah, how dare you play this kind of a part—your father will just die." Instead she said, "Tallulah, honey, you're just precious, Sugar. You're just like you were when you were a child. Remember your tantrums?"

7.

Tales of London Town

"ALL MY MOTOR-CARS"

SIR GUY LAKING BEQUEST

TO MISS BANKHEAD

Under that heading the London *Daily Mail* said in October of 1930:

Probate has been granted of the will of Sir Guy Francis Laking, third baronet, of Eubry-street S.W., who died in St. George's Hospital, Hyde Park Corner, on August 4, at the age of 26. By his will, which is dated November, 1925, he left "to my friend Tallulah Bankhead all my motor-cars."

Headline and story had a single flaw. Sir Guy Francis Laking didn't have a car to his name. It was a posthumous prank. He was the greatest mischief-maker in all England. Witty, malicious, petulant, he was the son of Sir Guy Francis Laking, a former Keeper of the King's Armoury, the grandson of Sir Francis Henry Laking, surgeon to the Royal Family. Under any biological classification I must describe his gender as neuter. He lithped. He was happiest when he could break up a party by inciting the guests to riot and rebellion with his innuendoes, his slanders. At one time Lady Diana Manners and I were the only women in London who would speak to him.

There were times I wouldn't speak to him. He was a born trouble-maker, worshiped me in sisterly fashion. On opening nights he would flood my dressing room with flowers. When I had my house in Farm Street, Francis would inflict himself on me for days at a time. The servants invariably gave notice within twenty-four hours of his arrival.

Most of my life I have avoided answering telephones. I have thus escaped hours of boredom. One day in a careless moment I did answer. It was Francis, twittering like a sparrow though I had warned him never to darken my door again.

"Hello, dolling! Dolling, what're you doing tonight, dolling?"

"It's none of your goddam business."

"You muth tell me, dolling! What're you doing tonight? I'm so interethted in your career."

"What I'm doing tonight has nothing to do with my career. Leave me alone."

"Oh, Tallulah," he gushed on, "when my mother died you promithed you'd look after me. Dolling, pleath? Are you going to wear the diamond brathlet or the mink coat? Pleathe tell me!"

"Well, Francis, if you must know, I'm having supper with the Earl of Latham and Gladys Cooper."

"They're no good to you, dolling," he cried. "Oneth got conthumption and oneth got a matinee."

Francis' grandfather had saved Edward's life when he was Prince of Wales. He had performed an emergency appendicitis operation on the Prince as he was about to succeed his mother, Victoria, on England's throne. His grandson—my bogus benefactor—was the first child born in St. James's Palace since James II. He was brought up in the royal household.

Although I did not inflame him with desire, he was jealous of any man in whom I seemed interested. When Tony Wilson and I were on the brink of wedlock, Francis surpassed himself in offensiveness. Tony and I and Monica Morrice had driven down to Brighton for a week end. We went slumming in a cheap night club, with a crooked *chemin de fer* game upstairs. We were having a drink at a balcony table, when I spied the evil Francis nearby with Audrey Carten. Knowing Francis would be at his poisonous worst under such circumstances I cut him cold. Shortly Tony was handed a note by a waiter. He bounded to his feet, strode over to Francis' table, and said, "Come outside, Francis, I want to talk to you." Tony was a good six-feet-four. Francis was wispy and shrill. As I came over to learn the cause of the commotion Audrey rose from her seat to greet me. Francis pulled her down into his lap and screamed at Tony: "You can't hit a woman! You can't hit a woman!"

Why was Tony furious? Francis' note had read: "You're a pimp." That night we tracked him down in his hotel room. When we walked in he drew back and yelled: "You can't tuth me, you can't tuth me, I'm on Tom Tiddleth ground!" In English lore a man on Tom Tiddler's ground is immune from attack. When Tony relaxed Francis grew waspish. "Wait a minute, wait a minute," he shouted, "until I can think of something that will make me mad." With that he hauled off and swung on Tony, knocked him halfway across the room.

Tony had thought to badger Francis. Now he was aroused. He really belted the bibulous baronet. His eye was shuttered. Fearful Tony had injured Francis, we bundled him into our car and started back to London. Francis was undismayed. He chattered like a magpie all the way back. We took him to an all-night chemist's and had him patched up, then to my house for a reconciliation bracer. After two jolts he turned insulting again, and foiled all attempts to get him out. His sniping so aroused Tony I insisted he leave.

"All right, I'll leave," he said. "Where's my hat and my overcoat?" Then Tony, to employ a phrase I've picked up on the sports pages, pulled a rock.

"Oh, you *have* an overcoat? And a hat?"

"Yeth, I have a hat, and a coat, and a thick, and a baronetthy, and a thousand poundth a year," he sallied as he swept out.

His rebuttal had insulting significance. Tony had no income of his own. As a second son he boasted no title. His father, Sir Matthew Wilson, for all his acres, was shy of sterling. Although Tony could boast he was the grandson of the Earl of Ribblesdale, Francis was a baronet in his own right. Thus he did throw his rank at my hero.

I heard the street door slam but I was sure Francis had not left the house. So certain was I that he had hidden himself for some later deviltry, I woke my butler and my cook, alerted my maid. The five of us searched every cranny of the house. No Francis! It was a very small house, with small rooms. A flea could not find cover in it. I persisted in the search even while the others pooh-poohed me. Where did I find him? On the floor of my maid's closet, buried under a pile of coats and frocks. When I fished him out he whispered warningly: "Get rid of Tony. Get rid of Tony."

Sir Francis was loathsome in many ways, yet his pranks and his talent for troublemaking fascinated me. More than once I went around to the Bow Street jail to ransom him when he had been plucked from the gutter by a bobby. Even in death he was fantastic. My friend, Gwenn Farrar, the cellist, went to the family home to pay her respects and mine. I was playing in Birmingham and couldn't come to the funeral.

Gwenn told me his sister, Joan, kept crying: "He died of a broken heart. Tallulah killed him." Gwenn found this hard to take. As Joan went on berating me, Gwenn wheeled and said, "Enough

of that! If it wasn't for Tallulah, Francis wouldn't be alive today."
This was an odd defense since Francis was lying stiff and stark
upstairs.

When I left England in 1931 someone loosed the canard I had
been deported. This brazen tale, of course, never found its way
into print, either in New York or London. But it won wide credence
in the half-worlds of Broadway and Piccadilly. I had been exiled,
said my traducers, for adult delinquency, for practicing voodoo
without a license, because my arrears in income tax outraged the
Chancellor of the Exchequer.

Utter poppycock! I had been similarly slandered when I sailed
for New York to see Jeanne Eagles in *Rain*. Like an addlepate I
rejoiced in these rumors. They inflated my reputation as a *femme
fatale*. The *Rain* excursion was a ruse to throw authorities off the
scent. That was the story, once I was at sea. My romantic adventures
with Tony Wilson set off another.

A London newspaper ran a story that due to their binge with a
well-known American actress, two young students at Eton had been
disciplined. Overnight it got around that I was the actress who
had flouted the headmaster and the provosts. Who else? I must
admit I was briefly in love with Tony. But my ardor waned when I
learned he was but nineteen, while I was twenty-four. I had been
to Eton but twice. Once I'd driven down with Lady Wilson. The
second time I had driven down with Tony and his elder brother,
Martin. It was on a Sunday. We picked up Tony's fourteen-year-
old brother, Peter, and another child, and took them to a place the
Café de Paris had set up on the Thames to cater to their Sabbath
customers. After lunch we took them punting on the river. It's
quite possible Peter and his classmate violated the rules in leaving
Eton on Sunday—missed chapel or something—but since they were

taken by two old Etonians, I couldn't see why I should be sand-bagged.

This innuendo mushroomed into the tale that my plays had been declared out-of-bounds for all Eton students. Indignant, I instructed my counselors, Lewis and Lewis, to write to the head-master and demand a letter that would clear me of kidnaping and corrupting. In time my barristers received a formal note from Eton saying that the penalties inflicted on the truants had nothing to do with any American actress. This statement was given to the press.

Don't think I snatched Tony off a campus. When we went to Brighton he was supposed to be down in Cornwall learning to pilot a plane. He had overstayed his leave. He was so worldly, so urbane, I was sure he was all of thirty. Those English youngsters confuse you.

I had still another romance in London that involved me with a small boy. I had been in England four years when I met Lord Beaverbrook, the newspaper publisher. His interest in me, I may say, was purely paternal. A little gnomelike man, Max loved to entertain. He had great love for the theater, never failed me when I sought advice. Between engagements I often was a week-end guest at his country place. Max introduced me to Michael Wardell. Michael was one of the great beaux of London, and one of Beaver-brook's top executives. He had but one eye. Over the other he wore a menacing patch. He had lost the eye while hunting, or while leaning over to pick up a lady's handkerchief in Vienna, or a fusion of the two.

We hit it off in great fashion. He looked like a swashbuckler from the Spanish Main, behaved in the same fashion. A very exciting person! Since he was rash and impulsive we were soon engaged. To Beaverbrook's delight almost at once we were dis-

William B. Bankhead with his daughters Eugenia and Tallulah, 1904 (Courtesy of the Alabama Department of Archives and History, Special Collections)

Tallulah at age 4 (Courtesy of the Alabama Department of Archives and History, Special Collections)

Tallulah at age 8 (Courtesy of the Alabama Department of Archives and History, Special Collections)

Tallulah at age 14 (Courtesy of the Alabama Department of Archives and History, Special Collections)

Tallulah at age 16, during the period in which she played in *39 East* on Broadway. She also played in *The Squab Farm* (1918) and appeared in two silent films, *Thirty a Week* (1918) and *The Trap* (1919). (Courtesy of the Alabama Department of Archives and History, Special Collections)

Tallulah in 1923, shortly before sailing for England to play opposite Sir Gerald de Maurier in *The Dancers*. De Maurier was considered one of the greatest theater directors and producers of his day. (Courtesy of the Alabama Department of Archives and History, Special Collections)

Charles Bickford, Paul Lukas, and Tallulah in the film *Thunder Below* (1932) (Courtesy of Jerry Ohlinger's Movie Materials Store)

Gary Cooper and Tallulah in the film *Devil in the Deep* (1932), directed by Marion Gering (Courtesy of Jerry Ohlinger's Movie Materials Store)

Tallulah hugging her father, William B. Bankhead, ca. 1940 (Courtesy of the Alabama Department of Archives and History, Special Collections)

Charles Dingle, Dan Duryea, Carl Benton Reid, and Tallulah in the stage production of Lillian Hellman's *The Little Foxes* (1939). Tallulah considered her role as Regina Giddens as one of the greatest of her theatrical career. (Courtesy of Jerry Ohlinger's Movie Materials Store)

The Greatest Play of the Generation!

HERMAN SHUMLIN
PRESENTS

TALLULAH
BANKHEAD
"The
LITTLE FOXES

LILLIAN HELLMAN'S DRAMATIC TRIUMPH
with
FRANK CONROY
STAGED BY MR. SHUMLIN

LANIER HIGH SCHOOL AUDITORIUM
Thursday, February 13 at 8.30 P. M.

Playbill for a February 13, 1941, production of *The Little Foxes*. The performance took place at Sidney Lanier High School in Montgomery, Alabama. (Courtesy of the Alabama Department of Archives and History, Special Collections)

John Emery, William B. Bankhead, and Tallulah in 1937. Tallulah and Emery were married on August 31, 1937, in Jasper, Alabama. (Courtesy of Jerry Ohlinger's Movie Materials Store)

Tallulah as Sabina in
the stage production
of Thornton Wilder's
The Skin of Our Teeth
(1942) (Courtesy of
Jerry Ohlinger's Movie
Materials Store)

John Hodiak, Walter Slezak, Hume Cronyn, Tallulah, Mary Anderson, Heather
Angel, Henry Hull, and Canada Lee in the film *Lifeboat* (1944). This film was
directed by Alfred Hitchcock from a story by John Steinbeck, and Tallulah won a
New York Film Critics Circle Award for her performance. (Courtesy of Jerry
Ohlinger's Movie Materials Store)

William Eythe and Tallulah (as Catherine the Great) in *A Royal Scandal* (1945), directed by Otto Preminger (Courtesy of Jerry Ohlinger's Movie Materials Store)

Donald Cook and Tallulah in a 1948 stage production of Noel Coward's *Private Lives*. Originally produced in 1944, the play was a smash hit in which Tallulah toured for several years. (Courtesy of Jerry Ohlinger's Movie Materials Store)

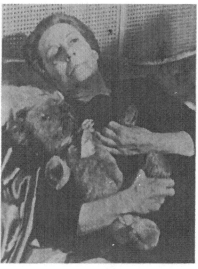

Tallulah in her last major film role in *Die! Die! My Darling* (1965), directed by Silvio Narizzano (Courtesy of Jerry Ohlinger's Movie Materials Store)

As the Black Widow in the *Batman* television series, 1967 (Courtesy of Jerry Ohlinger's Movie Materials Store)

Publicity photo, ca. 1940 (Courtesy of the Alabama Department of Archives and History, Special Collections)

engaged. Michael was a paragon of unpunctuality. He was always late, invariably offered his demanding hours at the Beaverbrook papers as an excuse.

On the opening night of *The Garden of Eden* he sent me a beautiful little eighteenth-century diamond brooch. But he missed the first two acts of the play. I was furious that he should be so careless. His alibi implicated Beaverbrook. He had been detained at the *Express* again.

For all the helter-skelter life I've led I have a phobia about being stood up, or of being late for an appointment. I've never missed a plane or a train in my life. I am always a good half hour ahead of time.

When I faced him after the final curtain, I blazed: "Look, Michael, if you're ever late again, I'm through with you. I'll never speak to you again. I *cannot* stand such nonsense!"

Two nights later he put me to the test. He was late again! By a good half hour! Having delivered an ultimatum I must live up to it.

"Michael, this is the end. It's happened day after day, night after night. I cannot take it," I raged.

Captain Wardell took the verdict nonchalantly. The next morning he rang me up. "Tell him I'm in my bath," I told my maid. I instructed all the servants—this was when I was in the chips in Farm Street—to say: "Miss Bankhead is in her bath," every time the Captain called. Michael was a determined type. He rang me up half a dozen times a day for two weeks. He seemed to think it quite normal for me to live in the tub.

But Michael was a man of resource. Returning home after a matinee two weeks after our split, I encountered a stranger in the bathroom. "Who are you, and what are you up to?" I roared.

"I'm installing a telephone in your bathroom," he said. "On

whose orders?" "On the orders of Captain Michael Wardell," he
replied. I routed the intruder along with his wires and pliers. But
that wasn't the last strategy of my Captain.

Michael's nine-year-old son was one of my favorites. Because of
ill health he didn't attend public school. He was being educated by
tutors, and was sophisticated beyond his years. He frequently sent
me notes signed "The Man with a Load of Mischief," the title of
an Ashley Dukes play. Thus I was not astonished when Simon
called me up one day: "Tallulah, darling! Could you lunch with
me tomorrow?"

"Sure, Simon, I'd love to. Where shall we lunch?"

"Anywhere you like, Tallulah. How about one at the Embassy.
I'll fetch you. Jolly fun, I think."

At the Embassy he escorted me to the bar, stood me a champagne
cocktail—he wasn't having anything, naturally. Then he took me
to our table upstairs. We had just started lunch when Michael
strolled in. Casually he paraded past, then turned to say, "Oh,
hello, Simon." The plot was Machiavellian. I couldn't berate
Michael in front of his own son, so for the next half hour we
engaged in airy chitchat.

I've always loved little boys. I completely ruined Sister's son,
Billy, when he stayed with me for a summer in Westchester. When
Billy came up from the deep South he talked like Amos, partner
of Andy. Then Sister took him abroad for two years—to Paris and
Algiers in North Africa. When next I saw him he was talking and
acting like Maurice Chevalier, down to the last shrug.

Sister, too, had her hour on the stage. Idling between marriages,
and unbeknownst to me, Eugenia got a small role in *The Barker*,
the comedy about carnival life in which Claudette Colbert had
made such a hit in New York. It had a tryout engagement in Manchester. There the critics of the *Empire News* got so worked up

over the prospect of a second Bankhead loose in the island he devoted his whole revue to Sister. Hear how he carried on:

While Tallulah Bankhead creates storms of hysterical frenzy among the gallery girls, Eugenia Hoyt disturbs masculine hearts. There is no need for her to wear scarlet garters on her shapely legs, though she does so very effectively. She has large dark eyes, and a husky drawing voice to betoken the passionate nature which she throws wholeheartedly into her acting.

Facing another Bankhead confused the Manchester reviewer. Confident no Bankhead would settle for less than the leading role, this gentleman had mistaken Sister for Claudette. Sister's only contribution was a hula-hula she wriggled in the last act. I went to the opening in London with Alan Parsons, critic of the *Daily Mail*, and husband of Viola Tree. His report the next day was chiefly concerned with my emotional reactions as I sat in on Sister's debut. She carried off her role with Bankhead zest. But she had no heart for it. She had other fish to fry. After two weeks she left the company without notice, without even asking for her salary, and went back to Paris. Sister was later to give some spectacular performances —but not on the stage.

Warmest and most generous of the Americans I met in London was Al Woods. He had made millions out of bedroom farces in New York. He called everyone sweetheart. I first met Al Woods in 1924, when convalescing from *Conchita* and *This Marriage*. As usual I was low in funds. I was low in spirits, too. We were fellow guests at a luncheon at the Savoy. He was leaving for America the next day.

On being introduced he said, "How are you for money, sweetheart?"

"I'm fine, darling. Everything's okay," I lied.

The next morning there was a letter from him at my flat. Out of it dropped a five-hundred-dollar bill, pinned to this note: "You don't fool me, sweetheart."

Five years later the stock market crash wiped Woods out. He was abroad at the time of the disaster. He felt secure, since he had over a million dollars in his safety deposit box. But the box was the joint property of Woods and his wife. She had been sucked into the market. Caught in the crash she had used up all Al's cash in an effort to salvage stocks bought on margin. When I returned to New York Woods was shattered. He ate in little Sixth Avenue delicatessens. He avoided his friends, rebuffed those who sought to cheer him up.

One day I received a note from him.

"Dear Tallulah," he wrote, "I hate to do this, but do you remember the five hundred I loaned you?" I was shocked that this man who had given away thousands could be in so desperate a plight. I knew how tortured he must be to ask for the return of something he had given me.

But I was elated that I could oblige him. I sent him my check for five hundred, with this note: "Darling, I hope you don't need this as badly as I did when you loaned it to me."

Sam Harris told me Woods broke down when he received my check. "After all the things I've done for people! This girl whom I hardly know is the only one except you who has helped me. And she didn't even owe it to me," he said to Sam. A gallant gentleman, Al Woods. He deserved better at the hands of the theater.

Threshing about in the past, I may as well introduce Criminal-at-Large. That's what I called Archie Selwyn, who with his brother Edgar long flourished on Broadway. Together they reared up a mess of theaters, amassed fortunes, lost fortunes. In the end Archie wound up behind the darkest of eight-balls which seems to be the common end of producers. Woods, Ziegfeld, Charles Dillingham, the Selwyns, Arthur Hopkins—all ended in the scuppers. Those gallants used to put up their own money for productions. Today a producer who invests so much as a quarter in his own play is looked upon as a mental case, a traitor to his class.

Archie Selwyn was a fascinating rogue. He was a man of enormous vision, of reckless expenditures, a gambler. He was a caller at my Farm Street house in London, too. To show his talent for paradox, he denounced me for my extravagances. It was Archie who baited me into signing a contract for a phantom comedy by Frederick Lonsdale, a miscue which led to me being hooked in *Blackmail* and *Mud and Treacle*, two of the worst plays ever to fog the footlights.

"You're a fool, Tallulah, to be spending all this money," said Archie, as he looked about my living room awash with champagne. "You've got to think of the future. Why don't you make these free-loaders give you something for this new home of yours?"

"Come, come, Archie," I said. "I can't impose a toll charge on my guests. Bottoms up, my brave! And to hell with the future!"

But Archie was insistent. "All right, why don't you start it?" I said.

"Agreed," said Archie. "What's the most expensive thing in your house?"

"My bed," I said. "It cost me three hundred pounds."

Whereupon Archie wrote me out his check for three hundred pounds. It came in handy. The bed was unpaid for. Two years later Archie was beggared by the stock market crash. There was an aftermath to that bed business. A week after his gesture he and I were guests at a charity bazaar. Freddy Lonsdale was officiating. Midway through the proceedings he swayed to his feet and said, "And now, ladies and gentlemen, you'll hear from that wayward American, that sterling citizen, Mr. Archie Selwyn, the man who gave Tallulah Bankhead her bed." The rumor-mongers relished that crack. In my time I've scrambled many a commandment, upended many a statute, but I've never been a kept woman! You can lay to that, Long John Silver!

So long as I'm in my bread-upon-the-waters mood I may as well cite Frank Hunter, one of the greatest doubles players ever to pace a court.

Frank was that rare thing, a wealthy tennis player. He and Bill Tilden won the doubles championship at Wimbledon in 1927. In 1928 I went with him to Paris for the Davis Cup matches in which the Three Musketeers, Cochet, LaCoste and Borotra, mowed our boys down, four matches out of five. For a summer Frank and I were *en rapport*, if you will excuse the euphemism. We had a lot of fun. On leaving for America, and aware of my financial status, he said:

"Now look, Tallulah! You have to live by your talent and your looks and your health. I'm very rich. I can't spend all my money. I play tennis because I love the game. Tilden does it because it's his life. Should you ever be in straits, just send me a cable. There'll be no strings attached. It will mean nothing to me. It might mean much to you."

Now for a splash of irony. When I returned to New York in '31, crawling with money because of my Paramount contract, Frank's fortune had been wiped out. Didn't have a sou. Writhing with embarrassment, he wrote that he was in dire straits. Could I let him have a thousand dollars? Should I be able to oblige him, he insisted I accept a legal note and six per cent interest. I sent him the thousand with a note: "Thank God you know who your friends are."

Lower the curtain to denote the lapse of six years. It is New Year's Eve of 1937. I have just been kayoed by Cleopatra, I've been married to John Emery for four months. We are down to our last can of pemmican. Broke, bemused and bewildered! Happy New Year indeed!

But the luck of the Bankheads held! Asked to a party at "21," we needed no second bidding. When we entered the private room on "21's" third floor, the first man I bumped into was Frank Hunter. "Come here, you bastard," I shouted. "Where's that thousand bucks I loaned you? I could do with it right now."

"My God, Tallulah," said Frank, "don't tell me I never paid it!" With that he dove into his pocket, pulled out two five-hundred-dollar bills and placed them in my hand. Frank had recouped his fortunes. He was the agent for all liquids consumed at "21." My loan to him was a blessing. Had I not made it, the thousand would have been gone long since. Loaning it to him was like putting it in a bank.

Have I darkly hinted that for eight years I cut a great swath in London? Well I damned well did, and it was all a spur to my ego, electrifying! London beaux clamored for my company. To be seen with me in the supper clubs, in the after-hour hideaways, the Paris boîtes on delirious week ends, confirmed their midnight note. I created quite a stir wherever I went. I rejoiced in this harum-scarum attention to the hilt, perhaps a little beyond the hilt. I had ecstatic flings with many of these braves, but I was incapable of sustained ardors. Sufficient unto the day was the night thereof, if I may corrupt an adage.

Remember Kimbolton, that haunted castle in which I shivered early in this chronicle? It is the ancestral home of the Duke of Manchester. What was I doing there? I was the house guest of Lord Mandeville, son of the Duke. Mandy six times offered to make me a Lady. My nays were gentle but firm.

My name was readily identifiable from Soho to the Strand, from

Limehouse to Chequers. Beaverbrook used to say that there were only two people in the realm who could be identified by any costermonger on hearing their given name—Steve and Tallulah. Steve was Donoghue—great English jockey. In headlines and on sandwich signs, the newspapers found "Tallulah" a satisfying and sufficient tag. Anything said or done by the Prince of Wales, Bernard Shaw or Tallulah rated page one, continued Max.

Get a load of Reginald Arkell in *London Calling*:

Everybody knows that Tallulah is one of those girls who could lure a Scotch elder into any indiscretion. Positively! Her lips are as scarlet as a guardsman's coat, and her diamonds make the flashing signs of Piccadilly look like farthing dips. She plays "He loves me, he loves me not" with pearls that are as big as potatoes.

Reginald worked himself into that lather after accompanying me to Leeds for a dress rehearsal of *Her Cardboard Lover*. In mock indignation he berated the burghers of St. Pancras. Why hadn't they rolled out a red carpet for me?

How will the stubborn Scots in Glasgow take her? This was the query of a lady journalist who came upon me in *Her Cardboard Lover*. Then she volunteered a reply:

Down go the lights and up goes the curtain, and in a few minutes Tallulah—in a sheath of ebony ring velvet shoulder-strapped with diamante—insinuates herself onto the stage. The famous husky voice with the break in it is there, the swift, lithe movements of body, and the rapid and disarming changes and hair tossing and tearing to chuckling, wheedling tenderness. As a vivid, irrational, emotional Frenchwoman she carries the vein of unrestrained farce without a moment's departure for subtlety. Beautiful? Oh, quite! Feline? Yes, with the broad, languorous movements of a blue Persian kitten whose claws are never far concealed. She can scream, too, not unlike the wail of a cat in the night.

That kind of talk might have turned the head of a Helen of Troy, much less a you-all miss from Jasper, Alabama.

164.

The English were great ones for throwing charity balls, garden parties, costume charades. At the drop of a Homburg all of London's *jeunesse dorée* would tog themselves out in masquerade. At these routs I might be Jean Borotra, Cleopatra, one of the Medicis. I had a lot of fun at these *chichi* carouses, but the parties I enjoyed most were Beaverbrook's. Sometimes he'd give them at his private office in the Express Building, sometimes at his town house, sometimes at his country estate, sometimes at a smaller place he had near Maidenhead.

Rarely did he have more than ten or twelve guests. Usually he had the same people—Lord Ivor Churchill, Perry, later Lord Bronlow, Edward's equerry up until his abdication, Jean and Richard Norton and Michael Wardell. When the occasion called for an outsized rout, Max would hire a couple of private rooms at the Savoy, bring in an orchestra and such headliners as Sophie Tucker and Rudolph Valentino. All Bohemian London would turn out and such somebodies as the Aga Khan, Lord Balfour and Sir James Dunn.

Max was but thirty-two when knighted in 1911, six years later became Lord Beaverbrook. Born William Maxwell Aitken in Canada, he had affection for invading Americans. He loved parties, loved to entertain people of talent. He is a brilliant conversationalist and has a remarkable memory. I learned of his talent as a spellbinder when Sister and I were week-end guests on his yacht. I was croaking with laryngitis, and sought to delay the trip. Max brushed my protests aside. "The sea air will be good for your throat. You can relax. I'll send my car for you and Eugenia."

We sat down to dinner that night with Lord Castleross, then writing a daily column for Max, and Lord Birkenhead, sometimes Chancellor of the Exchequer and Secretary for India and one of the greatest orators in the realm. Dinner over Max took the floor.

A magnum of champagne in his hand, he circled about the room, talking constantly and entertainingly on an amazing variety of subjects. One minute he'd be deep in the Old Testament, the next in a recital of the flight of Sweden's Charles XII to Turkey after his defeat at Poltava by Peter the Great. Max was smallish, built like a brownie, but he kept us fascinated until daylight, uninterrupted. I tag on uninterrupted to befuddle those oafs who swear I'm incapable of listening. Faced by my betters, I can hold my tongue. Ambushed by clods, I prefer to deliver the address.

During Sister's visit she and I went down to Beaverbrook's great country place—formal gardens, swimming pool, statuary, tradition and history—"Charkley," near Leatherhead, Surrey. There we were photographed for one of London's illustrated weeklies. When the pictures appeared they were headed:

TALLULAH'S COUNTRY HOME

Country home indeed! My digs were a small service flat in Curzon Street. All the tenants in a service flat building have access to cook and butler. They serve meals in your room if provided with the essentials. They go with the rent.

Richard Norton was a familiar at Beaverbrook's parties. He was a high-ranking executive in one of London's movie studios, witty and ingratiating. As such he had not endeared himself to one worker at the studio. To indicate his distemper this rebel scrawled "Richard Norton is a bastard" on the waiting-room wall. Norton had just become Lord Grantley when confronted with this slur. Undisturbed, he drew out a pencil, struck out Richard Norton, inserted above it "Lord Grantley."

When I opened at St. Martin's in *Scotch Mist,* Max gave me a party. *Scotch Mist* was a play by Sir Patrick Hastings, K.C. and M.P. I played a wild baggage, wife of a British Cabinet minister,

166.

who was trying to lay waste all Downing Street. Upset by its plot, the Bishop of London denounced it from his pulpit. The Lord Bishop changed a failure into a long-run success. Nothing like a clerical blast to buck up a sagging box office! Beaverbrook footed the bill for my party, but let me invite anyone I chose. Catholic if capricious in my choices, my guests ranged from princes to paupers, from riffraff to the rare refinements of Burke's Peerage. To Max's astonishment all of them turned out. If consumption of champagne is a criterion, all had one hell of a time.

Coincident with this shindig, Beaverbrook put my integrity to the test. Aware that *Scotch Mist* might be manhandled, he whispered: "Would you like me to speak to my critics?" Now I like an enthusiastic review as well as the next waif, but I don't want an instructed verdict. I gave Max a flat no. I think he thought better of me for it.

My talent as a rumor-provoker bore fruit shortly after I met Max. Paged while dancing at the Embassy, one of the morning papers asked me to confirm a story Max and I were engaged. Shortly the same question was put to me by a reporter from Max's own paper. Although he never confessed, I'm sure Max instigated the rumor. The only one who took this hoax seriously was Rebecca West. She took time out from her literary activities to write Max a letter of protest. She had a soft spot for Max, was annoyed at his concern with a pretty face.

Beaverbrook could be up to mischief when he scented an exclusive story, one that might stimulate circulation. He offered Perry Cust and me a thousand pounds if he could announce our engagement, another thousand when he would announce we had broken our troth. Perry was engaged at the time to Kitty Kinlock so the plot ran on a reef. I could have used a thousand pounds then, brother! So could Perry.

Max took me to Winston Churchill's country house where we found him deep in brick-laying. That's the only time I ever met him. But there were other Churchills. I'll get around to them shortly. It was through Max, too, that I met Lloyd George. In the fall of 1925 we went to Lloyd George's place, "Bron-y-de," in Churt, Surrey. We met the great Welshman in his garden. I was impressed with his charm and his gallantry. He cut a rose and handed it to me. Then he took us into his living room. Spread on the floor were the London reviews of *The Green Hat*, the Armenian mishmash in which I had opened at the Adelphi the week before.

Since I'm on a name-dropping binge, let's subpoena Ramsay Mac-Donald. I first met him at luncheon at a friend's house. He was then Prime Minister and I was duly impressed. I was even more impressed when he asked me to have lunch with him at the House of Parliament. Sure I'd have lunch with him. After lunch he drove me to my theater. The bobbies all recognized him. I got a great kick tooling down Piccadilly, the Prime Minister by my side.

When I opened in *Mud and Treacle* I invited him to a performance. It was one of those pro-and-anti-labor harangues. He was about the only man in the audience. The critics had slated this sermon, and theatergoers avoided it as they would a mine field. After the performance he came back to my dressing room. We split a pint of champagne. When we left he was gracious enough to autograph the programs of my gallery gang squealing at the stage door. It wasn't often they could bag Tallulah and a Prime Minister in one swoop.

Those other Churchills? Drop up to my chalet in Bedford Village and I'll show you a diamond brooch and my bust by Dobson. They're souvenirs of my friendship for Lord Ivor Churchill, son of the Duke of Marlborough. His mother was Consuelo Vanderbilt. His elder brother is the current Duke of Marlborough. Ivor and I were sympathetic. His chief interest was art and he had an astonishing collection of paintings. His idea of a gala was to lunch at Knoedler's Galleries, spend the rest of the afternoon anchored before this picture or that.

One picture fascinated him. It was a Vermeer, a small exquisite canvas for which Andrew Mellon later forked up something like $300,000. For all his titles and acres the Vermeer was beyond Ivor's purse. I had spent some six or seven afternoons with Ivor and Lord Bronlow, mooning over the Vermeer, when I thought up a diversion. Ivor was coming to my service flat of a Tuesday for tea. I connived with the management of Knoedler's to lend me the Vermeer. I wanted to hang it on the wall of my living room, thus dumbfound my guest. When Ivor looked upon the Vermeer in my flat his emotions should be something to behold. Knoedler's fell in with the plot. They took the precaution of stationing two plain-clothes men at the entrance to my flat so long as the Vermeer was in my possession.

I hung the Vermeer directly over my fireplace, the most conspicuous spot in the room. Ivor came to tea, stayed for an hour and a half, then departed. Without so much as the flicker of an eyelash did he indicate he had noticed the apple of his eye. His calm in the face of this taunt was maddening. Ivor was one of those fabled Englishmen who is beyond surprise. He would rather be consumed in flame than give any manifestation of curiosity.

Randolph Churchill? The first time he stood for Parliament I was playing in some atrocity in Manchester. He called up to ask if I'd campaign for him. I thought it would be a lark though I knew nothing of his pledges or his policies. Three or four times I bounced up on a platform and pleaded with the audience to put young Mr. Churchill in Commons. I found my candidate a trifle boring, a dash humorless, a little too hearty. His hints that our alliance might be mutually intoxicating did it proceed beyond the campaign left me cold as a cod. When he continued to call me on my return to London, I put an end to this escapade. "Listen, darling, it wasn't you, it was Manchester."

Did you happen to be browsing through the *New York Times* in late November, '28, you might have seen this item under a London date line: "Tallulah Bankhead, American stage star who has been playing in London these past five years, will shortly be married to Count Anthony de Bosardi, Italian businessman now resident in London."

Five months later the *Times,* eager to keep its clientele in touch with the conflagration, quoted me: "Tony and I have agreed to disagree." The *Times* went on to say it had been rumored the Count was to settle $500,000 on his bride.

I first met Tony at Brighton, while romping around with my friend, Monica Morrice. At dinner one night Monica spied him at a table with a girl. "Write him a note and ask him to come over," urged Monica. I wavered. "I can't send a note to a man I've never met," I protested.

"But I'm crazy about him," she argued. "He's so fascinating! Please?"

Eager to oblige a friend in flames, I waited until another man joined Tony, then sent this note by the waiter:

"If you are free, we'd like to have you come over for a liqueur with us."

Tony was over like a shot. He took one look at me, then started to act like Nelson at Trafalgar. Tony was handsome, possessed of great charm, and the last word in confidence. He was an amazing dancer. He had great love of music and a colossal nerve. When he got back to London he sent me a note. He stated brazenly he was going to marry me. With the note he sent an antique wastebasket, just to get my guard down. Three days later he moved into my home, announcing to the butler, "I'm not leaving here until she marries me."

Tony was British-born and hadn't seen Italy until he was twenty-five. That $500,000 bonus! Moonshine! But he oozed small gallantries. He was a born show-off. On impulse he'd charter a plane that we might fly to Paris for luncheon of a Sunday. When he said he wasn't leaving until I conceded, he wasn't fooling. His first directive was to my butler. "You can have the day off!" I didn't know how to cope with so rugged a Romeo! When he slipped a diamond necklace about my neck, I veered off my course. To accept this bauble from a brave to whom I was not engaged seemed reckless, even though he was sleeping in my home. Newspapermen had started to queue up at my door. So I capitulated.

Tony had a great knowledge of food and wine. He was smart, crafty, and a bit twisted. At Winchester he had starred on the cricket team. He had won a scholarship at Oxford. Once he won a gold medal for a poem in competition with so stout an opponent as Rupert Brooke. He never documented this poem. He could give a good account of himself on the golf course, the tennis court. He tossed money around with abandon, talked of it and his ability to make it in soaring terms. He was a brilliant linguist. He handed me a Rolls-Royce with the same nonchalance with which he offered me a cigarette. In retaliation I gave him a watch flecked with diamond numerals. But he was too damned dynamic! A composite of Frank Merriwell, Chesterfield, Captain Bligh and Brillat-Savarin.

His arrogance when crossed was unnerving. He loved me, I think, as much as it was possible for him to love anyone. It inflated his vanity to bag so pursued a belle as your correspondent. He was a calculating opportunist, full of prunes and punctilio.

My decision to forego Tony came after our safari to Berlin. He was up to some hanky-panky with UFA, the German film company, and I became convinced I was being used as a front, even a decoy. Other doubts churned me when I learned he had been previously married to a gal from Chicago, and had been divorced in the United States. The marriage was valid enough by British conventions, but the divorce was debatable. Did we get married he might have been hauled up on charges of bigamy.

He stayed on in Berlin when I went on tour in *Her Cardboard Lover*. I phoned him from Scotland. "I can't marry you, Tony," I said. "I don't want to. Besides it wouldn't be legal." Tony didn't sob or threaten to throw himself into the Spree. Insouciant as ever (That's what I said, Buster. Insouciant!) he only asked that I delay news of the breach until he could wind up his Berlin business. In terms of commerce the rift might make him look a touch frivolous. He'd been engaged to two other girls shortly before I met him. I agreed. After a decent interval, that he might face up to UFA in style, I phoned my friends on Beaverbrook's *Express*. I urged them to exert a little restraint, to avoid crediting me with any of that marriage-and-a-career-don't-mix nonsense.

That is how I took the Count, to say nothing of losing the only Rolls Royce I ever owned. Or did I own it? The only trophy I salvaged was the necklace. Perhaps I'm headlong in boasting I bagged the Count. It would be closer to the truth did I say he damned near bagged me.

In my eight years in London I appeared in sixteen plays. *Conchita, This Marriage, Blackmail, Mud and Treacle* and *He's Mine* were ridiculous, inept messes, fated for quick disaster. *The Creaking Chair, Scotch Mist, The Garden of Eden* were little better. They outraged all the rules of plot, dialogue and construction, but prospered in varying degrees, aided, I immodestly submit, by the contributions of your violet.

Starting with *The Green Hat* in 1925, I starred in five plays that had previously enjoyed great success in New York: *The Green Hat*, in which Katharine Cornell played Iris March at the same time I did; Sidney Howard's Pulitzer Prize Play, *They Knew What They Wanted*, with Pauline Lord the original Amy; *The Gold Diggers* seven years after Ina Claire impersonated Jerry Lamar at the Belasco; *Her Cardboard Lover*, in which Jeanne Eagles established priority rights, and, finally, Rachel Crothers' *Let Us Be Gay*, the comedy in which Francine Larrimore flourished at the Lyric in New York. *Let Us Be Gay* was my last London play. It was ironic that I should be echoing the Francine Larrimore whom I had supported in *Nice People* ten years earlier.

Those were eight crowded and exciting years. In my second play I achieved the actress's ultimate, stardom. But the critics chanted that, aside from *They Knew What They Wanted*, I had not had a play worthy of my yet untested talent. For all my reputed beauty, my excitements, my ability to stimulate box-office trade, my position in the theater was yet to be established.

Because of my spendthrift ways, my scorn for tomorrow, I was never in a position to sit back and wait for a good play. Who in the theater can afford that luxury? Pressed for money, I had to take the first thing offered me. Always in debt, I was nagged by necessity. I couldn't take time out to pause and reflect.

My salary had steadily risen until I could ask and get five hundred pounds. Had I been smarter, I could have topped that figure. I did top it when, with the consent of the management of *The Garden of Eden*, I made my first and only British film, *His House in Order*. This was a silent version of the old Pinero stage success. It enabled me to earn another five hundred pounds a week. The English press said I was being paid the highest salary ever given a film star in the islands. This was an exaggeration. I spurned quite a few film offers in England. I looked upon the screen as an unworthy upstart. Once, deviled by debt, I appeared in a vaudeville sketch at the Palladium. Whatever my role, whatever my play, whatever my success, I was always shuttling to and from the pawnshop. When Paramount waved a fancy, long-term contract at me I was in no position to haggle. If ever my books were to balance, this was the time to strike.

The critics were my partisans, but that did not lead them to a blanket endorsement of my antics. In London as in New York, the reviewers are notorious for their conflicting opinions. When I impersonated Iris March in *The Green Hat* the savant on the *Express* wrote: "Miss Bankhead is a genius. She does not act Iris March. She *is* Iris March." But his brother on the *Daily Mail* dissented. "Miss Bankhead neither walked, talked, looked nor acted like a member of a County family, but more like a member of the county jail," said he. I made a discovery the first day I rehearsed in Michael Arlen's play that escaped all the reviewers. It is reminiscent of *La Dame aux Camelias*. This suspicion became a conviction when I impersonated Marguerite Gautier in the Dumas work in 1930.

Camille was a risky do, if I may employ a dab of London slang. Heralding the revival, one London paper headed the story with TALLULAH TO FOLLOW IN FOOTSTEPS OF BERNHARDT AND DUSE. I was about to validate Shakespeare's "comparisons are odorous." I was very fetching in hoopskirts and crinoline, but James Agate wrote in the *Times* that my Marguerite was so chaste as to be downright painful. This was the same Mr. Agate who said I had "the spark of Bernhardt" after seeing me in the stinker called *Blackmail*. By way of atonement Agate later dug up the Rome and Paris judgments on both Duse and Sarah, when first they locked horns with Miss Gautier. I was solaced to read that both girls had been slapped down by the reviewers. My fanatics in the gallery remained loyal. They sobbed deliriously as I went through my death convulsions at the final curtain.

Here I'd like to intrude an estimate of my acting I treasure. Ivor Brown, still one of England's top drama critics, ridiculed the plot of *He's Mine,* an adaptation of a French farce in which I played a fake Serbian princess, but lauded your reporter. Wrote Mr. Brown:

> Miss Tallulah Bankhead's amazing energy and command of a dozen swiftly variable moods gives some sort of life and lustre even to this stuff. Miss Bankhead hits off the toughness and tenderness, the cheek and the charm of the husband-hunters with an easy passage up and down the scale of waywardness. Easy, it seems, but the effort must be enormous. Miss Bankhead never walks through a part; her simulations of caprice are triumphs of conscientiousness. Like all great players she is not so much the public's servant as its drudge, and I never see her act without respecting the diligence as well as the virtuosity of one who gloriously seeks to please.

Succumbing to Paramount while still playing in *Let Us Be Gay,* I decided to sell my Farm Street home, since my Hollywood phase was to cover, in theory, at least five years. The Maharanee of Cooch Behar was the leading bidder. Checkmated by edict, she compromised by signing up John Underdown, my butler, and spiriting him off to India. The die cast, I crated up my furniture, gave the Bentley back to its co-owners, and fled for Southampton and the *Aquitania.* Leaving England almost eight years to the day of my arrival, I had feasted on fame, rejoiced in stardom, reveled in page-one note.

Professionally I had advanced from comparative obscurity to international recognition. Fiscally I had receded. I had a letter of credit for a thousand dollars on my arrival; on my departure I had less. I left a lot of debts behind me, a few income tax arrears. But I left a lot of friends behind me, too. My eight years in London were the happiest and most exciting in my life.

8.

Portraits and Pranks

My most valuable possession is my Augustus John portrait.

I first met this great man of a midnight at the Eiffel Tower, an after-closing rendezvous in Soho. Doodling on a piece of paper he sketched out my face, soon thereafter asked me to pose for him. I was not familiar enough with John's fame or the customs of his rarefied world to realize the scope of this compliment. Blithely I brushed him off. My hairbrained excuse? I couldn't sit still that long! Sporadically over the next few years he renewed his offer. Finally I gave in. Damned white of me, wasn't it? I shudder belatedly at my audacity.

Even in agreeing to sit for John I had to haggle. Before I would consent to immortality I made John agree to sell me the portrait for a thousand pounds, once it had been exhibited. Save on matinee days I went to his studio each afternoon for two weeks. I became fascinated by the art and technique of the man whom many regarded as the greatest living portrait painter. He was a Bohemian, something of an eccentric. He wore jade earrings and was supposed to be the inspiration for *The Constant Nymph*, Margaret Kennedy and Basil Dean's play about an unconventional artist and his heretic household, adapted from the novel of the same name.

I was to learn that he was famous for "The Smiling Woman" and "The Way Down to the Sea," as well as for his portraits of many of the great in the literary and social world, George Bernard Shaw and William Butler Yeats among them. A defiant gypsy, John long had feuded with the Royal Academy. He had refused to show his pictures under its auspices. The membership was squeamish about admitting him because of his unconventional private life. Eventually it backed water.

John had just started to outline my face when the canvas was seen by Lawrence of Arabia. The author of *The Seven Pillars of Wisdom*, the man who had led the Arab revolt in Syria in World War I, was then identified as Aircraftsman T. E. Shaw. He had a fierce desire for anonymity and stubbornly flouted honors and offers of advancement from a grateful nation. I first met him when I was sitting for the sculptor, Dobson. Lawrence was experiencing his first artistic fever. He haunted Dobson's studio. When I ran out of "gaspers," he'd chug off on his motorcycle to get me cigarettes.

His enthusiasm for the portrait was something to see. In cavalier fashion he told John that he must have it in its unfinished state. When John demurred, Lawrence pointed out that it would be easy to start another. John ignored this request, much as he disliked disappointing a hero.

Enter now, stage right, the Viscount d'Abernon, noted art connoisseur and collector, and the British Ambassador to Germany. He was sitting for John for his own portrait. On seeing mine he made a fabulous offer for it. He wanted to present it to the Tate Gallery. To complicate matters Lord Beaverbrook wrote John: "You're a fool to give this to Tallulah. You could get twenty thousand pounds for it. Shortly John asked me to release him from our agreement. He wanted the picture for himself. He said that he would do another of me. I held John to his promise.

Other John canvases in that year's show were portraits of Lord d'Abernon and Sir Gerald du Maurier. I had a finger in the hanging of the last named. One afternoon while sitting for John I blurted out, "You've got to do Sir Gerald. He has such a wonderful face." "Oh, I did him some years ago," said John. "It's here some place. I'll try to find it." On my next visit he had dug up the du Maurier portrait. It was wonderful. When John expressed indifference, I tossed him this threat: "I'll not sit one more day for you, unless you show Gerald's picture at the Royal Academy." Quite a hellion, wasn't I? I should have been spanked. But Sir Gerald was hung.

When shown at the Academy my portrait created a great stir. John had done me in pale pastels, after the manner of El Greco, said one critic, wispy, a little gaunt and eerie. One judge called it "the greatest portraiture since Gainsborough's 'Perdita.' "

After Tallulah had been suspended at the Academy, she was crated up and brought to my house in Farm Street. Only then would John sign it, on my insistence. He felt his portraits were so distinctive they needed no identification of the artist. He was teetering on my bed, about to affix his signature, when a woman from Beaverbrook's *Express* arrived to hear me say, "My God, it's beautiful." A headline in the *Express* the next day read: TALLULAH SAYS "MY GOD! I'M BEAUTIFUL!"

The painting moved producer Arthur Hopkins to a flattering compliment. The John portrait, he said, showed the world what he had long suspected. I had a soul. Flattery is fine, if you don't inhale, to quote Adlai Stevenson.

Sir Gerald did not like his portrait at all. He gave out stories saying he had no intention of having so fearful an apparition looking down at him in his bedroom. I was astonished at this reaction. Shortly Audrey Carten and I were at a shindig called The Green Room Rag. It was not unlike the Lambs Gambol in New York.

A horrid little caricature of Sir Gerald was being auctioned off. We bid it in, then sent it to Sir Gerald with this note:

Patron of the Arts:
In view of the injustice done you by the brush of that second-rate artist, Augustus John, who had the impertinence to paint you as a mere genius instead of the Hampstead gentleman that you are, we wish to present to you this masterwork.

My insistence on getting the John portrait, even though I had to go in hock, was due to an earlier disappointment. Some years before I had sat for Ambrose McEvoy, who had a great vogue in London as well as connections at Court. He had an odd technique. He painted me in profile while looking at my reflection in a mirror. My sideview brought him a stack of sterling. Since I had sat for him as a favor, McEvoy painted me a second time, full face, with the promise that the portrait would be mine once he had shown it. Shortly thereafter he died. The day my likeness was hung, along with that of Princess Pat, I had a matinee. When I got to the Leicester Galleries the next day I was shocked to find that McEvoy's Tallulah bore a red seal. This meant it had been sold. But out of respect for his family, I didn't start a donnybrook. After all, ours had been only a verbal agreement.

When I learned it had been purchased by Anthony Rothschild, of the British branch of that house, I called the gentleman up. Although I didn't have a guinea to my name I said: "I know you bought the McEvoy portrait for six hundred pounds. I'm prepared to purchase it from you for something more than that." Mr. Rothschild was gentle but firm. McEvoy was his favorite painter. He had a room full of McEvoys, and he was particularly fond of the Bankhead, me in a pale blue dress against a pale pink background, slightly unfinished in the McEvoy style.

That was when I was engaged to Tony Bosardi. I hoped to give it to him as a wedding present. I have yet to meet Anthony Roths-child but I still have hopes of getting the McEvoy. I'm a bitter ender.

Leaving London, I was still indebted to John. I had been back in New York only a month or two when I was approached by an agent of Sir Joseph Duveen, the fabulous art dealer. He said a client whose name he could not reveal was prepared to pay one hundred thousand dollars for the John portrait. This confirmed Beaverbrook's advice to John. It convinced me I owned something valuable. I waved Duveen's man aside. It was no grandstand wave. Even though I get down to living in a hall bedroom and cooking on a Sterno I'll never part with that picture.

What did I have to challenge the palettes of John and McEvoy? Now hear this, as we used to say in the Navy.

"Tallulah is a wicked archangel with her flowing ash-blonde hair and carven features. Her profile is perfectly Grecian, flow of line from forehead to nose like the head on a medallion. She is Medusa, very exotic, with a glorious skull, high pumice-stone cheek bones, and a broad brow, and she was equally interesting sculpturally when she was plump as she now is cadaverously thin. Her cheeks are huge acid-pink peonies. Her eyelashes are built out with hot liquid paint to look like burned matches, and her sullen, discon-tented, rosebud of a mouth is painted the brightest scarlet, and is as shiny as Tiptree's strawberry jam."

A modest little tribute, eh? Cute of him to toss in a commercial at the finish! The author? Cecil Beaton, now the Royal Court photographer.

I moved into my own home in London in 1927. I had been holed up in service flats ever since my three-day stay at the Ritz. The opportunity to have my own house gave me a feeling of importance, a mistress-of-the-manor tingle. The house had been a mews—stable to you—then a garage. Converted into my home, it boasted five rooms on two floors, and was hard by a Catholic church.

The entrance was directly on the street. On the lower floor was a mirrored hallway, off which were the kitchen, largest room in the house, and a bedroom, shared by my butler and cook, legally, I'd have you know. A curved staircase spiraled up to the second floor which embraced my living room, dining room, bedroom, and Edie's room. Edie was my secretary and confessor. It was decorated by Syrie Maugham, Somerset's squaw. The furnishings and decorations cost me a pretty penny. A pretty penny in this instance means $15,000 a sum I could then ill afford. Then? Even now!

I didn't really own the house. I had a ninety-nine-year lease. It wasn't roomy enough for large routs. Add six people to the more-or-less permanent inmates and it was as crowded as a Bronx Express. The neighborhood was nobby. It was near Berkeley Square. Gilbert Miller, the theatrical producer, had a home across the street. You'll find small homes like it tucked in fashionable streets all over London. Since the Englishman's home is his castle, he takes a dim view of the threshings of commerce. When the Ritz Hotel made overtures to purchase the house of Lord Winborne because the Ritz management wished more ground, Winborne made a counter offer. He needed a tennis court. What was the asking price for the Ritz?

You've seen British butlers in those imported drawing-room comedies? Stiff and formal? Formality was flouted in my ménage! Because of cramped quarters my butler and the cook had to be wedded. The first pair to have their training tested were Arthur and Florence Meredith. It's an old British custom, dating back to Ethelred the Unready, to address butlers by their last names. That formula was pied in six hours. Arthur and Florence were cockneys and their accents, h-less and tangy, were right out of Dickens. Arthur had buttled for nobility. He and his wife were upset by my irregular hours, meals and conduct. His indignation reached its peak when I bought a refrigerator. This contraption led to an ultimatum. In all his years of service he had found the old-fashioned icebox most satisfactory. He wasn't having any electric substitutes. He was quite blunt about it: "Either the Frigidaire goes or I go!"

I fondly recall John and Mary Underdown. John was a Lancashireman and you could have spread his accent on a bun. John entered into the helter-skelter life of the house without batting an eye. He had a sense of humor, was not above caricaturing my visitors. "Modom, I have served a Queen," he said, the first time Ethel Barrymore dined with me. Ethel, for a summer, had a handsome country home outside London. Against her better judgment, I persuaded her to move in with me for a week. This led to complications. I gave Ethel my room. I moved into Edie's room, Edie moved into the room with the cook, Mary, and John, dispossessed, slept on the kitchen floor. Ethel's two young sons, Sammy and Jacky, were parked on a lounge in the living room. All very clubby and confused. Every night was Hallowe'en.

He's Mine had just laid a West End egg. I had no new play in prospect. I was in debt up to my ears. The London fog had not lifted for a week. I was depressed. Seeking to cheer me up, Edie handed me one book after another. "This is very gay," she'd say. "Try it." "Give me something morbid and depressing," I countered. "Something even more depressing than me." This was John's cue.

Gravely he approached me. "Read this, Modom. It's exceptionally depressing."

He had handed me Wheatley's Book. This was the ledger which the wine shop sent me each month. In it were entered my purchases along with the sum of my indebtedness. He was quite right. I owed Wheatley's four hundred pounds. The English, as you know, are suspicious of patrons who pay cash. They discourage the trade of such ignoramuses. Encouraged by his mistress, Underdown developed a talent for mimicry. He could give hilarious impersonations of some of my guests.

Of all my London friendships, that with Edie Smith proved the most enduring. Edie is reliable in storm and strife, understanding, loyal. My secretary for fourteen years without interruption, she rejoined me in the summer of 1951. To identify Edie as my secretary is blunt and unsatisfactory. She is much more. Cool, humorous, nonchalant in the face of whatever conflagration may menace us, she is what reporters call a pillar of strength.

Edie was one of my first gallery fans. Well-mannered and reserved, she never waxed hysterical over my performances, never tried to throw herself under the wheels of my Bentley. She's as well qualified to write these confessions as I. She has a better, and a more accurate, memory.

She had been in the queue at four or five of my London first nights. More than once I stopped to chat with her on leaving the stage door. One day I received a note asking if she might speak to me alone. Her request was simple. She had seen me leaving the theater with Gordon Selfridge, son of the head of the famed department store. Would I intercede with him in her behalf? She wanted a position. Within a week she was working in the bakery department.

Shortly my elderly maid got ill. She found my hours difficult to cope with, and wanted to go back to Scotland to her mother. At once I thought of Edie. She always looked like a scrubbed apple. She had a charming presence and a lovely speaking voice. She was about my own age. She wasn't the type who would be short-circuited by early morning commotions. I sent for her, told her the risks and rewards of the job. I gave her a week to make a decision. I didn't prod her since she had a steady position at Selfridge's. My own employment was far from steady. She said it would be impossible for her to live in. Her parents would frown on it. I thought the matter was closed. She was back in a week, remained up to and through *The Little Foxes*. Edie's serenity complements my eruptions.

Edie has a nickname for me. It is *Die Donner*. In German it means "the thunder." Those familiar with my vocal potential will be aware of its significance. This nickname years later led to confusion in the Paramount Studio in Hollywood. Mechanics, cameramen, directors, their allies and sycophants, thought Edie was addressing me as Madonna.

Entangled in this libretto, Edie reminded me of the time we routed Bea Lillie out of her hotel room at the Savoy at one in the morning. Napier, Princess Natasha Paley, now married to producer John C. Wilson, Cecil Beaton, Oliver Messel, Marian Harris, the blues singer, John Sutro and I had returned from a performance of the Russian Ballet. Caught up in the graces of that artistic riddle we felt we should celebrate. We couldn't celebrate properly without Bea Lillie, as funny a woman as ever stood in shoe leather.

Bea was having none of it. "Teeny's tired," she said. "Besides, I'm in bed." But we beat down her resistance. She slipped a coat over her nightgown and came over in a cab. By that time attendance had picked up. Shortly, unbeknownst to any of us, Bea went off to my bedroom, lay down and slept for five hours. The pitch of the proceedings was so high her flight went unnoticed. We thought Bea had come in, saluted and returned to her cot at the Savoy.

It was six in the morning and only three guests in top hats remained when I went to my bedroom in search of a lost garment. There was Bea, sleeping like a cherub.

Once Bea was upright we set off for the Savoy. Now Miss Lillie,

184.

in more regal circles, was Lady Peel. Her husband's great-grandfather, Sir Robert Peel, had started the London police force. London's bobbies are derived from his first name, Dublin's peelers from his last.

There is nothing more snobbish, more stuffy, than a British hotel clerk. Trailed by my three toffs, I approached the desk with assumed dignity. Bea was half asleep. I felt incidents might be minimized did I act for Lady Peel, rather than for Bea Lillie. The entrance of an actress at that hour might give the Savoy a turn. For a Lady it would be *de rigeur*. Icily I addressed the gentleman behind the desk:

"Give me Lady Keel's pee, please!"

The man's aplomb was shattered. But he made no move. I repeated: "Lady Keel's pee, please!" Whereupon Bea chirped up: "My pee, my good man, my pee!" It was only then I realized that I wasn't as sober as I thought I was. Nor was Bea!

Without design, Bea Lillie and I collaborated on many a Mayfair commotion. Aided and abetted by Aimee Semple McPherson, we all but upended Fleet Street in mid-October, '28.

Fresh from her conquests among the heathen in Los Angeles, Aimee came to London hell-bent on redeeming the British. Under the sponsorship of The Four Square Gospel Churches of the British Isles, she started a set of revival meetings at Albert Hall. At the invitation of Charles Cochran, who must have had a finger in her pie, Bea and I sat through one of her afternoon demonstrations, after the collection went back to see her. Aimee had beautiful eyes and lovely skin, but her hair was badly dyed and she had the body of a peasant. On leaving, I invited her home for a drink. Bea and I were curious about her piety, her sincerity. Were they genuine or sham? Aimee resorted to evasive action. She invited us to have a

185.

drink with her at the Cecil. We agreed. The next day Bea, Leslie Howard and I invaded her chambers. No drinks were served. Instead she showed us pictures of her temple in Los Angeles, baroque and vulgar.

Aimee was fascinated by Bea and her witty sallies and comments. That night she went to see the final rehearsal of *This Year of Grace*, the revue in which Bea and Noel Coward were to appear in New York a month later. This was a little rash. Her sponsors frowned on bobbed hair and attendance at the cinema. On invitation, Aimee came to my house after my performance of *Her Cardboard Lover* the next night. Gwenn Farrar, Leslie Howard, Audrey and Kenneth Carten, and I tried in vain to trick her into admitting some peccadillo. We admitted to depravities and excesses—mostly invented—to test her tolerance. She shrugged them off. "I don't mind those things so long as you don't hurt anyone else by doing them," she said.

Aimee expressed concern because she had not seen Bea Lillie before her departure for Southampton. I had a quick solution. It was only a little after midnight. Why didn't we all drive down in my car to say good-by to Bea? Aimee was agreeable. She wanted to give Bea a signed copy of the Bible. Bea was sailing on the *Leviathan*, scheduled to leave at dawn.

Ordinarily the drive from London to Southampton can be made under two hours, but we had to crawl along at a snail's pace thanks to an impenetrable fog. It was nearly six when we reached the *Leviathan*. It, too, had been delayed. All of us, save Aimee, toasted Bea, bade her Godspeed. Coming back the fog was even thicker. We didn't get back to London until two in the afternoon. Aimee was disturbed. The delay had caused her to miss an appointment with her sponsors.

But Aimee was more disturbed when she read this headline on page one of Beaverbrook's *Express*:

MRS. MC PHERSON'S

ALL NIGHT

MOTOR JOURNEY

ACTRESS FRIENDS OF THE

EVANGELIST

RETICENCE OF HER

COMPANIONS

The ensuing story hinted Aimee had been joyriding with rowdies, an excursion contrary to her call. On the way back from Southampton, we had all agreed to keep quiet about the trip. We liked Aimee and didn't want to incriminate her in a teapot tempest. But we reckoned without the newsmen. They were badgering all the excursionists within an hour of our return. We hadn't anticipated this hubbub, hence gave conflicting stories. Aimee would only admit to being out riding all night and not having any sleep. Gwenn Farrar denied that she'd been on any party. This put her on the spot because Audrey Carten told the same reporter: "You'd better ask Miss Farrar about the party." I confessed I had seen Aimee aboard the *Leviathan* but denied that she had driven down or returned with me.

These contradictions spurred the reporters. The *Express* played the story up as the biggest scandal since Guy Fawkes tried to dynamite Parliament. Headed "The Vanishing Lady," Beaverbrook let fly with this editorial:

Mrs. McPherson has one of the greatest qualities of the electric light bulb, she arouses the most interest when she goes out. She went out on the California seashore some years ago, and people are still dazzled by

187.

her disappearance. When the Home Secretary announced his decision to admit her to these shores, it was discovered that she was already here and in seclusion. . . . It's all the greatest possible fun, but Mrs. McPherson must remember that if a light goes out too often, and stays out too long, people are apt to get used to the darkness.

In this crisis Aimee took a powder, was next heard from in Glasgow. There she confessed she had gone to Southampton to see Bea off and present her with an autographed Bible. She had driven down with me and my friends, she said, although we were seeing someone else off.

To wring the last drop from this tidbit, Beaverbrook radioed Bea aboard the *Leviathan*. That antic lady, at sea in more ways than one, came back with this dissent: "My friend, Mrs. McPherson, did not give me a Bible, but a copy of her book, which I find very interesting."

Mr. E. J. Phillips, secretary for the Four Squarers, when treed by an *Express* reporter, was understandably bewildered.

"I can only say that it seems very strange. I do not understand Sister McPherson's actions. I can only suppose she went after Miss Bankhead and Miss Lillie because she thought they would be good catches."

Thus endeth *l'affaire McPherson*. I have always thought that Cochran, a glutton for publicity, tipped off the press. Had she received all that notoriety before opening at Albert Hall, Aimee might have had a capacity engagement. An ill-timed adventure.

9.

Duels with the Screen

Eight years an exile, I was in the pink on my return to New York in January of 1931. That I might appear at my best, thus impress both the press and Paramount, I had dieted violently, denied myself all nectars. I was dressed to the nines. Swathed in a mink coat, looking ethereal and mysterious as all getout, I came down the gangplank eager for such homage as was available.

The reception committee was the flower of the Confederacy, called to the colors by Daddy, and reporters. Florence, Daddy's wife, was the first to greet me.

"Tallulah, honey, you're just precious, but you look downright haggard."

While presiding over the opening of my luggage, she turned to me and said: "Tallulah, honey, do *Camille*." She was a little hurt that I didn't make with Marguerite on the pier. Had the newspapermen backed her up I'd have done it, too.

I moved into a hotel suite with Edie, then sat down to hold court, flanked by interviewers and free-loaders without portfolio. To one of Mr. Hearst's slaves I confided: "Although Englishmen are the most divine creatures in the world, I want to see something different. I hope to find some nice chap in America." Ever hear such drivel? To Mr. Pulitzer's man from the *World*, I was equally gracious. "I'm going to make a million in the movies, then marry and settle down."

Generously I consented to be interviewed by the *Telegram's* Douglas Gilbert while coursing across the Queensboro Bridge from screen tests in Astoria.

Mr. Gilbert was properly impressed. In his report to Roy Howard he said: "Tallulah Bankhead is about as sweet and sentimental as a third rail." In the next paragraph Doug dropped all formality— we were still on the bridge—was calling me Tallu, and informing the parish that, since my return, I had received more souvenirs, orchids and billets-doux than did Lillie Langtry in the palmy days of Prince Edward. Off the bridge and in Manhattan he really warmed up: "Her entire attitude towards life, towards herself, is a supreme insouciant flip, a charming and electrifying go-to-hell. She has faced more gossip than Garbo. But the girl behind the whisper can never be found when Tallulah steps out. Hers is a voice with a baritone croon; and she carries a wisecracking wallop in every phrase."

Paramount didn't delay putting me to work. Within a week I was up to my ears in *Tarnished Lady* in Astoria, L.I. By the terms of my contract I was assured of $50,000 for the ten weeks necessary to make the picture. Thereafter I was linked to a chain of options which, had they been carried out to the last decimal place, would have seen me getting an annual wage of $400,000 five years hence.

Tarnished Lady was the work of Donald Ogden Stewart, a literate and amusing writer. I was fortunate, too, in that it was to be directed by George Cukor. Both Stewart and Cukor were stage veterans. All three of us were having our first fling on the talking screen, pioneers in a garrulous new medium. In the back of my skull stewed the notion that the fifty grand I would pick up in ten weeks would enable me to return to England, scotch the rumors that I had abdicated under pressure, wipe out my debts. A lot I cared if Paramount exercised its options. I was fated, or so I thought, for loftier adventures.

Tarnished Lady will never be listed with *The Birth of a Nation, Broken Blossoms, The Informer,* or *Mr. Deeds Goes to Town* in any list of bests by cinema historians. But I'm backing into a verdict. Was it any good? In a word, NO! Though it had a fine director, a first-rate writer, and a luminous, er, star, it was a fizzle. Why? For the same reason that though the eggs, the cracker crumbs and the salt used for a soufflé may be topnotch the resultant dish may be rancid. The picture was made by trial and error. What appeared on the screen showed it.

There was still another factor. Paramount was running a financial fever, teetering on the brink of bankruptcy. Many of its high brass were fearful of dismissal. Paramount's corporate jitters were reflected in their products. As filmed, the story of *Tarnished Lady* was banal. That's still the rule in screen colossi. The effort and skill put into it by Cukor, Stewart and my favorite actress, was not confirmed in the result. Patched, scissored, and victimized by all sorts of hocus-pocus, *Tarnished Lady* wound up a mess. And so, too, did *My Sin* and *The Cheat,* the two other *opera* I made for Paramount at Astoria, under the direction of the skilled George Abbott.

In *My Sin* I was a notorious hussy loose in the Canal Zone, up to some erotic nonsense in a cabaret. It was flubdub, but it led to an international contretemps. Argentina, yet to bask under the benevolent rule of Colonel Péron, banned it when the Minister from Panama protested that the film sullied the dignity of his homeland. His Nibs had something! Panama wasn't the only thing smirched.

I had voiced a grievance before the Panama protest. Dropping into the Paramount Theatre of an afternoon, I was floored by an advertising trailer following the feature:

COMING! COMING!

TALLULAH THE GLAMOROUS

TALLULAH THE MYSTERIOUS

TALLULAH THE WOMAN

WE GAVE YOU MARLENE DIETRICH

NOW WE GIVE YOU TALLULAH BANKHEAD

Thinking in terms of my London eminence, I was shocked by my employers' boast that Dietrich preceded me. The next afternoon I bearded Walter Wanger—producer of *My Sin*—in his hutch.

"This is an outrage," I ranted. "You can't do this to me! In London Marlene is called the second Tallulah Bankhead."

Wanger, no stranger to such eruptions, brought me to earth.

"Don't worry, Tallulah," he said. "The trailer will be changed. Hereafter it will read: 'We Give You Back Tallulah Bankhead.' "

Paramount picked up my option with alacrity. After the three mishaps cited, I was shuttled off to Hollywood where, successively, I was starred in *Thunder Below, The Devil and the Deep* and *Faithless*, the last-named for Metro, to whom I was loaned by Paramount for some shady doings with Robert Montgomery. In all six of these fiascos I was a wicked woman, inclined to be promiscuous, double-dealing and dark of design. To conform with the screen's moral code, I was always repentant at the final fadeout. I can't blame Paramount for this. On the stage in London the same procedure had been followed. There, too, I had invariably been the *femme fatale,* adulterous and deceptive. I seemed sentenced for life to playing tarts, reformed tarts or novice tarts.

Critically I didn't suffer from my demonstrations in these didos.

Listen to Percy Hammond, a critic who rarely could be persuaded to face a film.

"I revel in Miss Bankhead's smooth veneers and varnishes and agree with her managers in their pronouncement that she is as mysterious and as potent an influence on motion pictures as Will Hays or any of the Warner Brothers."

Let's have no nonsense about logrolling. I never had so much as a highball with Mr. Hammond. And he liked highballs. I can't say as much for critic Richard Watts, Jr. Over the years I've clinked many a glass with him. But I applauded Dick when he wrote:

At least they have photographed the eminent Miss Bankhead properly in "My Sin." It remains, nevertheless, another mean trick to play on a fine actress and a brilliant personage who is waiting for a part worthy of her. It is little short of magic to see England's favorite American star acting away resourcefully and honestly in a photoplay which is neither resourceful nor honest.

Magic? My favorite word!

Despite these salutes, I began to realize that no matter how flattering my reviews they added up to nothing. When a picture was judged guilty, all concerned must share the guilt. I was also becoming conscious of the till, the box-office "take." Unless things took a turn for the better I'd be marked a pictorial hoodoo. Would California change my luck? We'd see.

In preparation for my descent on Hollywood, sometimes called the land of the lotus-eaters, I went on a clothes-buying spree. I barged into Hattie Carnegie's and laid that salon waste. I'm still like that. I have to be prodded with hot needles before I'll consent to enter a shop, but, once in, I run amok, stagger out with loads of knickknacks I will never wear.

Through Paramount's agents I arranged to take over the Hollywood castle of William Haines. I took along my friends, Audrey and Kenneth Carten. In my subconscious I may have thought of them as witnesses for the defense. They could return to London and report how I was roughing it in the Far West, where the deer and the antelope played on the lawn!

For my mistakes in Astoria I had been rewarded with $150,000. For the first time in my life I was solvent. I was to get $5,000 a week for my first year in Hollywood. Did I stay on my fee would be tilted a thousand a week each year. Faced with all this loot I found I didn't have time to spend it. I was netting $2,500 a week after paying off retainers, settling bills, toting up the bites put upon me by friends and foes whom fate had elbowed.

Thunder Below was my first Hollywood film. It was directed by Richard Wallace, whom we called "Pops." He had once operated a merry-go-round in a carnival; in his youth had been a medical student, later an undertaker's assistant. He was fascinated by cadavers. Once, after a trying day at the studio, he took me to a morgue. Pointing out the departed on the cool slabs, he said: "Tallulah, this should cheer you up. See how peaceful they are." He was a divine man. Don't wince at my adjective. It hasn't intruded often on this saga. For all Wallace's divinity, for all my vitality, *Thunder Below* was a double-jointed dud, maudlin and messy.

I grew morose. *The Devil and the Deep* didn't cheer me up. In this gem I was the wife of Charles Laughton, playing fast and loose with Gary Cooper in a submarine. Laughton, Cooper and I were supposed to be some hundred fathoms down throughout the action of this illusion. *The Devil and the Deep* never surfaced. And no wonder.

I learned one thing from those screen mishaps. Too many people were involved. No one had the authority to fuse conflicting elements. Cameraman, star, director and writer worked at cross purposes. They reminded me of humorist Stephen Leacock's knight who jumped on his horse and rode off in all directions.

The producer, as often as not, was the culprit. Drawing a fancy fee, he felt obliged to contribute to the jigsaw. As a rule his offering was negative, consisted in mutilating or deleting the work of his betters. Had there been one over-all authority, one competent judge, some order might have come out of the chaos. Usually the nabob with the most authority—he might be a bank executive toying with a mortgage—was the least qualified of the posse to speak either up or out. Did that deter him?

Don't think I had any illusions about my share in these errors. I was no great shakes. I was victimized by the mechanics of the whole business. In Hollywood you do nothing for yourself. You don't even apply your own make-up. You are awakened, taken to the studio, made up. I was a set-up for that formula. You play your roles in snips and driblets, harassed by delays, interruptions and stupidities. Over the proceedings hangs the pall of indecision, the fear of the studio swami that the work may in some fashion upset a coal miner in West Virginia, a lama in Tibet. Timidity was the screen's curse. It still is. In its effort to please everyone, it succeeds in pleasing no one. It's the most easily frightened industry, art form or opiate ever to solicit favor. The screen is scared of the churches, of Congress, of the Benevolent Order of Elks, of the American Legion, of the D.A.R., of its own shadow. But what it fears beyond all else is ideas. It's devoted to the past, to the tried-and-found-wanting, to the museum and the reactionary. When one of its practitioners blurts out the truth, he is looked upon as a madman.

I had no regrets about that year in Hollywood. I bagged a quarter of a million. I lived in splendor, did my share of skylarking between pictures.

On my return to New York in December of '32, I told Ward

Morehouse of the New York *Sun* I wasn't completely pleased with my Hollywood pictures, but the fact that they were bad wasn't intentional. There's a lulu. Who ever made a bad picture purposely? Those cameras must have done something to my mind.

I had gone to Hollywood on a train that carried Joan Crawford and Douglas Fairbanks, Jr. Joan couldn't have been sweeter, more democratic. She invited me to her stateroom, volunteered the names of her hairdresser and masseuse. Just before I became entangled in *Thunder Below*, she sent me a note asking me to dinner. Strictly informal, she said. Just five or six friends. Taking her literally I turned up in slacks, only to find Joan rigged out as if she were going to the Metropolitan with Berry Wall. To add a casual note to this soiree, there were place cards on the table. Whatever Joan's notions of informality, she could be prankish. Over the telephone she told me that she had a surprise dinner companion for me, someone she was sure I would like. Now I prefer to rely on my own prejudices in such matters. But I didn't wish to seem churlish. Unfamiliar with local tribal customs, I made no protest. My dinner companion? Jackie Cooper! Flanked by his mother. He was all of eight. I had seen him five times the year before in *Skippy*, and cried my eyes out. Now I almost cried them out again, for different reasons. That Joan! Cute, *n'est-ce pas?*

Earlier I had used Jackie to advantage. In New York the previous winter Walter Wanger invited me to the opening of Bea Lillie's new revue, *The Third Little Show*. At the last moment he called up to say he couldn't make it, but he was sending an attractive young man in his place.

I called him seven kinds of a swine. How dare he be so impertinent? If he couldn't come, didn't he think I should have the option of naming my companion? I didn't lack for friends. One tinkle of the tocsin, and I'd have ten beaux at my door. But Wanger had a twinkle in his voice. I knew he wouldn't risk my wrath by sending up some clod. My curiosity aroused, I conceded. Who should my squire be but Gary Cooper. Wanger knew I thought Cooper the handsomest man on the screen. Strong silent type!

Silent is right. Gary never opened his trap throughout the evening. Perhaps he was self-conscious and nervous! When I'm nervous and self-conscious I cover up with torrents of words. I chattered away like a magpie, while my hero remained sealed. The next day a columnist, noted for his scorn of syntax rather than his accuracy, wrote that Gary and I were engaged. Reuters, British equivalent of the Associated Press, sent me this cable: CONFIRM ENGAGEMENT TO GARY COOPER.

Our columnists are a headlong lot. Shake hands with a man publicly, and they scream you're engaged to him. Their English opposites are more reserved. They only hint at an engagement when they discover the couple in the hay.

Thinking to twit Reuters I cabled:

YOU HAVE IT ALL WRONG. AM ENGAGED TO JACKIE COOPER.

One London journal, taken in by this hoax, inflamed its front page with:

TALLULAH ENGAGED TO JOHN COOPER.

Fleet Street doesn't go in for such corruptions as Jackie. To prove its point the paper dug up a picture of a mustached John Cooper in its morgue, identified him as the lucky man. John turned out to be a retired golf pro.

It was a dull week in Hollywood when my engagement wasn't announced to one man or another. Did I go to a party with a likely looking brave, the next day we were practically at the altar. One of these canards linked me with Ronald Colman. In this instance the inventors violated their own ground rules. For all my respect for Mr. Colman's skill, I had yet to meet him.

Before I got to Hollywood the busybodies were trying to foment a Bankhead-Dietrich feud. Marlene was one of Paramount's top star, I the rash intruder. Vendettas are food and drink for fan magazine writers and Hollywood correspondents. They had thrived on the Pola Negri–Gloria Swanson caterwaul for years. For all I know they coined it. I first saw Marlene at the commissary at lunch. In a flame-colored tea gown she was presiding at a table over which hovered the flower of Paramount. I was snookered behind a pillar. On seeing me she came over and welcomed me to the studio, was all candor and charm. When I asked if I might come and watch her work, she readily consented. Marlene's concern was for her eight-year-old daughter, Maria. She was in deadly fear of kidnapers, had her home guarded by detectives, day and night. That eight-year-old is now Maria Riva, one of the ablest young actresses to be seen on television screens. Marlene is now a grandmother. We girls are getting on, sho 'nuf.

When I was at grips with Robert Montgomery in *Faithless*, my studio neighbors were the Barrymores—all three of them. Ethel, Lionel and John were filming *Rasputin and the Empress*, the first and only time in their careers that they worked together, on stage or screen or in the armed forces. It was eerie to huddle with the Barrymores at seven in the morning. I had often been up that late, but never so early in pursuit of my trade.

I first met Greta Garbo at the Hollywood home of Salka and Bertold Viertel. He was the German producer. Once he had been kind enough to edit one of my Astoria pictures. The mystery surrounding Garbo was as thick as a London fog. Though I admired her work on the screen tremendously, I was a little awed in her presence, consequently I clowned outrageously when we sat down to dinner. Hell-bent on being the life of the party, I did everything but my slack wire act. "This is the first dinner party I've been to in years. I have enjoyed myself thoroughly," she said.

While prowling underseas with Laughton and Gary Cooper I gave a small party to which I asked Salka and Garbo. Dinner was about to get under way and no Greta. Edie Smith and my cook were desolated. Inwardly irked, outwardly cool, I was pleased when she showed up in jodhpurs. Later Ethel Barrymore joined us— Ethel who ordinarily would not step into the next room to meet a composite of Rachel and Nell Gwynn. We all got along famously. I stayed off the trapeze. We went in for charades and danced to phonograph music. Garbo complimented my cook on the dinner. That jade, in a display of loyalty rarely encountered in Hollywood or the Aleutians, had a snappy comeback.

"Glad to meet you, Miss," she said. "Next to Miss Bankhead I think you're the finest actress on the screen." Forget all the bilge about Garbo. She's excessively shy. When at ease with people who do not look upon her as something begat by the Sphinx and Frigga, Norse goddess of the sky, she can be as much fun as the next gal.

In that year in Hollywood I didn't encounter much hell-raising. Their medium gone vocal, most of its inmates were too busy learning how to talk to engage in shenanigans. Save for a few convivial rebels most of the picture folk were too tangled up in taboos, option nets and other professional frights to relax. There was another deterrent to hi-jinks. If you have to face a camera at seven in the morning you think twice before opening the second quart of Old Grand-Dad.

Late in '32 the renewal of my option was the order of business. Remember '32? It was the year in which Florenz Ziegfeld, Minnie Maddern Fiske and John Philip Sousa died, that the bonus army marched on Washington, that Lindbergh's baby was kidnaped, that Amelia Earhart flew the Atlantic, that Jimmy Walker resigned as mayor of New York, that a man named Hitler ran second to Hindenburg in the German elections. It was also the year in which we hit the bottom of the depression. Banks were folding up like concertinas. Paramount had similar symptoms.

One of the firm's nabobs, Al Kaufman, relative of Adolph Zukor, called me up.

"Things, as you know, are bad, Tallulah. Would you consider staying on with us at your same salary?" Did they pick up the option I was assured $6,000 a week for my third term.

"No, Al dahling," I cooed, "I would not. I'm quite unhappy here. Let's call it quits."

Unhappy I was. The six pictures I had made were rancid. The whole set-up annoyed me. I could continue to make more than I had ever made in the theater. But money was a minor consideration now that I had $200,000 in my kick. For once I could be independent. So, independent I was. Paramount's plight was my pardon. But it survived my departure. It went on to larger and more lofty things once Franklin Delano Roosevelt pried open the bank doors.

As I left Hollywood a rash of rumors broke out that I had been sacked. That was the BIG LIE, later to be popularized by Hitler, Stalin and, on our own shores, Joseph McCarthy of Wisconsin, our sewer Senator. On the news that Paramount and I were no longer wed, Darryl Zanuck and Hal Wallis, two of Warner Brothers' yogi, approached me waving sheaves of money. I was as flint. Then I was broached by the messiah at mention of whose name most of Hollywood groveled in the dust to indicate their unworthiness—Louis B. Mayer.

My appointment with the All Highest was at 2:30. I arrived at 2:25, after being certified as pure by a long line of menials.

"Please sit down. Mr. Mayer is busy. He will see you as soon as he has a moment free," said the last of these sycophants.

I wasn't buying any of that.

"He'll see me at 2:30 or he'll never see me," I said.

"But he's talking to Joseph Schenck in New York, Miss Bankhead," said his buffer, shocked that anyone could be so sacrilegious as to challenge her master.

"I'm leaving at 2:31," I said. "Tell the Panjandrum to hang up."

Through a leak in his office I learned he frowned on me because I wore slacks, and he thought my conduct smirched the fair name of Hollywood and/or Mayer. By his code I should be decked out in ermine, my hair full of gold dust. To appease him I donned all my finery, wore a mess of jewels I borrowed from Connie Bennett. Hence my defiance.

I was facing the master at 2:30 on the button. He was oily and patronizing. He told how he had redeemed John Gilbert and Wallace Beery through his strategies. He could do as much for me. To prove it he offered me $2,500 a week. That was just half of what I was getting in *Faithless*, which carried the Metro imprint. I had been loaned, you'll remember, to Mr. Mayer's cartel by Paramount. Metro and Mayer were one and indivisible. Goldwyn was thumbing his nose at Noah Webster.

Afire with virtue, Mr. Mayer started to grieve over the case of Jean Harlow. She had just started to make *Red Rust* when her husband had destroyed himself. Her sainted employer, offensively sensitive to the common weal, felt he must replace her. For reasons beyond human ken he felt her presence in the film would be an affront to the millions dedicated to the proposition that Mayer and the screen, in that order, were the last citadels of culture, honor and good will.

Would I care to replace Miss Harlow? I would not. To damn the radiant Jean for the misfortune of another would be one of the shabbiest acts of all time. I told Mr. Mayer as much. I tossed in a survey of the background of some of his box-office pets. He blanched. To distract me, he undertook to act out the circumstances of Paul Bern's death. He rose from his throne, became highly emotional, started to circle his desk, the better to ham up the scene. Purposely I misread his intentions. "None of that, now, Mr. Mayer," I said. "Stay on your side of the desk. I can visualize the scene. You don't have to demonstrate."

It would be twelve years before I'd face a motion picture camera again. It gave me considerable satisfaction to deflate this Nero in my final gesture.

10.

Touch and Go on Broadway

When the curtain went up on *Forsaking All Others* at the Times Square on the night of March 1, 1933, eleven years had elapsed since last I strode a New York stage. For all my overseas note, I was yet to be judged by my countrymen. Heady tales of my triumphs on the Thames had seared the cables, but New York settled for no alien endorsement. I must prove myself all over again. My screen scuffles were regarded as professional slumming.

My first efforts were snafued. The plays submitted to me were shockingly bad. I had yet to learn that practically all plays submitted by producers are shockingly bad. So are practically all the plays written by all authors from Aeschylus to Zangwill. Not one in a hundred is worth a second look. But I was impetuous. Broadway steamed with the rumor that I had been cashiered in Hollywood. To cancel this canard, I felt obligated to do a play immediately. But the nonsense submitted to me grew progressively worse.

Spurred by the furies, I finally came upon *Forsaking All Others*. It was light, frothy and amusing, and had a brittle Philip Barry quality. I was aware it was no masterpiece, but it was better than many of the séances in which I flourished in London. I paid the authors an advance royalty, then looked about for a producer to finance and present the comedy. It's no cinch to find a solvent producer. Do you find one it's unlikely that he will so far violate his oath as to put up any of his own money. He needs time to solicit funds from speculative friends.

While prospects were hemming and hawing, I grew increasingly jumpy. A month of this and I cast the die. I would produce the play myself. With my own money! I didn't realize at the time that such procedure on the part of an actress might result in her being hauled up before a sanity commission. Producing a play involves a lot of dickering with scene designers, directors, actors, theater managers and booking agents. I wasn't up to it. An old acquaintance, Archie Selwyn, with long experience as a manager, was idle. I engaged him as nominal producer of the play. He was to supervise the details of production, be my proxy in fiscal and professional matters. I didn't want this to leak out. The enemy would say Tallulah must be desperate indeed to produce her own play.

Eager to make my bow in style, I insisted on the best of everything. The bit players wore Hattie Carnegie clothes. Donald Oenslager designed the settings. Gilbert Miller, a perfectionist in the items of taste and production, told me the physical production of *Forsaking All Others* was the best of the year. Should I wish to continue as actress-producer, he said, he'd be glad to effect an alliance.

I had named Archie my producer because of that bed he bought me in London and the concern he had expressed for my future. His concern should have been for his own future.

Archie was a skilled professional, gay and deft. He did not quarrel with any of my judgments. But once the play was in rehearsal, Archie took a powder. He went off to bask in the Florida sun. I thought nothing of this. The contribution of a producer to any play is chiefly conversational, once he had raised the necessary money. Archie did play me one false trick. In a fit of loyalty he booked the play into the Times Square in West Forty-second Street, a theater he had operated in a happier day. When the Selwyns rode the crest Forty-second Street housed a dozen excellent theaters. But in 1933 it looked like the Bowery, cluttered up with flea circuses, grind picture theaters, orange drink stands and fake jewelry joints.

Ilka Chase played my bridesmaid in the comedy. She was a venomous witch full of suspicion and speakeasy brandy—the bridesmaid, not Ilka. When the company got to Providence, R.I., Charles Brackett, an old friend of Ilka's, gave us an after-performance party. For reasons best known to himself Charley invited a lot of Back Bay toffs and their crusty wives, weighted down with dog collars and other symbols of wealth and antiquity. They were patronizing, acted as if they were on a slumming tour.

Eddie Baylies, of our company, was an old Bostonian who had fled Beacon Hill for the loose life of the theater. He introduced me to a forbidding old ruin. Unable to thaw her out with small talk, shortly I left in search of more convivial prey. This irked the frosty blueblood. She sought out Baylies.

"When is Miss Bankhead going to do her stuff? When is she going to let go?"

"Let go? Why, she's behaving much as she always does," said Eddie.

"Then to hell with it," said the old rip, "if she's going to behave like everyone else, I'm going home."

That's one of the troubles with a legend. You have to constantly coddle it or it will shrivel. I've had a cartwheel complex ever since I ruffled the Governor of Alabama. But I've never let fly with one in a ballroom, uninvited, unchallenged. If I'm to make an ass of myself, add to the rumor that I'm a chronic show-off, I want to choose my grounds.

Forsaking All Others had a stormy pre-Broadway tour. Two directors, Harry Wagstaff Gribble and Arthur Beckhard, went down the drain. The confusion slackened when I persuaded Tommy Mitchell to step into the breach. A gallant Celt, that Mitchell! He holds his liquor well, has wit and gaiety and Hibernian charm. He is never hornswoggled by the hocus-pocus of the theater. Eager for the esteem of the critics, I egged myself on even while sabotaged by booking offices, aides and allies.

Capping my out-of-town agonies and anxieties were the visits of Leland Hayward, then as now suffering from delusions of invincibility in malignant form. Mr. Hayward had parasitic tendencies. He was an author's and actor's agent, who fattened on the talents of others through his ten-per-cent cut of their incomes. The late Alva Johnson once described a Hollywood agent as a man who hesitated to drink tomato juice in public lest fellow diners suspect he was slaking his thirst with his clients' blood. When I was wavering about producing *Forsaking All Others*, Hayward urged me on. I needn't worry about money, he boasted. One flourish of his magic wand and investors would stampede to my door. He had himself confused with Emerson's mousetrap, Ralph Waldo's, not Fay's. Hayward proved one of the most elastic reeds I was ever to lean on. Not a cent did he or the Midases he was to hypnotize raise.

As my play careened through its tryout, Hayward continued to assure me. He would fly to whatever town we were playing, paint tomorrow's prospects in glowing colors, then depart, but not before collecting at the box office his plane and hotel expenses.

It would be sixteen years before I collided with Mr. Hayward again. In September of '49 he approached me with an offer to play the leading role in *Rat Race*. Having amassed a fortune as a huckster, Hayward had turned square. He was now a producer and over a brief span had shown considerable talent in setting up popular plays. But I was still suspicious.

In conformity with my fees from other producers I asked for

fifteen per cent of the weekly box-office receipts, and twenty-five per cent of the profits. As an agent Hayward had thrived through his ability to wheedle producers into paying the highest possible wages to his clients. Hayward, the producer, winced as if menaced with a belaying pin when Miss Bankhead asked her normal salary. Though Hayward blanched, I wouldn't retreat by so much as a millimeter. It's a good thing I didn't. When *Rat Race* opened in New York it was boiled in oil by the critics, one of the most pretentious flops of the generation.

Unwittingly I elected an evil day for the New York baptism of *Forsaking All Others*. That morning the banks closed with a bang that rocked Herbert Hoover to his basement. The opening-night audience was understandably jumpy. Cut off from funds, it was in anything but the frivolous mood demanded by *Forsaking All Others*.

Though I get indignant when charged with being superstitious, I plead guilty on a few counts. Ever since *The Squab Farm* a framed picture of my mother had graced my dressing-room table on opening nights. Unfailingly I would drop on my knees just before curtain rise and pray: "Dear God, don't let me make a fool of myself." Then I would open a split of champagne and my maid and I would drink to our good fortune.

Tallulah, the worry-wart, got to the theater an hour earlier than necessary. I was made up and dressed at seven-thirty. I had my usual feeling of doom, a hunch the night of my crucifixion was at hand. The dressing room was bursting with flowers, tributes from cronies. To distract myself I started to fumble through my mail, unread for weeks.

Suddenly I realized Mother's picture was missing. I interpreted this as an omen of disaster. Hastily I dispatched Rose Riley, my maid, to call Edie Smith before she left our hotel. She must get the picture to the theater before the curtain's rise.

Outside it was raining cats and dogs! Edie would never make

it. Shortly Rose returned to say Edie had already left for the theater. This paralyzed me. Again I started thumbing through my mail. While thus engaged, there was a tap on my door. The stage doorman handed me a small package. I was too upset to take note of this intrusion. A star's dressing room is out of bounds to everyone on opening night, lest some intruder scramble the delicate mechanism that is her nerves.

Absent-mindedly I unwrapped the package. In it was a picture of my mother as a child of four, lovely and innocent. With it was a note from a stranger.

Dear Miss Bankhead: I knew your mother well. Noting that you are opening in a new play it occurred to me that you might like to have this picture. It's possible you may not have it.

Let's not hear any scoffing about coincidence. I walked on the stage elated, exalted. I felt purged and cleansed! My panic vanished. On my entrance I received an ovation!

An ovation was more than *Forsaking All Others* received. Robert Benchley said the comedy should be called "The Bounder's Bride." In the first act I was left in the lurch at the altar when my intended came down with an attack of conscience. Mr. Benchley was the critic for *The New Yorker*, as gay and thirsty a gentleman as ever I encountered. I drew this comment from Brooks Atkinson, the *Times'* oracle: "This is Miss Bankhead's first appearance in this country since her canonization in England, so let's not be too peevish about her play. She's a dynamic sort of person, an amusing young lady who can fill an evening with merriment." Gilbert Gabriel took another tack: "Miss Bankhead has the sound and a curiously good deal of the looks, too, of a young Laurette Taylor, with mezzo-basso leanings. There is no withstanding her vitality, humor and her half-gam'n, half ladylike loveliness." Though the play was roughed up,

I glowed when I read Walter Winchell's verdict: THIS BANKHEAD NO BUST. MY FAVORITE VALENTINE! When first I met Walter he said: "Miss Bankhead, I've heard a lot about you." "Well, it's all true," I replied.

This was my first and last adventure as a manager, masked or otherwise. Since the banks had gone underground, Equity ruled producers could reduce salaries during the emergency. Box offices were accepting checks for tickets—sometimes on phantom banks. I scorned Equity's hint and careened on.

Defiant, I kept *Forsaking All Others* running for fourteen weeks. Since I was in the contrary position of being my own employer I worked for a new minimum wage—nothing a week. As a producer I would grab off all the profits. But there were no profits. I worked twenty weeks for exercise, lost $40,000 to boot.

But I had rewards, though they were on the intangible side. Almost to a man the critics lamented that so gusty a gal should be betrayed by so rickety a vehicle. Little did they know that I had selected my own vehicle, compounded the error by producing it.

After *Forsaking All Others* it was fifteen months before I got on a payroll again. But what am I saying? I wasn't on the payroll of *Forsaking All Others*. Remember?

A dud as a producer, I didn't chew too long on the cud of regret. A month after the closing I agreed to play Julie Kendrick in Guthrie McClintic's production of Owen Davis's *Jezebel*. Julie was a Louisiana hothead who had been helling about Europe for three years in an attempt to forget a quarrel with her cousin, Preston. On her return, dripping repentance, she was knocked for a loop on learning her kinsman was sealed to another. Julie was a jealous rip. To avenge Preston's perfidy she prodded him into a duel with the crack shot of the county. Preston was about to join his ancestors when his brother volunteered to substitute for him. This brother, a second Daniel Boone, drilled his opponent deftly. Then a yellow fever epidemic raged through Louisiana. This flattened Preston. But when he was hauled off to the pesthouse Julie went with him, while his wife took off for the Nawth. Quite a plot, brother! Add ten commercials and it would make a hell of a soap opera.

I liked Guthrie. Hadn't he tried to get me into one of Maeterlinck's confections? He was the husband of my old playmate in *Nice People,* Katharine Cornell. Rehearsals were to start in July. So I hopped out to Hollywood for a month's rest in one of those bungalows which fringe the Garden of Allah, the most gruesomely named hotel in the western hemisphere. In neighboring bungalows were Robert Benchley and Vincent Youmans. Benchley didn't like to go to bed early, either. I used to sit by the hour and listen to Youmans play the piano. He was as good as Jerome Kern or George Gershwin or Richard Rodgers. Remember "Tea for Two," "I Want to Be Happy," "More Than You Know," "Rise 'n' Shine," "Time on My Hands," and "Hallelujah"? He composed them all.

Housed in a near-by bungalow with his wife, Jill Esmond, was a young actor slated for fame and knighthood, Laurence Olivier. He had been brought to Hollywood by Metro to be Garbo's leading man in *Queen Christina.* Louis B. Mayer had decided that John Gilbert's voice was not up to the demands of the vocal cameras. Miss Garbo resented the fashion in which Gilbert, long her leading man, had been erased. So she exercised her veto. Even Mayer couldn't risk the Garbo frown. Metro solved this impasse by sacking Olivier. Crushed, Olivier vowed he'd never return to Hollywood. He was to keep that vow for seven years. When he returned it was to give stirring performances in *Wuthering Heights* and *Rebecca.* He has gone a long way since then. Sir Laurence Olivier, no less!

After rehearsing in *Jezebel* for five days I became violently ill. It was mid-August and the play was scheduled for a September opening in New York. Guthrie told me to take a day off, but I grew sicker. My doctor, Mortimer H. Rodgers, brother of that Richard Rodgers who wrote the score for *Oklahoma* and *South Pacific,* ordered me into Doctors Hospital for observation. My stomach was swollen up like a basketball. At first it was thought I had an intestinal cold, caused by sleeping under an electric fan. Rehearsals were delayed a week and the traditional rumor popped up: "Bankhead wants to get out of *Jezebel,* and has resorted to the ruse of the invalid." These vicious stories never found their way into print—but they had wide currency in Sardi's, the Algonquin and other water holes frequented by gossips and backbiters.

Guthrie was in an awkward position. He couldn't suspend rehearsals, pending my return, and he didn't want to replace me. Laurette Taylor had told him I was the only one who could properly play the role. The Lunts concurred. Since Julie was both Southern and evil, it was not the role for Mrs. McClintic. Horizontal for five days, I felt better. Guthrie brought the male leads to my bedside to rehearse. The next day my costumes were brought to the hospital and I was propped up for fittings. Two nights later my doctor dosed me with codeine and I was permitted to go to the theater. There I watched a rehearsal, with Guthrie reading my part. Through this makeshift I could become familiar with the stage business, positions, crossings. I was letter perfect in my lines before I was flattened.

On my return to the hospital my temperature had vaulted to 104. I was sicker than ever. What ailed me? The doctors were baffled. I started to lose weight alarmingly. Finally I was packed off to Lenox Hill Hospital. There I was operated on in early November. I was living on mush and custards and was down to seventy-five pounds. I could almost have crawled through the proverbial keyhole.

Unless you shy away from clinical statistics you may be interested in knowing I was on the operating table for five hours. What they found in my abdominal cavities and adjacent areas was hair-raising. There was a technical name for the contortions of my innards, but I can't remember it. My trunk lines were matted, meshed and fouled up. To climax my woe I developed as pretty a set of chilblains as you'll ever lay eyes on. To this day I wince at the sight of an ice-bag. I was hospitalized for fifteen weeks.

My illness cost Guthrie a pretty penny. What it cost me was devastating. I was paying rent on a fancy hotel suite. What with nurses, hospital bills, specialists and the various surveys necessary to determine the cause of my malaise, I was nicked to the tune of $40,000. Outlay was at its flood, income at its ebb.

There was another episode born of my sickness which history should make note of. When my temperature was at its peak, my weight at its all-time low, a reporter for one of New York's great newspapers called the hospital to ask the nurse: "Is it true Miss Bankhead is having a baby?"

So help me, Hannah, he did! "So help me, Hannah," is not the phrase I used when I learned of the impertinence. Had I been able to get to my feet I would have tracked him down and drilled him with my derringer. Two jumps ahead of an autopsy! My blood still boils!

What happened to *Jezebel?* Guthrie sued for a truce. Equity conceded it. With Miriam Hopkins as Julie, he placed it in rehearsal again. Miriam was an old Georgia gal, with accredited drawl. Guthrie felt Julie might be her mutton. *Jezebel* popped open on December 19. The jury brought in a verdict of guilty as charged four weeks later. I'm not trying to pin the rap on Miriam. Had I been in it *Jezebel* might have lasted five weeks.

As soon as I was able to totter I fled the hospital, five weeks after I had been carved. "Don't think for a moment this has taught me a lesson," I said to Dr. Rodgers. I wolfed down a thick steak and a double order of mince pie, and felt better. But my legs weren't up to my ardor. For weeks I was jelly-kneed. I did get strong enough to go to Jasper for Christmas with Daddy and his wife. It was my first visit to Alabama since my return from England. When I arrived, pale and interesting with rouge-slashed lips, I created something of a rumpus. All six of my pictures had been shown in Jasper. They had caused a lot of "I knew her when she was only knee-high-to-a-grasshopper" guff. I had only been back a week, was still wobbly, when the manager of the movie theater aided, I'm sure, by Daddy, asked me to make a personal appearance.

Whatever the verdict of Hollywood and Vine, whatever the judgments of the screen critics, in Jasper I was a screen star. I wasn't going to let them down. I decided to dress as they felt a screen star should dress. I togged myself out in a daring black gown, sprayed myself with gems and sallied forth with Daddy, his wife and Edie Smith.

When we mounted the platform in front of the screen Daddy turned to the audience and said, "Well, folks, this is my little girl." With that he stepped back into the audience. There I was, high, dry and bejeweled! I wasn't dismayed for long. Words rarely fail me when I have an agreeable target.

I cooed, and I gestured, and I tossed my mane. I even tossed in a few of those come hither looks. A lot of water had eddied under the bridge since I had spouted "Old Ironsides" in a schoolhouse fifty yards away. I ended by saying Daddy had never let me forget I was still an Alabama hillbilly. Ah shoa was, and I was proud of it.

But my return to Jasper was flecked with sorrow. Daddy had just had a second heart attack. Though he was supposed to rest he was forever jumping up to do things for me. The gallant fashion in which he attempted to shrug off the nature and implications of his trouble touched me. On my arrival in Jasper I was haggard and pale as the ghost of Hamlet's father. But I felt well. I had a ravenous appetite. Within four months I had regained fifty pounds. I started to reduce again.

During my convalescence I came to the conclusion that I was hoodooed in my own, my native land. It had been over four years since I returned from England. What did I have to show for it? Six bad pictures and one bad play. Prospects were not enchanting. The theater was about to go into the summer doldrums. This meant idleness until fall. I consoled myself thinking I had left England only because of the fabulous salary offered. Hadn't it always been my intention to return?

Early in the spring of '34 I made up my mind. I'd go back to England and stay there. I'd had my share of bad plays in London, even of failures. But there I had prestige, a loyal following. I had been happy there even when my fortunes were at their lowest. Though still a bit shaky, I packed up—it would be more accurate to say that Edie packed up for me, since as a packer-upper I'm a washout—and sailed for London around May 1. I holed up in the Hotel Splendide. After a month I was fortunate enough to get the house of my friend, Dola Cavendish, in Regent Park. Dola had been called to Canada to iron out her estate in British Columbia. Surrounded by old friends, and with a satisfactory bank balance, I shook off the melancholia which had sporadically gripped me in New York and Hollywood, and had a rip-roaring good time.

I hadn't been in London more than a month when Jock Whitney called me on the transatlantic telephone. He wanted me to star in *Dark Victory*. Jock wasn't the producer of *Dark Victory*. He was the silent partner who put up the money. I knew all about *Dark Victory*. I had been baited by one producer or another to play it for three years. It must have been rewritten twenty times. That many producers had held options on it. All of them had badgered the authors into changes in plot and dialogue. Even did it fail as a play, I had been told in Hollywood, it would be a great screen vehicle for me. I thought otherwise. Why? I had read it. I had read it in at least six of its variations.

For all my qualms about *Dark Victory*, for all my conviction it was a dramatic dud, I was finally won over by Jock. Maxwell Anderson, he said, had done some furtive rewriting. It was to be given a very plush production. So great a man as Robert Edmond Jones was scheming the *décor*. All the auspices, save one, were favorable. The exception? The play.

Among the gentlemen who greeted me on my return from London was A. J. Liebling, then a crack reporter on the New York *Telegram*, now the author of "The Wayward Press" in cherished issues of *The New Yorker*. Wrote Mr. Liebling:

Miss Tallulah Bankhead arrived last night on the liner "Europa" with her two Pekes, Sally and Ann. She wore a blue dress with lumps on it by Schiaparelli, and was apparently transfixed by a long pin with a head like a polo mallet, but demonstrated, on request, that the pin merely passed through her belt, missing her body entirely.

Two hours after I had convinced the customs men I had yet to take up smuggling, I was in rehearsal at the Plymouth. Edie and Ann and Sally were stashed away in an East Side hotel. And I was headed for another catastrophe. *Dark Victory* was not the critics' dish. When, clarioned the critics, would Miss Bankhead get a play worthy of her mettle? Why were the playwrights so derelict? The prankish Percy Hammond didn't help matters. "Miss Bankhead is the daughter and niece of two of America's most important statesmen, the Alabama Bankhead brothers, Phil and Bob." It pleased Percy to confuse Alabama and Wisconsin.

As everyone in the theater knows, the box office comes down

with an attack of the bends in the interval between Thanksgiving and Christmas. Business with *Dark Victory* was erratic from the start. By erratic I mean bad. You know? Stinking! After Thanksgiving it got worse. But the management, leaning on Jock Whitney's bank roll, felt that if the play could weather the storm until Christmas it would prosper during the holidays.

Dark Victory never made Christmas. Why? Its heroine was stricken again. I was becoming The Fabulous Invalid and/or The Doctor's Dilemma, with proper credits to George S. Kaufman, Moss Hart and George Bernard Shaw.

On the night of December 20 Laurette Taylor, Estelle Winwood, Dame Sibyl Thorndyke and I were gathered in my suite at the Gotham, shredding a few reputations, griping about the theater. Between us we had only a quart of champagne—Estelle and Dame Sibyl were teetotalers. All save Laurette had matinees the next day. This precluded any whoopla. We adjourned around three, with Estelle occupying my other bedroom. When I awoke, Ann and Sally draped across my quilts, I found to my horror I couldn't talk. Horror, indeed! The company manager had told me the night before the matinee was sold out, the first time we would enjoy such popularity since the opening night.

Estelle paged Dr. Reeder, my ear, nose and throat man. Like all doctors who cater to the bewitched people of the theater, he was aware of our slogan: "The show must go on." He told me to spray my throat, stop trying to talk, and he would see me in my dressing room before the performance. Thus encouraged, I was able to bathe, dress and get to the Plymouth by one-thirty.

Although suffering no pain, my face was swollen to twice its size when I got to the theater. My mouth and lips were distorted. The skin across my cheekbones and forehead was stretched taut. One look at me and all hands agreed I couldn't go on. Even had I been able to totter out on the stage, I could only have played in pantomime. My voice had vanished.

The audience was dismissed. The stage manager got me into a cab and took me back to the Gotham. I had picked up some bug so deadly and progressive that for a time the doctors thought it might be necessary to cut away my upper lip to keep the infection from spreading to my brain. Later Dr. Reeder told me that had I made up for the matinee it might have cost me my life. The rouges and oils and salves involved would have aggravated the infection. The Bankhead luck was getting no better in a hurry. Faced with a capacity house I was flattened. Hexed I was, and no mistake!

For two weeks I could only take liquid nourishment through a straw. I shed weight rapidly. I dramatized my illness by receiving friends with the lower half of my face draped in one of those half-masks which make Moorish and Turkish maidens so provocative. Even after my face had receded it was with regret I parted with my veil.

My illness sealed the fate of *Dark Victory*. I had been confined to quarters for two weeks when I received an invitation to a cocktail party from Joan Payson, Jock Whitney's sister. Irked at my imprisonment I was hell-bent on going. The doctor relented after exacting from me the promise I would not use any lipstick, that I would only stay an hour. Now I would just as soon attend a party naked as a jay bird as to face my friends without lipstick. My lips are whiter than my face, thanks to chronic anemia. Without lipstick I look like a circus clown.

I have good reason for remembering Joan's party. At it I met James Thurber, the brilliant cartoonist, writer and humorist. When I had first seen his misshapen dogs in *The New Yorker* their humor escaped me. Eager to be hep, boastful of the wit and gaiety of *The New Yorker*, I was baffled by Thurber. My brighter London friends found him convulsing. On my return to America Thurber's famous "War Between Men and Women" series was running, but I remained immune to his sardonic humor. But about the time *Dark Victory* went into rehearsal, I became a Thurber fan overnight.

A single cartoon converted me. A formless oaf of a man was facing his dowdy wife. Nearby one of Thurber's lumpy dogs was staring dejectedly at the two. The caption read:

YOU ARE DISENCHANTED. I AM DISENCHANTED.

WE ARE ALL DISENCHANTED.

"Thank God! At last I'm on to James Thurber!" I cried.

Introduced to Thurber at Joan's rout by Bob Benchley, I confessed my long bewilderment.

Thurber was gallant. He said he'd give me the drawing which had penetrated my coma. Agog at the prospect of owning a Thurber original, I reckoned without the Thurber vagueness. Years went by and no drawing. High, I'd call Thurber, brand him an Indian-giver. Once I called him to ask how I should frame his drawing. "What drawing?" he asked. "The one you promised and never sent." "I think a black frame would be best," he said, and hung up.

Five years later a press clipping said that in an exhibition of Thurber cartoons in London the one marked, "Loaned by Miss Tallulah Bankhead," was voted the most amusing, the most typical of the artist. Eventually I treed him in his summer retreat in Cornwall, Connecticut. "Now that I've loaned you the cartoon for ten years, would you mind returning it?" That did it. The disenchanted trio, framed as the Master wished, now adds gaiety to my living room.

The Payson party over, I threw caution to the winds. I ignored Dr. Reeder's ruling. The people there had been gay and provocative. The potables, too, inflated my enthusiasm. With Benchley and two other rebels I went out for a night on the town. We barged into night clubs and speakeasies flirting with padlocks and had ourselves a romp. I didn't hit the hay until thirty hours later. I awoke the next morning, fresh as a daisy.

Dark Victory convinced me my jinx was still working. My appearance in the revival of *Rain*, six weeks later, did nothing to dissipate that alarm. Spurred by frustration, I charged into rehearsals of *Something Gay*, as misleading a title as ever was hung on two hours of plot and dialogue.

An old comrade-in-arms directed it. But neither singly nor together could Tommy Mitchell and I get blood out of this turnip. Again the critics chanted "When is Miss Bankhead to get a good play?" Percy Hammond edged his chant:

Miss Bankhead is one of the most popular stage witches of our time. In this flimsy weaving of ropes out of sand she lets loose all her seductive forces. She is ladylike, rowdy, wheedling, pathetic and comic, innocent and guilty, feeble and strong, which in the argot of dramatic criticism is running some gamut. She goddamns and s.o.b.s., but always with a disarming Alabaman delicacy.

Something Gay was liquidated after nine weeks, unwept save by the Adelaide Heilborn who wrote it, by the Brothers Shubert who produced it.

This mistake subdued, I did a little summing up. It was two and a half years since I had fled Hollywood. Over that span I had drawn but twenty-one weeks' salary. Perhaps I should have *stood* in London. If it hadn't been for Jock Whitney and his damned transatlantic calls I might now be rioting in the West End instead of sulking in a New York hotel. My reflections brought on another discovery. Termites had gotten into my bankroll. I'd better haul in the mainsail, mix a new batch of metaphors and scud before the gale. After all I was a grown girl of thirty-five. It was time I pulled myself together. Or relaxed.

Relax? It was one of the longest relaxes on record. My siesta developed into a sabbatical. A year elapsed between the closing of *Something Gay* and the first rehearsal of *Reflected Glory*. Production was delayed interminably because playwrights and producers were at loggerheads over monies from sales of motion picture rights. The authors demanded sixty per cent of this loot, the producers thought they should be content with fifty. The authors won out.

In an attempt to exorcise myself, I decided to open *Reflected Glory* in San Francisco. I reasoned, if you can use the verb so loosely, that could this comedy play six or eight weeks out of town, there would be ample time to iron out such imperfections as might develop. Practice makes perfect, I muttered. Dedicated to a pre-Broadway skirmish I was determined to get as far away from New York as possible. So I elected San Francisco.

Those cool July nights in San Francisco were tonic after the swelter of New York. The city itself is exciting. Golden Gate harbor is something to remember. So are those evenings atop the Mark Hopkins. San Francisco is one of the very few cities that lives up to its billing.

I had still another reason to rejoice in *Reflected Glory*. Through it I met George Kelly, author and director. There is no man in the theater for whom I have more respect or affection. He is the perfectionist. He's singularly free of the vulgarity and brashness which often sullies even the ablest people in the theater. His attitude toward life is Olympian. He could no more perform a petty act, or lend himself to a shabby device, than he could debase himself by writing down to what the theater so often misjudges, popular taste.

Both he and Thornton Wilder have a cloistered air that sets them apart from the playwrights with whom I've had traffic. Never have I seen Kelly waver in his professional code. He is a gentleman! To the tips of his fingers!

George Kelly was the first top-drawer dramatist I had encountered since my return to the New York stage. His first play, *The Torchbearers*, is the most devastating satire on amateur theatricals ever written. I had seen it just before I bolted to London in '23. Shortly thereafter he set New York to laughing with *The Show-Off*. A year later he was to win the Pulitzer Prize with *Craig's Wife*, a relentless caricature of the possessive wife. *Daisy Mame, Behold the Bridegroom, Maggie the Magnificent* and *Philip Goes Forth* were to follow. In all of these he was expertly concerned with the follies and lunacies of his fellow men. Before he'd written *The Torchbearers* he had seen fourteen years' service as an actor. He had learned his trade in the dog-eat-dog competition of vaudeville.

Opening in San Francisco in late July we traipsed across the continent until he arrived at the Morosco, where I had been entombed in *Something Gay* the year before. Whereas in *Forsaking All Others* I had been mousetrapped into producing the play myself, now I had three producers. Allied in the adventure were Lee Shubert, Homer Curran, the San Francisco impresario, and Joseph M. Gaites. A treacherous knave, that Gaites, now with his ancestors. Fired with the notion that their contents would inspire his press agent to feats of derring-do, he borrowed all my scrapbooks, handsome albums in which were recorded my triumphs on the Thames, my duels with the screen, my off-stage antics. I've never laid eyes on them since. This chronicle would have more form were those volumes available. A posthumous pox on Mr. Gaites.

In *Reflected Glory* I was an emotional actress torn between an urge to forsake the theater and settle down, and the desire to add to her professional fame. In the end she elected the theater. By Kelly's terms it seemed like a sound decision. *Reflected Glory* was one of George Kelly's lesser plays, and the critics flayed it. Had it been written by a lesser playwright, I think they would have cheered it. Kelly was the victim of his own high standards. *Reflected Glory* prospered in moderate fashion for sixteen weeks, then toured until June in the larger cities. In it Chicago saw me for the first time, and vice versa.

The modest success of *Reflected Glory* tricked me into believing I had been de-haunted. But I was living in an opium world. Shortly I was to commit my master *faux pas,* resort to a role in which I was to be skinned alive, not, may I add, without provocation. But before I go into the details of that ambush another item must intrude on this report.

The item is John Emery. I married him on August 31, 1937. To telescope my marital statistics, and ease suspense, a Reno judge granted me a divorce on June 13, 1941, on the grounds of mental cruelty. A gentleman, Mr. Emery didn't offer any rebuttal. It's just as well.

When first I laid eyes on my future husband he was impersonating the Captain William Henry O'Shea who blasted the career of Irish patriot Charles Stewart Parnell, when he named him co-respondent in a divorce suit. Parnell, it seems, had taken time out from his Home Rule activities to play footsie with O'Shea's provocative Kitty.

In June of that year I met Mr. Emery formally. Rehearsing *Reflected Glory* in Los Angeles, I went backstage at the Biltmore Theatre one evening to greet Katharine Cornell. She had crossed the continent that Southern Californians might see her as George Bernard Shaw's Saint Joan. John was playing the Earl of Warwick, the dastard who purchased the Maid from the Burgundians. He was concealed behind a luxurious set of stage whiskers.

Either as Captain O'Shea or the vengeful Earl, John Emery was a fine young romantic actor. He had style and eloquence and was completely at ease in costume drama. In July of that same year I was to see him as Lord Peter Wimsey in *Busman's Honeymoon* at the Westport Country Playhouse in Connecticut. As is the custom in summer theaters, his engagement was for only a week. He'd had but a week of rehearsal, yet he gave a deft and amusing performance. At the time I was living in a rented house on Long Island Sound, ten miles from Westport. It boasted a swimming pool and free liquor. There I held open house for the likes of Anna May Wong, Clifton Webb, Estelle Winwood, Vincent Price, Louisa Carpenter and a lot of other friends, overloaded with leisure.

I got a sizzling crush on John on seeing his Wimsey. After the performance I went back to see him. Would he care to spend the week end with me? John readily agreed. I found him intelligent, amusing and exceptionally good-looking. He had good manners and seemed a good listener. This last marked him a rare bird in the set in which I traveled.

But when John asked me to marry him, I looked upon his offer as an impertinence. Wasn't he getting presumptuous on short acquaintance? Yet I was fascinated by his impulsiveness. No pussy-footing with Emery. He was a direct actionist. In this dilemma I consulted my sibyl, Estelle Winwood.

"Why not?" she said. "I think everyone should be married at least once. You've always wanted to try everything. This will round out your experience. Besides, it's not irrevocable. It's a calculated risk."

Calm, cool Edie Smith! When I told her how attractive I found John, she recognized the symptoms. "You wouldn't marry him, would you, *Die Donner?*" "My God! An actor! You must think I'm out of my mind," I shouted. However impertinent I thought the late Captain O'Shea, the recent Earl of Warwick, I consented. John was three years my junior but I didn't stop to quibble about this discrepancy. So I must have been out of my mind.

"I've always wanted to make a trip to Reno," was Edie's comment.

Despite my reputation for long and loose conversation, we kept our engagement secret for a week. Then we flew to Birmingham in a chartered plane, from there took a car to Jasper. We were to be married in Daddy's house. On our entrance Daddy was talking to London, long distance. There had been a leak in our communications. The London *Express* wanted a quote from my sire. He gave them one. "My daughter has on a little French dress and a little string of pearls. . . ." Like any good actor he was an improviser. He didn't know what I was wearing. The Episcopal minister in Jasper was desolated because he couldn't marry us. John, you see, had been divorced. A judge officiated. When John and I were one, Daddy asked if he might read the ceremonial as my mother would have liked it, the "Dearly beloved" and all the rest. He had been startled when he learned I was to marry. He thought Sister had a monopoly on the sacrament.

Only witnesses to our union were immediate members of the family: Uncle John and his wife, Daddy and my stepmother, and a passel of cousins. After the ceremony I went upstairs to primp up. Some of the more enthusiastic townspeople had gathered outside, and Daddy felt I should make a speech. Their votes might come in handy the next time he was up for re-election. When I came down Daddy and John were on the lawn doing a scene from *Julius Caesar.* John was the "lean and hungry Cassius," Daddy was going all out as Antony. Have I told you John's father had been leading man for both Ethel Barrymore and Minnie Maddern Fiske?

Just ten years before this, egged on by Beaverbrook, I had said in his London *Express*: "I should want my husband to be a sportsman in the true sense of the word. One who plays tennis and would not mind getting his shoes dirty, who would leap over a five-bar gate for the sheer joy of doing it, and could be alone with Nature and not be lonely. I would like him to know what it feels like to have the rain blowing in one's face and enjoy the buffeting of the wind, without crawling into the nearest taxicab or putting up an umbrella on the heights of a Yorkshire moor. . . . I believe that few stage marriages are really happy, unless the wife forsakes her profession. A stage life is so indefinite."

Pretty highfalutin' talk, eh? Well, the rain was blowing in our faces when we drove back to Birmingham. When we learned our flight was canceled we stayed the night at the Tutwiler Hotel. John didn't hurdle a fence on the whole journey. He was still shaken at meeting a roomful of Bankheads, all talking at once. When I presented him to Daddy, John blurted out, "How do you do, Mr. Squeaker?" Daddy was the only one who introduced me as Mrs. Emery in the four years of our marriage. He called John "my son."

Had I fled a nunnery, my marriage couldn't have created a greater hubbub in the newspapers. Back at my house on Long Island Sound for what we thought would be a two-week honeymoon, things started to pop. Reporters moved in on us in squads, remained to celebrate long after they had forgotten what they were celebrating. The reports they filed were incoherent. Through most of them ran a vein of sympathy for John. There were numerous tributes to his courage. Some of them hinted he was the most promising candidate for martyrdom since Lord Essex. I was credited with some of the most drooling nonsense ever to find its way into print. One addled scribe had me saying John "looked like a Greek god," still another that I had married him because he looked like John Barrymore.

I didn't help matters. When a reporter asked me if marriage meant I contemplated retirement, I raged: "For goodness' sake," if you'll pardon the fraudulent expletive, "if I wanted to retire, you idiot, would I marry an actor? Who would support me? Or us?"

After we were divorced, John said he first suspected there might be flaws in our union when I urged him to have a Planter's Punch for breakfast. What a quibble! A Planter's Punch, loaded with orange and pineapple slices, a cherry or two, is rich in food value, a most invigorating tonic. John could never escape the suspicion he had married an institution, rather than a woman. So long had I been in the public domain, he felt himself an intruder. He best expressed it on the opening night of *Antony and Cleopatra*." Asked by our mutual friend, Eddie Baylies, what he was doing after the performance, John said: "I don't know, but I think I'm going up to Tallulah's." He'd only been married ten weeks. Where the hell else would he go? Or should he go? Couldn't he have said, "I'm going home?"

Here's another Emery reflection: "Tallulah is the only woman I ever knew who could carry on a conversation, listen to the radio, read a book and do her hair at the same time." It was Mr. Emery who described my accent as "half British, half pickaninny." Questioned by one of Mr. Henry Luce's scouts when I was tapped for a *Time* cover, John was most co-operative. Asked how it felt being married to your historian, he said: "In a way it was like the rise, decline and fall of the Roman Empire." John may not have been able to top a five-bar fence, he may have been a stranger to the fairways, but he was as understanding as any male in view of what he had to cope with.

For the record, if I may lift a line from Al Smith, it wasn't John's

226.

fault our marriage failed. My interests and enthusiasms are too random for sustained devotion, if you know what I mean. Other actor pairs have loved and married and endured. Witness the Lunts, Vivien Leigh and Laurence Olivier. Witness John Emery and Tamara Geva. Miss Geva is John's wife and has been these past ten years. She's a damned good actress, too.

After twenty years of unbridled freedom, of acting on whim, I couldn't discipline myself to the degree necessary for a satisfactory union. I had roamed the range too long to be haltered. Don't think John tried any such nonsense. He went into the maelstrom with his eyes open but he overestimated his recuperative powers. It may sound like the all-American bromide but we're still good friends. When I toured in *Foolish Notion* in '45–'46 John and Donald Cook were my leading men. Both of us oozed *noblesse oblige*—John and I, that is.

I have no regrets about my marriage. John and I were to survive greater crises, as I shall now demonstrate. Our honeymoon over, the reporters back on their jobs, together we resumed professional practice.

Now that I've been wooed and wed, let's get back to that *faux pas* I was muttering about. More than once I've boasted of my ability to stimulate a soggy box office with the vim and vigor of my performance. Now I'll reverse my field. Here's how I curdled a classic.

Since Shakespeare coined *Antony and Cleopatra* back in 1607 a great many actresses have tackled the seductress, among them Lillie Langtry, Constance Collier, Edith Evans, Jane Cowl and Julia Marlowe. Although I had been twenty years in the theater I had yet to appear in a play hallowed by time. *La Dame aux Camelias* was only weatherbeaten. Shakespeare, Ibsen and their like had never challenged me. But the plays in which I fumed after my return from England made me susceptible when it was suggested I impersonate Cleopatra.

The producer must have had an inkling of what was to come. His name was Rowland Stebbins, but for this venture he chose to operate under the alias of Lawrence Rivers. Stebbins-Rivers gave the play a very flossy production. That I might have ample time to master its complexities, its rhythms and poetic flights, he booked it for six weeks on the road prior to our New York opening. There was another reason why I was eager to come to grips with Cleo. The producer and director agreed with me that John Emery would make a capital Octavius Caesar. Did we succeed in *Antony and Cleopatra,* John and I might move on to other joint triumphs —as had the Lunts. It was a pleasing prospect. Only I was vile.

On Armistice Day, 1937, I received the worst critical lambasting I ever experienced. There was no dissenting verdict. My old friend Richard Watts, Jr., wrote in the New York *Tribune*: "Miss Bankhead seemed more a serpent of the Suwannee than of the Nile." John Mason Brown, later to caress me with superlatives, mowed me down: "Tallulah Bankhead barged down the aisle as Cleopatra and sank. As the serpent of the Nile she proves to be no more dangerous than a garter snake." "Miss Bankhead played the Queen of the Nil," spit out George Jean Nathan, then took time out to warn the compositors that "Nil" was no typographical error. Even staid Brooks Atkinson joined the posse. "The Serpent of the Nile is definitely not Miss Bankhead's dish," he wrote in the *Times*.

Did I bristle and bite back? I did not. No use denying I was desolated. As Octavius Caesar my husband emerged from the melee unscathed, but my plan to emulate the Lunts was wrecked. I scorned suggestions that I hide out in a stone quarry until the hue and cry died down. Recently Miss Vivien Leigh took on Cleopatra, twice. She played that mercurial vixen in Shaw's *Caesar and Cleopatra* and in Shakespeare's *Antony and Cleopatra*. I wished her well. Matter of fact she was in no need of my benediction. She and her husband, Sir Laurence Olivier, packed the St. James in London and the Ziegfeld in New York in the two plays. All of which goes to prove that matrimony is not necessarily fatal to a tilt with either the Bard or the Beard. As far as I'm concerned Shakespeare should have left Antony and Cleopatra in Plutarch, where he found them.

Bringing Vivien Leigh into this serial touches off an explosion in my memory. Miss Leigh, you'll recall, played Scarlett O'Hara in *Gone with the Wind* after producer David Selznick had scoured the continent from the Yukon to the Yazoo in quest of a maid to defy Sherman and soothe Rhett Butler. It may have been the greatest girl hunt in all history. It certainly was the most expensive.

I was in San Francisco in *Reflected Glory* when first I collided with Scarlett. Though one of the longest novels of all time, I gulped it down in one sitting. Immediately I was inflamed with the desire to play Scarlett. I felt I had qualifications beyond any of the hundreds of candidates. I had the looks, the Southern background and breeding, the proper accent. There was one flaw in my equipment. I was thirty-four, a touch old for Scarlett. But through dieting, self-denial and discipline, I was sure I could come up to the pictorial mark. I knew I could *play* the pants off Scarlett.

There was another fly in my ointment. I was in no sense a picture star. My screen career was four years back of me. At its peak I hadn't caused any box-office hubbub. And I had still another discredit. For all my London acclaim, I had yet to star in a stage hit in America. I would have felt cockier had I already played Regina Giddens in *The Little Foxes*. My record didn't match my confidence.

The Scarlett hunt was boiling when I reached Los Angeles. So was I, although I masked my fevers. My maid roused me from a nap one afternoon to tell me George Cukor was on the telephone. Mr. Cukor had directed me in my first picture in New York. As all the world knew, he was to direct *Gone with the Wind* for David Selznick. Here was a friend at court. On my way to the telephone my wishes jelled into a conviction. I was sure his call had to do with Scarlett.

There was an exultant note in George's voice.

"Tallulah, the most wonderful thing has happened. It's out of the blue, and it's none of my doing. Selznick saw you last night in *Reflected Glory* at the Biltmore. He called me up first thing this afternoon to say, 'I've got our Scarlett.' "

George Cukor's call was proof to me I had the occult touch. From the moment I read the novel I had a feeling I was fated to play Scarlett. My Muriel Flood in *Reflected Glory* had a lot in common with that minx. Muriel ran an emotional gamut. Now she was gay, now despairing, now torn with conflicting desires. How fortunate Selznick had seen me at my best. I had been on my toes the night before, eager to show friend and foe the ex-Paramount player had what it took.

Exulting in the endorsement of producer and director, I felt consecrated. I looked upon myself as a symbol of the South, the fine flower of its darkest hours. Henceforth I would be humble and simple and austere. Temple bells rang in my head, and I whiffed the scent of magnolias.

For the seven weeks that *Reflected Glory* ambled eastward, I was on tenterhooks. Since a fortune was to be spent on the picture every detail had to be worked out after long research and study. A month after the New York opening, Cukor called me from Hollywood. What was the first possible moment I could come out for photographic tests? Equity contracts provide that attractions playing in New York or on the road may lay off the week before Christmas, when business hits an all-season low. I told George I could fly out on Saturday night after the performance, that I could spend two days in Hollywood.

No word of my probable choice for Scarlett had leaked into the newspapers. I had kept my mouth shut. That was part of my enforced discipline, that I might be worthy of Margaret Mitchell's heroine. In the mid-West our plane plunged into an electric storm and we were forced to make an emergency landing in Lincoln, Nebraska. Desolated by this delay, I called George Cukor.

"Take it easy, Tallulah! Relax!" said George. "We're going to take two tests by two different cameramen. We'll shoot the first tonight, the other tomorrow."

After my arrival in Hollywood I had time for a massage. I looked my best. At the studio I was placed in a make-up chair, a ritual without which no screen venture can hope to start. I was about to submit to this going-over when someone said, "You were in Louella Parsons' column this morning, Miss Bankhead."

You've probably heard of Louella. The writer of a syndicated screen column for the Hearst newspapers, she terrorized most of Hollywood, was flatteringly called "The Gay Illiterate."

Thus spake Louella:

Tallulah Bankhead breezed into town last night to take a test for Scarlett O'Hara in "Gone with the Wind." George Cukor, her friend, is going to direct; Jock Whitney, another friend, is backing it, so I'm afraid she'll get the part. If she does I, personally, will go home and weep, because she is NOT Scarlett O'Hara in any language, and if David Selznick gives her the part he will have to answer to every man, woman and child in America.

Jolly, eh? A salute from the screen's sibyl. An unpredictable witch, that Louella! Seven years later she was cooing over me like a pigeon. "Tallulah can out-talk, out-think and out-act anyone in Hollywood," she wrote, after seeing me in rushes of *Lifeboat*, the picture I made for Alfred Hitchcock. From this I could only conclude either I had purged myself to her satisfaction, or that she had repudiated the nation's men, women and children.

Into my two-day stay in Hollywood were crowded three tests. I was fit as a fiddle for the first, rested, calm and assured. I was tricked out in the clothes Garbo wore in *Camille*, since the styles of the periods were similar. When it was over I suggested we dispense with the second. I argued that we had had a crack photographer, that I would never be better. Cukor vetoed this proposal. When we made the second test, reaction had set in. I was fatigued. My eyes were bloodshot from loss of sleep. But I was grateful to George when the two tests were run off.

In the first, taken when I was fresh as a daisy, I looked a fright, old, unattractive. In the second, made while I was down and dumpy, I looked radiant, fascinating. Later I was to learn the secret of this contradiction. It is a matter of lighting. Cameramen can work miracles when their subject is properly lighted. But the best of them can botch an assignment when lights and shadows are clumsily played. The third test, in color, frightened me stiff. Color was then in its infancy. It may still be for all I know. I looked a fright. My heart went into my boots. If I tangled with Scarlett in the spectrum, I might touch off another war between the states. But in black and white, in that second test, I was something to cheer up the Confederacy.

For months thereafter I was cited as leading the field in the Scarlett Derby. Selznick and his aides kept looking in treetops, under bridges, in the Social Register and on lists of parolees from reformatories. An actress who hadn't been mentioned for the role felt humiliated. My bones told me I wouldn't get the part. I pay attention to my bones. Once they'd communicated with me, I ceased to worry about the role and the picture.

Vivien Leigh, who grabbed the brass ring, won the Academy Award for her effort. But I'll go to my grave convinced that I could have drawn the cheers of Longstreet and Beauregard and Robert E. Lee had I been permitted to wrestle with Rhett Butler.

And that, my sweets, is why Tallulah never got to Tara.

My emotions shot up like a geyser when I saw *Gone with the Wind* on the screen. As Sherman put Atlanta to the torch my blood boiled. In this state I was further outraged when the gentleman directly behind me applauded furiously, then cut loose with a couple of bravos. I swiveled about and spat out, "You dirty Communist!" though "carpetbagger" was what I meant. Too late I discovered it was Amos Pinchot, father of the lovely Rosamond, and an old friend of mine. He had timed his outburst to test my conduct under fire, though aware his action might incite a riot.

Once the hue and cry over my Cleopatra had died down to minor border incidents, I felt it safe to come out of the cellar. Since there was nothing in the penal statutes to cover my offense, I was let off with a reprimand. Having hocked everything I owned, I had to borrow money. All that Hollywood plunder was gone. With François Villon I might have cried out, "Où sont les neiges d'antan?" but I wasn't familiar with François' concern with snow.

In mid-April, 1938, I was scraping bottom. Scarlett had been denied me. I had a husband, a handful of pawn tickets, a nervous landlord and an offer to appear in *The Circle*, a seventeen-year-old comedy by the Somerset Maugham who clipped me from behind when I was on my way to a touchdown in *Rain*.

I was in no position to air a grudge. If I didn't find employment pronto, I might become a public charge. When William A. Brady beckoned me to his museum, I jumped at the opportunity to play the role my old friend, Estelle Winwood, had played seventeen years earlier. John, growing a little gaunt, was but a jump behind me. Grace George, in private life Mrs. Brady and one of the ablest comediennes of our time, was to play the leading part, created by Belasco's famous redhead, Mrs. Leslie Carter. Mrs. Carter once swung from a bellclapper in *Shenandoah*. Remember? Neither do I.

When he felt a spring revival coming on him, Mr. Brady did not think it politic to pamper his players with high salaries. His judgment couldn't be faulted. An impecunious lot, actors, faced with a summer of idleness, are in no position to haggle over fees. Set up in Mr. Brady's own theater, *The Circle* endured until wilted by hot weather—a run of nine weeks. Who was I to jeer at a nine-week run? I had cooled off Cleopatra in five performances.

For all its brevity I have reason to remember *The Circle*. In it I was reviewed by Wolcott Gibbs for the first time. Gibbs had succeeded Bob Benchley as *The New Yorker*'s critic when my sometime drinking partner bolted that magazine to cut up before Hollywood's cameras. A brilliant stylist, Mr. Gibbs can be venomous when his eyes and ears are affronted.

"Miss Bankhead is a brilliant and turbulent actress (an intelligent man's guide to irony and adultery), whose interpretation of her role makes it hard to believe that she would hesitate for a moment between a dull husband and a fascinating lover even though the honor of every Campion-Cheney, living or dead, was at stake."

Ten years later I would repay Mr. Gibbs, in part, for his tribute.

Stricken with some pestilence, he was pining at the Lenox Hill Hospital when I raided his chamber one afternoon. Eager to divert him, I put on a one-woman floor show designed to cure or kill. The nurses swore it was the most exciting vaudeville ever seen on the floor. Without music, too! After the drubbing I had taken in Cleopatra, Gibbs' words had been nectar. I would have married him on the spot, had not the venture involved double bigamy.

John and I were still strapped when *The Circle* came apart at the seams. Almost at once we plunged into *I Am Different*, a Hungarian mishap by Lily Hatvany. Zoe Akins had decoded it for American consumption. Defying the thermometer, it opened in Chicago in August, by Thanksgiving Day had edged as far east as Washington. There it collapsed from public lethargy. It had been a shambles from the start. It toured three months only because Lee Shubert believed in miracles. Mr. Lee, as he is known in the trade, was hard to convince. Basking at Cannes the following summer, he said he would bring it into New York with Constance Bennett in the role which had floored me. Cooler heads—among them Miss Bennett's—prevailed. New York has had its share of indignities. It could well be spared that one.

Though I didn't know it at the time, that Thanksgiving Day was the end of a six-year ordeal. I was about fed up. I had scorned that easy Hollywood swag because I was discontented, frustrated by the tripe in which I was obliged to appear. In the theater, I reasoned, I would be a free agent. I could elect my own plays, have something to say about direction and casting. It hadn't worked out that way. In those six years I had been starred in eight plays. Two of them were revivals, one never got to New York. Lumped together, the seven that faced the music ran a total of sixty-three weeks. You needn't be an Einstein to figure out that since I fled Paramount I had averaged nine weeks a year on the New York stage. Over that span I had spent almost as much time in the hospitals. Thanksgiving Day, eh? A lot I had to be thankful for! But I didn't give way to an orgy of self-pity. This was no time to moon over my plight. Nibbling at my cranberry sauce I found solace in one of Daddy's favorite proverbs: The hour is darkest just before the dawn.

236.

11.

Regina and Sabina

My creditors had started to keen in chorus when Herman Shumlin sent me the script of Lillian Hellman's *The Little Foxes*. A taut and unhappy man, Shumlin was a director and producer. In both capacities he gave the utmost of his uncommon industry and ability. Shumlin thought I would make a desirable Regina Giddens in this devastating play about the predatory Hubbard family, as they plotted and plundered in the deep South at the turn of the century.

Regina Giddens was a rapacious bitch, cruel and callous. Etched in acid by Miss Hellman, who at first thought I was too young for the role, she was a frightening opportunist who stopped at nothing to further her prestige and fortune. All in all, Regina Giddens is the best role I ever had in the theater. So *The Little Foxes* is the best play I've ever had. Up to this time most of my roles had been on the light and larkish side. Though generally playing a woman who didn't give a fig for the commandments, I usually had redeeming qualities—gaiety, a racy and rowdy attitude toward life. Regina permitted no such compromises. She was soulless and sadistic, an unmitigated murderess. For profit she would have slit her mother's throat, but not before so staging the crime that the guilt would be pinned on another.

Regina fascinated me, as did Lillian Hellman's searing prose. Here was a role which cried for an actress of stature. Its demands were far above and beyond those of the flibbertigibbets I had mirrored. Regina was a challenge that I welcomed—even though I was to play a woman with a seventeen-year-old daughter and wear corsets. There were compensations. The role permitted me to use my authentic Southern accent. I didn't need much prodding to accept Shumlin's bid.

But before we went into rehearsal we were victimized by a fiction. The play was scheduled to open in Boston on January 23, 1939, but Frank Conroy, who was to play my doomed mate, was tangled up in some Hollywood assignment that delayed practice a week. One morning I picked up the *New York Times* and read in the theatrical news column, written by Sam Zolotow, that the delay in starting rehearsals was due to the fact that I had had a row with Shumlin.

This charge was damnably false. Later I had rows with both Shumlin and Miss Hellman, but as yet all was serene. Shumlin was no man to take a charge like this lying down, even when it appeared in so august a journal as the *Times*. The story was all the more damaging because it appeared in the *Times*. It is generally recognized as the nation's greatest newspaper, as Mr. Zolotow is recognized as the ablest and most widely read of all the gentlemen who report on theater doings.

Together we bore down on Arthur Hays Sulzberger, president and publisher of the *Times*. We protested that the report was false, not to say harmful, since the theater looked upon Mr. Zolotow's reports as gospel. Mr. Sulzberger temporized. He said that the *Times* would print our denial. But we were looking for something more decisive. The *Times* should admit its error, rather than quote our rebuttal. By Sulzberger's suggested procedure we'd be put in the awkward position of defending ourselves against a charge of which we were guiltless. We scorned one of those "I do not beat my wife" devices which stir in the reader a suspicion that where there is so much smoke there must be some fire. When Sulzberger persisted in this elusive tactic, my language grew sulphurous.

To allay our anger, or get rid of us, Sulzberger resorted to a diversion. He sent us to Edwin James, his managing editor, to whom we repeated our grievance. James, too, was nimble. No matter how vehemently we protested the outrage, he would not concede the *Times*'s guilt.

Two or three days later Zolotow's column carried this item: "'The Little Foxes' is expected to open January 30, out of town, the January 23 booking at the Wilbur, Boston, having been cancelled. Tallulah Bankhead, the actress, indignantly denied that there had been a row between her and the play's sponsor, Herman Shumlin. She attributed the report to a mischief-maker."

Mischief-maker eh? I used a more violent epithet. Remember the Virginian's reply when thus rudely identified in the Owen Wister novel? "Smile when you say that, Trampas."

Newspapers, I've found, are slow on the retraction, when caught with their facts down. When I was playing in *Foolish Notion* in Baltimore before the New York opening of the play, columnist Danton Walker of the New York *Daily News*, wrote that author Philip Barry had been carted off to Johns Hopkins Hospital with internal hemorrhages brought on by a Tallulah tantrum. This was an outrageous fabrication. As soon as I read the libel I called Joseph Medill Patterson on the telephone. Captain Patterson was an old friend of mine. He often visited me in the theaters, always came down to the *Daily News* color studio to banter with me when I sat for a cover for his rotogravure section. He was editor and publisher of the *News*, had once written a play, *The Fourth Estate*.

I didn't mince words with Joe. Though I liked Patterson, I loathed the repulsive editorials in his newspaper, and never hesitated to tell him so. In my anger I yelled that the *News* was only read by followers of "Dick Tracy" and "Little Orphan Annie," that for all its nasty attacks on Franklin Roosevelt, it didn't sway the vote of one cab driver. His Mr. Walker had libeled me. I demanded a retraction. What if Barry should die in Johns Hopkins? Readers who delighted in Walker's bilge would think me his murderess, Barry's not Walker's.

Patterson laughed at my outburst. "Tallulah, you actresses are always working yourselves up into a tizzy. Cool off. These column writers have to do their job." "Their job?" I yelled. "Are you implying their job is libel? Did Barry say I put him in the hospital? Did I say it? No! Only Walker said it. Gossip columnists have no concern for fact. They thrive on suspicion, touched up with malice." I had a lot of other words for Joe, too explosive to set down here. I threatened him with a libel suit, then hung up. Some days later Mr. Walker, an old friend of mine, wrote that Mr. Barry was recovering at Johns Hopkins. That's as close as I ever got to a retraction.

The Little Foxes justified my hopes. Overnight it blotted out memory of the bad plays in which I had been imprisoned. It was both a critical and a popular success. My Regina won applause that warmed my heart. At long last, said my judges, Tallulah had a play worthy of her, and, having it, knew what to do with it.

The Little Foxes ran for a year in New York, for another year on tour. It provided me with more weeks' employment than all the other fifteen plays in which I had appeared in my own country combined. But it did something more. It established me as a dramatic star, an emotional actress worthy of the critical halos voted me. (Someone has said that a halo only has to slip eleven inches to become a noose.) *The Little Foxes* did me still another service.

Since I received ten per cent of the weekly box-office receipts, it enabled me to wipe out my debts, walk out of the stage door after a performance without fear of a bouquet from a process server.

But *The Little Foxes* was not to be an unalloyed joy. My phantom brawl with Shumlin, invented by Zolotow, flowered into reality in November of 1939. And it was to embrace Lillian Hellman. At its peak it was one of the finest Donnybrooks of that or any theatrical year, with no quarter asked or given.

It was provoked by Soviet Russia's attack on Finland. I thought the Russian invasion the brutal act of a bully. The people of the theater, their emotions inflamed by this wanton assault on a small and peaceful neighbor, were quick to volunteer aid for the victim.

My indignation can boil as high as the next man's, or the next woman's, when I see the weak bludgeoned by the mighty. I protested at the top of my lungs. Miss Hellman and Shumlin thought otherwise. Challenged, Miss Hellman said, "I don't believe in that fine, lovable little Republic of Finland that everybody gets so weepy about. I've been there and it looks like a pro-Nazi little republic to me." Shumlin concurred.

Violently as I disagreed, I respected their right to express their opinion. It took courage to take the stand they did, since American sympathy was overwhelmingly for the Finns. Eager to do my bit, I announced that I would give a benefit performance of *The Little Foxes*, the entire receipts to be used for Finnish relief. Miss Hellman and Mr. Shumlin promptly vetoed this proposal. As author and producer of the play, there was no appeal from their decision. I raged with anger. I expressed my scorn for their attitude in no uncertain terms. Our *entente cordiale* was scuttled forthwith, our conversations reduced to nods.

My anger at Shumlin and Lillian Hellman didn't hit its peak until later, when my road tour in *The Little Foxes* was over and I was being subjected to the caprices of Billy Rose in *Clash by Night*. This Clifford Odets drama was in its tryout phase in Philadelphia when I came down with double pneumonia. I had a temperature of 105 degrees when spirited off to the hospital by Mr. Rose after the opening performance. He registered me under an alias. News of my grave illness, he felt, would react badly on the box office. For fiscal reasons, he hoped I might make a miraculous overnight recovery.

I spent two weeks in an oxygen tent. For three days it was touch and go. I had just emerged from this fog, was still luxuriating in the tent, when I picked up a copy of *The New Yorker*, to become engrossed in a profile of Miss Hellman, written by my old Algonquin playmate, Margaret Harriman. In it Miss Hellman said she and Mr. Shumlin had prevented me from giving a performance of *The Little Foxes* for Finnish relief because "Miss Bankhead and the cast had refused some months earlier to play a benefit which Miss Hellman had asked them to give for the Spanish loyalists."

On reading this, I blasted a vent in the tent. The charge that I had refused to play a benefit for Loyalist Spain was a brazen invention. Neither Shumlin nor Miss Hellman ever asked me to do any such thing. Nor did anyone else. Both were champions of Loyalist Spain, both were desolated when Barcelona fell. *The Little Foxes* was rehearsing on that black day. I remember taking Lillian to my dressing room and giving her a shot of brandy to ease her anguish. I had adopted two Spanish children, hungry and homeless because of Franco's fury. The children were twins, grandchildren of the famous Spanish composer, Granados. I also contributed money that their father, a noted cellist, might find haven in this country. I made a visit to the Commissioner of Immigration that his entry might not get snarled up in red tape. I wasn't too familiar with the politics of the civil war in Spain. But I was concerned with the plight of the widows and orphans, innocent victims of the bloody business.

Miss Hellman and I have not faced each other since, an omission which I have survived without difficulty. I think she is one of our ablest playwrights. As a playwright I have tremendous respect for her. As a person she is not my cup of tea. I was still simmering over Miss Hellman's deception three years later when I picked up a copy of *Time*. In a John Hersey dispatch from Moscow I read that Miss Hellman, in Russia as the guest of VOKS, Soviet Cultural Society, had said in an address: "I don't like the theatre very much. . . . An actor doesn't make much difference to a play."

At first I thought this statement was born of too many swigs of vodka. But I couldn't let it go unchallenged. A week later the Letters department of *Time* carried my answer:

I loathe Lillian . . . a remark like that is beneath the contempt of an actor. She doesn't know what she's talking about. I'd like to see what some of her plays would be like with a second-rate cast. Of course she's really a wonderful playwright, and a good play that has a good part is awfully hard to find. If Lillian had a good play right now I'd do it, even though I hate her.

Communication with Russia being laggard in that winter, Miss Hellman's reply wasn't aired until three weeks later. It read:

Time misquotes me as saying at a Moscow reception that the actor doesn't make a difference to a play. As one hundred guests and the stenographic record will testify I said that although many actors have made plays successful, no actor has ever made a good play into a bad play, or a bad play into a good play, which is a very different statement and should quiet the excitable Miss B. Accustomed to yearly public greetings from the well-bred daughter of our plantation South I think the time has come to say that hate from Miss Bankhead is a small badge of honor, and praise undesirable. Miss Bankhead will never act in a play of mine again, only because I can stand only a certain amount of boredom.

That last sentence left Miss Hellman open to charges of plagiarism. Only a month before I had branded her a bore in a New York interview. I had priority rights in this reciprocal smear. Our exchange led one idler to term the fracas "The Battle of the Bores." I don't think either one of us got around to thanking *Time* for letting us use its columns for a shooting gallery. In my professional relations with Shumlin he behaved with integrity. He treated me handsomely, denied me nothing I asked. I am indebted to him and Miss Hellman for my finest role. No verbal brawl can cancel out that acknowledgment.

Didn't Billy Rose intrude on this memoir three or four hundred words ago? You remember Mr. Rose, to be sure? I had just started to compose this confession when he came romping out of his tepee, with his blanket down, screaming, "The publicity will ruin me." His plaintive whoop was brought on by the arrival of a squad of newspapermen at his wigwam atop the Ziegfeld Theatre on hearing that a young woman had committed an indiscretion in his bathroom with a razor blade.

The newsmen thought his lament the most ironic utterance of our generation. Mr. Rose, they exulted, had been hoist by his own petard. Long a worshiper at the shrine of publicity, indeed the product of it, it seemed to them, as it did to me, that he could have resorted to a happier phrase in his romantic crisis.

Mr. Rose, as I told you, was the producer of *Clash by Night*, the Odets play in which I found myself after *The Little Foxes*. (How many of you know the derivation of that title? It was Dorothy Parker's contribution to Miss Hellman's play. It can be found in the Bible in the Song of Songs: "Take us the foxes, the little foxes, that spoil the vines. For our vines have tender grapes.") How odd to get Billy Rose and the Bible tangled up in one paragraph! I bristled the first time ever I met the man flatteringly described as "the basement Belasco." He had delusions of infallibility. Since he had charmed the unwary in Texas, Ohio and Flushing with his alfresco tableaux, he was convinced he had invented the theater. He approached the Odets play as if he was putting on a rodeo.

I smoldered through rehearsals, burst into flames when I reached Baltimore where the play was to open. The electric sign over the marquee spelled out:

BILLY ROSE PRESENT

TALLULAH BANKHEAD

Modestly he had his name in letters no larger than mine. With characteristic taste he had neglected to mention the name of the play, or its author. Aside from his grammatical lapse—"Billy Rose Present"—he had airily omitted Joseph Schildkraut and Lee Cobb. In the play I was the wife of the last named, but was up to some extramarital didos with the first. This detour led Cobb to track down Schildkraut in his projection booth and strangle him with his bare hands. I was a Polish flower wilting under the boredom of life on Staten Island.

I seethed at Rose's effrontery. I called his manager and delivered an ultimatum in rich, ripe words. "Unless that 'Billy Rose Present' comes down immediately, there'll be no performance tomorrow night. If your foul employer insists on 'Billy Rose Present,' then you need only add, 'Tallulah Bankhead Absent.' Who does he think they're coming to the theater to see? Fannie Brice's ex-husband?"

"Billy Rose" came down, and the curtain went up. But the whole engagement was a mess, thanks to Rose's intrusions and omissions.

True, *Clash by Night* was the work of the Odets of *Waiting for Lefty*, *Awake and Sing* and *Golden Boy*, but it lacked the vigor and rebellion of his earlier works. It was stained by Odets' collusion with Hollywood. It languished in New York for six weeks. Never did a final curtain fall on a more relieved actress. Did his ability total up to a tenth of his ego, Rose would be a composite of Stanislavsky, Shakespeare, and Pontius Pilate.

I first played the citronella circuit in the summer of 1940. Solvent by an eyelash, I felt that I'd better shore up my bank account. *The Little Foxes* wasn't to resume its tour until September. In increasing numbers stars were seeking employment in renovated barns and silos. Few of them could afford to loiter for three months, regardless of their note and glitter. I had long scorned these sorties into the sumac. I looked upon summer theaters as shabby deceits, swindles contrived for naïve natives and gin-scented vacationists. Originally they were schemed to foster budding playwrights, serve as incubators for young players fired with the desire to inherit the mantle of Duse or Coquelin. This design went up in smoke in short order. Commerce raised its head. The promoters and dreamy-eyed idealists behind this hot-weather hoax found experimental exercises didn't pay off. Summer theaters were a variation of winter stock companies. Stars were engaged to insure box-office trade. These stars had to have a new barn each week, usually accompanied by their own casts. This spared them the necessity of rehearsal, but it raised havoc with low-salaried resident apprentices.

Trying to get on my fiscal feet I barged through a succession of straw-hats in *The Second Mrs. Tanqueray*, a relic from the pen of Sir Arthur Wing Pinero. Mrs. Patrick Campbell had rocked London when she created the title role nine years before I was born. I discovered that I had been too uppity about summer theaters. There was gold in those dells. In subsequent summers I was to knock off as much as $5,000 a week from June to September in roles I could have played in my sleep.

I had just said farewell to Paula Tanqueray and was about to start my tour in *The Little Foxes*. Sister and I were at the Lombardy Hotel in New York. We had the radio turned on to hear Daddy's speech from Baltimore urging the election of Franklin Delano Roosevelt for a third term. At the appointed time an announcement came over the air that because of the sudden illness of Speaker of the House Bankhead, Governor O'Connor of Maryland, would read his address. Sister and I knew at once. Daddy had had a succession of heart attacks over the past seven years. He dismissed these with characteristic flippancy even when their severity forced him into a hospital. I knew Daddy must be desperately ill. Nothing short of a stroke could have forced him to forego his opening speech for Roosevelt.

The telephone rang. It was Daddy's chauffeur. He was speaking from the Baltimore hotel from which Daddy was to address the nation.

"Miss Bankhead, you'd better come," he said.

Sister and I were in Baltimore within three hours. We spent the night outside Daddy's door. Neither of us entered his room. Had he regained consciousness and seen us, he would have known of the gravity of his condition. When we were admitted in the morning he was conscious, even cheerful. Asked by the doctor "Where is your pain?" he replied, "I don't play favorites; I scatter my pain." His concern was in getting back to Washington, to the Capitol where he had served his country for twenty-three years. His wishes were respected. Just before we parted I leaned over and kissed his cheek. "Daddy? Do you still love me?" He flashed his winning smile. "Why talk about circumferences?" It was the last time I was to see him.

Daddy died on the evening of September 15, 1940, at the Naval Hospital in Washington, while I was playing Regina Giddens on the stage of the McCarter Theatre in Princeton. That afternoon Uncle John phoned me to say the end was near. But I knew Daddy and his code of conduct. It would annoy him did I cancel the performance to speed to him. I would be failing a professional obligation, he would have argued. It was arranged for the Washington Express to stop for me at Princeton immediately after the performance. I reached Baltimore at three in the morning. My family met me at the station. Only then did I learn that Daddy was no more. With consideration and courtesy the newspapermen had withdrawn, that I might learn of Daddy's death from those close to me.

The next day most of official Washington came to pay their respects to my stepmother, to console Sister and me. I was deeply moved when Secretary of State Cordell Hull came to me, tears streaming down his cheeks. "I loved him so," he said. I had not seen Cordell Hull since I had ridden his Shetland ponies at Staunton, Virginia, twenty-four years before. Floor Leader Sam Rayburn, who was to succeed Daddy as Speaker, came to see us. So did James F. Byrnes, Robert H. Jackson, Frank Knox and a lot of others.

He was a gallant gentleman, Daddy! His exit, his last lines, his final curtain were as he would have had them. He was something more than a gentleman. He was a MAN. His place will never be filled, in my heart or in my mind.

I have said Regina Giddens was my best part, that *The Little Foxes* was my best play. I lean toward Regina and *The Little Foxes* because this was the role, this the play, that established me, demonstrated to the captious that I was something more than a skilled comedienne, a gaudy personality, an exciting rebel.

Those choices were neither hasty nor easy. For in the fall of 1942 I started to rehearse in *The Skin of Our Teeth*, Thornton Wilder's brilliant and controversial comedy that upended more than one critic, defied all the canons of the theater, confused the literal-minded. It was a gay delight to those with imagination as it was to those who rejoiced in nose-thumbing at tradition.

Jed Harris was the first producer to read Mr. Wilder's play. After a six months' trance he decided it was not his mutton. Impressed by his enthusiasm, Wilder tapped Michael Myerberg for the assignment. Short of the necessary funds, Myerberg solicited half the producers in New York for assistance. Howard Cullman, heralded for his ability to pick and back potential hits, dismissed it as a variation of *Life with Father*. So astute a producer as Gilbert Miller couldn't read it through. It baffled Vinton Freedley, a Harvard graduate, no less. The Theatre Guild thumbed it down as the caprice of a literary man engaged in a little leg-pulling.

The theater has always been the foe of change, of progress, of innovation. I'm surprised it ever conceded the electric light. It is the prisoner of precedent. When Mr. Wilder schemed *Our Town* without scenery, producer Jed Harris had been forced to cancel its second week in Boston because the American Athens shunned a play that flouted stage conventions. *Our Town* won the Pulitzer Prize as the best play of that year. More than one critic rates it the finest play ever written by an American.

The success of *Our Town* made the cavalier treatment of *The Skin of Our Teeth* all the more inexplicable. Wilder had already submitted evidence that he knew more about the theater, its variations and its origins, than any of his contemporaries. But the theater is suspicious of intelligence, of new forms, of deviations from the tried and true. Generally speaking, its slogan reads: "If it was good enough for granddaddy it's good enough for me." Producers should thaw out their minds, cease their worship of the *status quo*.

In the comedy I was variously Sabina, general utility maid in the household of the Antrobuses, an Ice Age family; Lilith, Adam's fabled first wife; Lily Fairweather, hostess in an Atlantic City bingo parlor; and Miss Somerset, an actress who, when the whim seized her or Mr. Wilder, addressed the audience. Mr. Antrobus had just invented the wheel. He had the nine muses as house guests. He was susceptible to Sabina's feminine wiles.

In general *The Skin of Our Teeth* was Mr. Wilder's tribute to mankind, its indestructibility, its resourcefulness in time of crisis, its lust for survival in the face of such horrors as the seven-year locusts, the flood, the double feature, war, famine and pestilence. Flouting formula, Mr. Wilder scrambled both time and circumstance. He thought nothing of having a dinosaur frolicking on the lawn while the Antrobuses were bemused by a radio commentator. All children understood it, but it escaped the ken of Adolph Menjou and most screen actors.

The legend has long persisted that Wilder wrote the play with Ruth Gordon in mind for his Sabina-Lilith-Somerset. Alexander Woollcott, close friend of Wilder's, was dedicated to Miss Gordon. Wilder told me he had toyed with the notion of playing *The Skin of Our Teeth* as broad farce, with Groucho Marx as Mr. Antrobus, Fannie Brice as Sabina. I was about the last actress considered for the role.

In naming Michael Myerberg to produce *The Skin of Our Teeth*, Wilder flouted all professional canons. Myerberg was an erratic, tactless man, lean as Cassius, who had been fiddling around the theater for a dozen years with little success. But above any other producer, successful or idle, he had enthusiasm for the comedy. Something of a rebel, Myerberg was attracted to the play by the very qualities which bewildered the more experienced producers he addressed. By what miracle he raised the money to produce it remains his secret. I suspect that had it not sold out in its tryout week in New Haven, we would have had to hitchhike to the next stand, Baltimore.

Myerberg approached me as a last resort. He was hipped on Helen Hayes for the role. Visiting the bedridden Edward Sheldon, one of the most venerated and respected men in the theater, Helen told him of the offer to play Sabina. He was quick to disillusion her. He told her he thought it a remarkable play which might be a great popular and critical success, but Sabina was not right for her. "The only person in the theater to play the part is Tallulah Bankhead," he added. Helen concurred. It was her recommendation that brought me to Myerberg, Thornton Wilder and Sabina. For the fifteen years prior to his death in '46, Sheldon's bed had been a shrine to which all the theater's elite went to pay their respects, to get advice and consolation. Sheldon had written such great dramatic hits as *The Czarina, Romance, Miss Lulu Bett.*

I was starred in *The Skin of Our Teeth* with Fredric March and Florence Eldridge, with Florence Reed giving a notable performance as a timeless sibyl.

The Skin of Our Teeth provoked storms of controversy starting with its first performance in New Haven. The fury of the debate rose as we visited Baltimore, Washington and Philadelphia. Many walked out on it, protesting it was a riddle beyond their range. The controversy was box-office fuel. We sold out in every town, leaving in our wake confused and/or ecstatic customers. We had a three-day recess before the New York opening. I took advantage of this lull to approach Myerberg.

In one scene Fredric March and I were up to some amorous antics in an Atlantic City cabana. Conforming with Wilder's stage directions this shelter was in the orchestra pit. Entrance to the pit was awkward since we had to descend a flight of stairs and squeeze by front-row customers. The space granted Sabina and Mr. Antrobus for their folly was so cramped as to preclude the full potential of the desired fireworks. I suggested to Myerberg the removal of two aisle seats would be a happy solution. Myerberg cringed. He wasn't up to removing seats he could sell for $4.80 a copy. I resorted to direct action. Armed with a carpenter's kit, I invaded the auditorium of a dark afternoon, while stage hands were wrestling with lights and properties, and started to remove the offending chairs. With that Myerberg capitulated. The seats were removed. Antrobus and Sabina were able to validate their ardors in satisfactory fashion.

My Sabina was sprayed with superlatives. Wolcott Gibbs wrote in *The New Yorker*: "The most brilliant and certainly the most versatile performance of Miss Bankhead's entire career." The aloof Louis Kronenberger wrote in *Time* that I played Sabina "with brilliant verve and vivacity." In less dignified vein humorist "Bugs" Baer wrote, "Tallulah plays a beauty-prize winner and flashes a swell set of gams."

Since the *Times*' Brooks Atkinson was off to the wars in China, the comedy was reviewed by Lewis Nichols. Cautiously he wrote it was "one of the best plays in many months." Warmed by this salute from so influential a newspaper, Mr. Myerberg inflamed the Plymouth's marquee with Nichols' verdict. This action enraged Woollcott. His hair on fire, he addressed this sizzling protest to Myerberg:

How dare you advertise "The Skin of Our Teeth" as "the best play in many months"? *There's* faint praise if ever I heard any. These foggy words did appear in the *Times*, but why should you quote them boastfully—you who ought to know that Thornton Wilder's dauntless and heartening comedy stands head and shoulders above anything ever written for our stage? It has been your rich privilege to produce the nearest thing to a great play which the American theatre has yet evolved and I begin to suspect that you don't deserve it. Don't point to that long line at the Plymouth box-office as proof of your shrewdness. It merely proves again that the public is not such a fool as it looks.

To add to the confusion Myerberg used the Woollcott letter as an advertisement in the newspapers. Alex saw the play many times. He stood to watch half a matinee the day before he was fatally stricken in a radio studio.

For all the comedy's spectacular success, for all the hubbub it raised, there were people who found it as baffling as the hieroglyphics on the Rosetta stone. Typical was the reaction of a Park Avenue debutante reported to me by a friend who had overheard a conversation in the lobby.

Shortly after the curtain's rise a slide flashed on a motion picture screen saying the cleaning women had collected articles lost in the auditorium, among them "a wedding ring, inscribed 'To Eve from Adam.' Genesis 11:18. The ring will be restored to the owner or owners, if their credentials are satisfactory." Another bulletin stated the wall of ice coming down from the North had pushed the Cathedral of Montreal as far as St. Albans, Vermont. Still others introduced Mr. Antrobus, inventor of the lever, and Mrs. Antrobus, inventor of the apron. Then the curtain rose to reveal Sabina dusting off the furniture in the living room of her employers. She was rattling off a monologue about her plight and the character of the Antrobuses, when she suddenly wheeled and addressed the audience:

"I hate this play and every word in it. As for me, I don't understand a single word of it. Besides, the author hasn't made up his silly mind as to whether we're all living back in caves or in New Jersey today."

At the intermission the Park Avenue birdbrain said to her escort: "I agree with Miss Bankhead, I don't understand a word of the play. I haven't any notion of what it's about. Have you?"

Her companion stammered slightly, then said, "Yes, I think so." "What?" she snapped. "Well, in general terms it's about the human race."

"Oh," jeered the belle, "is *that* all?"

Remember that mammoth I milked back in the first paragraph of this work? *Attendez, mes cheries!* Shortly after the episode just cited I confronted Mrs. Antrobus for the first time. After twitting me for letting the fire go out on the coldest day of the year—it was mid-August—Miss Eldridge turned to me and said: "You've let the fire go out. Have you milked the mammoth?" "Yes," I replied, "I've milked the mammoth."

The Skin of Our Teeth was directed by Elia Kazan—Gadge, to his cronies—a graduate of the Group Theatre. He had first attracted attention for his slangy cab driver in Clifford Odets' *Waiting for Lefty*. The Group Theatre was made up of dedicated young men and women who hoped to redeem the stage, restore it to the Grecian glory. Full of ideals and resolution, it collapsed when its successful members went over the hill to Hollywood. Kazan had some directorial experience with the Group. Myerberg, ever the gambler, named him for the job, I always thought, in proof of his contempt for common practice. Kazan was alert and eager. He reacted to the problems presented by the Wilder comedy courageously. He was handicapped by the absence of Mr. Wilder throughout the rehearsals. Thornton was a major in the United States Army, assigned to duty overseas.

Kazan and I had minor differences of opinion about the interpretation of Sabina during rehearsals. Such differences are productive, as often as not, of sharper performances. When the contending parties do not see eye to eye—actor and director—it is generally agreed free discussion of their differences clears the air. Kazan received a lot of kudos for his staging of Wilder's comedy. Afterward he was applauded for his directorial work in *Deep Are the Roots, A Streetcar Named Desire,* and *Death of a Salesman.* Browsing through the magazine section of the New York *Herald Tribune* two or three years ago, I tilted an eyebrow on reading a story: "Hits by Kazan" in which the author wrote:

"Kazan had been a competent director for three years, but he really hit his stride late in 1942 with 'The Skin of Our Teeth' which starred Tallulah Bankhead. It was also his first experience with the tempestuous Tallulah-type star. Quarrels were frequent, and finally Tallulah told the producer that Kazan would have to go—or she would."

"'Considering your investment, you'd better keep her,'" the author quoted Kazan as saying; then added: "But the producer insisted they both stay and try to get along. Two days later the battle raged again. Tallulah swung hard, but Kazan cut her down, and the play eventually went on as he wanted it. He and the star haven't exchanged a word since. . . . Essentially a peaceful and good-tempered man, Kazan says now that he wishes that he'd been more tactful."

Then this direct quote from Kazan: "But I guess that everyone has to have one fight that makes or breaks him. After that one, I knew I could handle anybody."

A pretty story, *mesdames et messieurs,* but it has a single flaw. It isn't true. Did I say my eyebrows arched? My mane stiffened! So Kazan and I hadn't exchanged a word since the opening of *The Skin of Our Teeth* on November 18, 1942, eh?

Six weeks after the comedy opened I observed an old Christmas custom. I commonly send Christmas gifts to the people associated with the play I happen to be in. I had sent Kazan such a gift—a gold bill-clip bearing a St. Christopher's medal. Unless my memory failed me, he had acknowledged it. I'm notoriously sloppy about correspondence. I rarely keep a letter or a telegram, regardless of the content. Now I scoured the house for Kazan's note, was elated when I found it. Here it is in its entirety:

My Dear:—
    I was very touched by your gift. I carry it around with me, like praise from someone I respect. I want to thank you for it, and while doing so, thank you for a number of things. Things that took place a number of weeks ago.
    Thanks for being right those times when I was completely wrong. Thanks for having the courage, being right, and the strength, being yourself, to battle for what you believed in—battle against inertia, and unconcern, and sometimes just plain dumb stubbornness. And thanks above all for a thing no one can thank you for—for your gifts akin to genius. What you have added to Wilder's play and to my production can only be reckoned one way—by sitting down and imagining what it would all have been without you.

Ever,
Gadget

Boy! Take a memo to Mr. Kazan. "Never write. Telephone!"

Around April seventh each year the members of the New York Drama Critics' Circle meet to name the best American play of the year and the best foreign play of the year. The membership consists of the critics of the New York daily newspapers, critics for such periodicals as *The New Yorker, Time* and *Theatre Arts*. It also includes a few veterans looked upon as authorities even though they may, for the moment, be without portfolio. In April of '43 these worthies came up with one of the most incredible verdicts of all time. They named Sidney Kingsley's *The Patriots* as the best

256.

play of the season. For this they should have been drummed out of the theater on the grounds of sheer incompetency.

This comment is not set down to castigate Mr. Kingsley. I imagine he was as surprised as anyone. Kingsley has written some very effective plays. His *Men in White* snatched the Pulitzer laurel in 1933, his *Dead End* was exciting theater, and as recently as 1951 his adaptation of Arthur Koestler's *Darkness at Noon* won and deserved high praise. But *The Patriots* was third-rate Kingsley, a confused story about the early years of democracy in America with actors in badly fitting wigs and words to match, profaning Thomas Jefferson and Alexander Hamilton.

Later I learned the reason for the malfeasance of the bogus Shaws and Beerbohms. No one of them had given a second thought to *The Patriots* until George Jean Nathan arose and denounced Wilder and *The Skin of Our Teeth*. He charged Wilder had lifted the play from James Joyce's *Finnegan's Wake*. Should they cite his play, they would be endorsing plagiarism. Now few of the twenty-odd critics assembled—and I mean odd—had ever read *Finnegan's Wake*. But they were intimidated. George must know what he's talking about, they assumed. Later Padraic Colum, the Irish critic and friend of Joyce, said Joyce had mined *Finnegan's Wake* from the works of the Spaniard, Lope de Vega, one of the most prolific dramatists of all time. Nathan's charge was as ridiculous as it would be to denounce Shakespeare because he found some of his material in Hollingshead's *Chronicles* and Plutarch. It's my guess Wilder is more familiar with De Vega than is Nathan with Joyce.

The Pulitzer Award committee was unawed by Nathan's smear. A month after the infamous decision, these gentlemen gave their vote to Wilder for *The Skin of Our Teeth*.

In the spring of '43 my irritation with the critics was salved by another of their decisions. Polled by *Variety*, the trade weekly often called the Bible of the theater, the reviewers named my perform-ance of Sabina the best of the season by an actress. If I had been validated by Regina Giddens, I was canonized by Sabina. Stout fellows, those critics, barring a lapse here and there.

For all the acclaim I received for Sabina, for all the awards showered on *The Skin of Our Teeth*, I was wracked throughout the engagement. This enables me to introduce my ulcer. When we were playing in Washington before the New York opening I was seized with violent pains in my back. The doctor who came to see me at the Carlton took my temperature. The reading floored him. It was 94 degrees. In a burst of frankness he said, "You should be dead." "Dead or alive, I must play tonight," I replied. The doctor said that did I insist on playing it would jeopardize his reputation. He could be accused of gross negligence. So I played that night, though I could scarcely raise my arm. Thus did I honor the old show-must-go-on hokum.

These intermittent agonies continued after *The Skin of Our Teeth* opened in New York. In desperation, I dropped in on the great diagnostician, Dr. A. L. Garbat. He had my innards X-rayed immediately. The next day he floored me. "No more cigarettes for three months. For the next forty-eight hours eat nothing. Drink only milk." Since I loathe milk unless it's ice cold, I con-ducted a short filibuster. In the end I submitted. I had a gastric ulcer. I was disappointed in the nature of my trouble. I had hoped for something more spectacular. Ulcers were things that waylaid Hollywood agents and similar trash.

For the first three months of the run I went from my bed to the stage, then back to bed again. On a diet of junket, milk, custards, rice, farina and similar pap, I started to gain weight alarmingly. This rankled me. In the Atlantic City scene I appeared in a bathing suit, which revealed my contours. I was proud of my figure. I fretted like a porcupine when I started to bulge out in the least attractive places. I complained bitterly to Dr. Garbat.

He waved my protests aside. "Tallulah, now I can tell you something," he said. "Until a month ago I thought you had an incurable cancer. Proof that you haven't is your gain in weight. You have recovered because you followed my orders explicitly."

Shocked at his first suspicion, relieved at his final judgment, I was elated. I was elated because I had won a victory. I had proved I could submit to discipline. I always felt that Myerberg's bickering, his petty tyrannies, his genius for arousing hostility, gave me my ulcer, just as I felt Billy Rose's heckling brought on my pneumonia.

I escaped *The Skin of Our Teeth* before its shabby end. All run-of-the-play contracts in the theater terminate on June 1. At that time the producer must renegotiate terms with all players holding such pacts. Much as I liked the play, much as I exulted in Sabina, I couldn't stomach Mr. Myerberg beyond the end of my obligation. The Marches took a powder at the same time. I would have liked to tour in the play, but not under harassment. Miriam Hopkins undertook to animate Sabina on my departure. Subsequently Myerberg, in a spasm of inspiration, elected Gladys George to banter with the dinosaurs and the muses and Homer and Moses, the two tramps who intruded on the first act.

The tour of *The Skin of Our Teeth* was an epic of disaster. Laureled with the Pulitzer Award, a citation tonic to the box office, the play opened in Boston, ran for one consecutive week and closed. Public apathy hit a new high. Myerberg had parlayed a gold mine into a dud. But he rates a salute for his courage. Of all the New York producers, only he saw the potential of Wilder's brilliant comedy.

12.

Chez Moi with Zoo

Aside from my ulcer and Myerberg's antics, I had another reason for escaping *The Skin of Our Teeth*. It had been open but a few weeks when I realized an old if vagrant dream. I bought a home.

In the summers that I had lived in rented houses in Connecticut, one at South Norwalk, one at New Canaan, I had grown to love the country. It reminded me of the English countryside—green, lush and inviting. Ever since my return from Hollywood I had periodic attacks of home-buying fever. These would rage for a week, subside as quickly. These enthusiasms are part and parcel of me. I have run similar agues over Dixieland musicians and second basemen, fighter pilots and lyric poets.

This time the desire to own my own home was more than an overnight rash. Save for my leased London home, I had never boasted a roof I could call my own. In the chips, most of the members of my profession grow ecstatic over the joys of country life. They get rhapsodic over rural tranquillity, the satisfactions of the soil, the morning hymns of the birds. In this mood they get poetic over the city's madding throngs and ignoble strife. Some of them go to the extreme of foresaking the tabloid columnists for seed catalogues. Usually they forget the idyllic business, once they've sobered up. The brake on their enthusiasm is the knowledge that the rewards of a home in the country are negative. An actor could live in his dream house only when idle. If idle he couldn't afford it. Vicious circle!

But I'm not notorious for my logic. In the summer of 1940, just before I was to start a nine-month tour in *The Little Foxes*, I bought a home near Nyack, on the Hudson, an hour from New York. It was two miles from the home of Burgess Meredith, not much further from the home of Helen Hayes and Charles MacArthur. (Miss Hayes once turned farmer. She told me that the milk which came to her table only cost about seven dollars a quart.) It was a reconstructed barn, in the best Bohemian tradition. It demanded additions and renovations and raids on my bank balance. An actor friend, Rollo Peters—he had played Romeo to Jane Cowl's Juliet—was living in it while he experimented with redecorations.

While chilling St. Louis with Regina Giddens, the Nyack operation went up in smoke—literally. A midnight telephone call informed me my shelter had burned to the ground. A boiler had exploded. Fortunately I had not moved my London furnishings into the house. But my budget got an awful mauling. The insurance didn't cover the extensions and improvements.

This conflagration checked my zest for life among the maples. It spouted up two years later while I was living in New Canaan, just before starting to rehearse in *The Skin of Our Teeth*. For weeks I scoured the back country. The houses I liked were too expensive. Any hutch costing over $1,000 would have been too expensive. But when Wilder's comedy put me back in the chips I renewed my search. As outlined to real estate men, my specifications must have seemed confusing. It must be within commuting distance of New York. It must have a swimming pool. It must have a view. It must have seclusion. It must lie within the confines of my purse. One agent suggested I was prospecting in the wrong part of the country. Save for the commuting problem he thought Idaho or Montana the terrain most likely to meet with my requirements. One house near Mt. Kisco fascinated me, but its price, $65,000, floored me.

Skidding through an accumulation of mail about a week before the opening of *The Skin of Our Teeth*, my eye fell on a circular picturing the interior and exterior of a house at Bedford Village, New York. I thought it attractive. It filled two of my demands. It was within commuting distance of New York, and it was available for $25,000. But $25,000 was outside my orbit unless the play was a success. I wrote the agent that I'd be up to see it within two weeks. By that time I'd know the fate of *The Skin of Our Teeth*.

The play was an immediate sellout. My share of the loot was close to $3,000 a week. On a bitter day I took off in a car for Bedford Village. The house was on a side road on a considerable elevation. I had to walk the last half mile in snow up to my navel. The walk brought out the pioneer in me.

As I mushed up the road the house seemed vaguely familiar. Had I been there before? I had indeed. It was the $65,000 white brick castle I had enthused over when scouring Westchester in August. Then it had been set off against walls of greenery, now it was bleak and snow-covered. But the view on that December day was enchanting. There wasn't another house within a mile. Did I purchase it I would be the mistress of eighteen acres. Its many small rooms were cluttered with windows. There was no swimming pool. Rash and impulsive, I closed for the house at once. The cost was assured by the pen of Mr. Wilder. Why had its price shriveled $40,000 in four months? The witness doesn't know—but is grateful.

I moved into Windows, as I called my home, on April 1. It wasn't the expanse of glass that led me to thus name it. Its christening derived from "my life is an open book." For twenty years I had lived behind transparencies. The world and his wife looked in on me. Regardless of translation, my home would justify its billing. It had seventy windows.

Built in the early 1930's, Windows had cost something like $85,000. Tallulah, generally credited with not knowing a dollar from a droshky, had come up with a bargain. A bargain? I was soon disillusioned. On the day I moved in I knew that I must re-do the whole house. Trying to remold it nearer my heart's desire I got into a jam. Knocking down walls, connecting windows, and other trivial changes, ran into a fortune. Since my ready cash had gone into the purchase price I had to go about my alterations piecemeal.

Fortunately I had much of the antique furniture from my house in London. It had been stored at Daddy's home in Jasper for years. My stepmother shipped it on to me. On its receipt I grew giddy at the realization that I could prance about amid reminders of my reign in the West End. Up, too, came my Augustus John portrait, my bust by Dobson, John's portrait of Gerald du Maurier, the sum of my tangible assets.

As I write this there's a Renoir over my bed, and a really beautiful Chagall in my dining room. I have two Eisendiecks, both very decorative; a Toulouse-Lautrec lithograph; two canvases by Max Bond; four of John Decker's caricatures in oil, one of which was reproduced on the jacket of Gene Fowler's *Good Night Sweet Prince*, tribute to his friend and drinking companion, John Barrymore. I also rejoice in a painting by the modern artist, Beatrice Lillie; a Grandma Moses primitive and an Ezard. Don't think from these boasts I pose as an art lover, even an art appreciator. I'm sensitive to design and color and imagination in oils as I am sensitive to those qualities on the stage.

My furniture, save for the London residue, represents an accumulation of gifts. My silver and linen testify to the good taste of my friends, the enthusiasm of an occasional admirer.

I take pride in my Louis XV console, in my Italian tables from the fifteenth and seventeenth centuries, in my Dutch chest, in my French provincials. Had I not married in such haste, I'm sure I would have bagged some valuable wedding presents. Thanks to my impulsiveness I drew a blank. But I've fared well since I became a landowner.

Are you curious about my sudden devotion to possessions? So am I. Save for my London furniture and souvenirs, I could have packed all my chattels into three or four trunks until I took over Windows. Is it a sign of advancing age that I rejoice in sleeping under my own roof? My professional life had been a succession of hotel suites, of bellboys, waiters and those haunted men who try to keep up with the confusions of room service. The roof is the symbol of security. There's a certain satisfaction in knowing that should one of my dogs decide to breakfast on an upholstered chair, the chair is mine, and the outrage will not lead to debates with an indignant management.

I made some hair-raising discoveries on taking over Windows. The water supply was a trickle. This called for another artesian well. The well could not be sunk in the vicinity of the house since it was set on solid rock. After expert soundings, readings of the sun, and other mumbo-jumbo, it was decided that the most likely spot in which to bore was in a declivity some 300 yards from my door, some 100 feet below it. The engineers fell upon this plot with a ferocity I have seldom seen. Reports on their progress were as harrowing as the travels of Ulysses. My boys burrowed down 185 feet, give or take a few fathoms, before they struck water. Once this thirty-gallon-a-minute geyser had been harnessed, it had to be piped up the hillside to my house. The cost approximated that of Grand Coulee Dam.

I had to have that swimming pool. When properly charged many of my guests felt the Gertrude Ederle urge; if males, dashed out in search of a Hellespont to conquer. In Hollywood a swimming pool can be gouged out in a week. You dig a hole in the ground, line its sides and bottom with cement, install a springboard and start to iron out your double gainer. No such nonsense was possible *chez* Bankhead. It had to be within an anvil's throw of my front door, otherwise few Bankhead guests could proceed to their morning dip under their own power. My swimming pool was the result of a month of blasting. The welkin rang with the explosions. Natives within a radius of five miles cowered in their cots, convinced Stalin had elected Bedford Village as a target for his A-bomb. The explosions did more than blast stone in the air. They blasted chunks out of my surplus.

In April I discovered that for all the view, for all the expanse of woodland about me, there wasn't a flower or a flowering shrub near my home. That is a slight exaggeration, a flaw you may detect in me when I wax enthusiastic or critical. There were three stunted lilac bushes, a blanket of wisteria, and a circle of juniper bushes. The berry of the juniper, I'm sure you must know, is one of the ingredients of both varnish and gin. As far as I'm concerned the liquids are interchangeable.

A country home without flowers was as contradictory as a television show without a cigarette plug. With the assistance and advice of Louis Venuti—he comes from eleven generations of Italian gardeners—I flung myself on the grounds like a fury.

Right off I let fly with 5,000 daffodils and set up what would be, in season, a riot of pink and white dogwood. In one plot I rooted

150 rose bushes; in another a swash of peonies. In tribute to my birth flower I planted a fan of that bell-shaped perennial, lily of the valley. On this color bender I planted 1,000 gladioli, great clumps of tulips, tuberoses, hyacinths, narcissi, rhododendrons, bleeding hearts, Canterbury bells, asters, dahlias, zinnias, double hollyhocks, red and blue salvia—the scarlet sage to you—phlox, Easter lilies. Most actresses would have settled for hollyhocks. I had to have double hollyhocks, just as I won't settle for less than a double daiquiri. I bought a lovely chestnut tree when told its flowers would be pink. They turned out to be white. Did I mention my nicotiana, a blossom for which I have a strong leaning? It only blooms at night. Yet I have a floral regret. No Southern magnolia raises its lovely blossoms. The climate is hostile.

Windows has five bedrooms. One, the shelter next to mine, I call the Tiptoe Room. One is the Monk's Cell! Still another is for Edie Smith. I have five fireplaces, a library in which you can commune with Kukla, Fran and Ollie, Marcel Proust or Zane Grey. Comes January and a flurry of snow, and it costs a small fortune to have my road ploughed. Whoever said, "It isn't the cost, it's the upkeep," knew the country. Though my digs cost but $25,000, I have sluiced another $100,000 into them, and keep right on sluicing.

My vegetable garden? Nothing to brag about. Just enough ground to raise chives for the *vichyssoise,* mint for the juleps. My respect for Louis Venuti and his skill and patience as a gardener persists in spite of a shocking weakness in his character. He is a Yankee fan. My butler, Sylvester, who can also do tricks at the wheel of the Cadillac, leans toward the Dodgers. Lillian, my cook and legally mated to Sylvester, can do miraculous things with fried chicken. She passed the final test when she prepared Southern dishes for Aunt Marie and Uncle Henry. Her table roused them to Rebel cheers. I'm not easy to cook for. Half the time I'm munching on head cheese in an effort to reduce. My meats have to be roasted or broiled for hours. Though it seems a paradox, I can't go red meat.

Seceding from *The Skin of Our Teeth,* I soon discovered what with the blasting for the pool, the boring for the well, the installation of new oil burners, the expense of odds and ends, I couldn't enjoy the luxury of a vacation. I'd damned well better go to work, or Windows would be papered with attachments and garnishee proceedings.

I was rescued by a complete stranger: Alfred Hitchcock. Mr. Hitchcock is the largest screen director alive. For all I know he may be the best. He has the equipment for his job. He learned it the hard way, through trial and error. He directed the first two good pictures turned out in English studios: *Blackmail* and *Murder.* *Blackmail* was that stinker in which I played in London in 1928. Remember? In making a first-rate film of it, Hitchcock displayed something akin to genius. Hitchcock directed the first talkie in England. The British, understandably, were suspicious of a film that talked. But Hitchcock stifled their alarms through exceptional industry. He wrote the picture, photographed it, directed it, cut it, developed the negative, schemed its *décor.* I suspect such a solo effort has advantages over the usual procedure when as many as thirty cooks may be contaminating the broth. Made by so able a man as Hitchcock, the finished product will have more style, form and unity, than will a film on the same theme begat and bludgeoned by a mess of authors, technicians, directors and relatives.

Hitchcock offered me $75,000 to play the leading role in *Lifeboat,* and off I dashed to Hollywood. It had been eleven years since I faced a camera, a rich trollop playing fast and loose with Robert Montgomery in *Faithless.*

Flouting the screen's bylaws, canons and taboos, Hitchcock confined the entire action of the picture to a forty-foot lifeboat adrift at sea. The plight of the passengers was the result of a U-boat torpedo. Although the derelict craft was supposed to wallow for days in the Atlantic, beset by hurricane, death and destruction, the picture was made in a studio with the drifters photographed against a bogus ocean. In the trade these are called process shots. In the picture the players were shivering from cold, but in its making I sweltered for fifteen weeks. I had to wear a mink coat. Blazing lights were focused on my every move. In a bow to authenticity, tons of water were sloshed over us at intervals.

I was black and blue from the downpours and the lurchings. Thanks to the heat, the singeing lights, the fake fog, submersions followed by rapid dryings-out, I came up with pneumonia early in November. Temperature 104 degrees, and rising.

A Dr. Fox dosed me with sulpha drugs. After three days I tottered back to the boat, rubber-legged and dizzy. Three more days amid the ice and brine and the bluster of the Nazi agent (Walter Slezak) who hoped to do us all in, and my temperature shot up to 104 again. Guess what this time? Another case of pneumonia!

This return engagement with Dr. Fox upset me. Only one more shot remained. I had reservations back to New York on the Super Chief. And here I was flattened by my idiot devotion to the show must go on drivel! Of course I'd returned to the studio too soon.

Sick as I was, I was frantic at this delay. There was no flying back to New York in December of '43. The armed forces had priority rights on all planes. So I steeled myself to go on with the picture, pneumonia or no pneumonia. To my delight and surprise Dr. Fox didn't argue. "You are letting me return without protest?" I said. "Why?" "Because I'm anxious to see what's going to happen to you. You're the most defiant, contradictory patient I ever treated. I think you're part yogi. You retard your pulse at will, speed it at will. You have the arteries of a girl of sixteen. I don't think anything can kill you. So co to the studio!"

So off went your germ-ridden heroine. Chest out, chin up, pain-wracked, oozing that old "the coward dies a thousand deaths, the hero dies but once" moonshine. I should have been sent to a mental institution.

But I was compensated for my marine acting, for my dual pneumonia. When the New York screen critics met to name the best performance of the year by an actress, Miss Bankhead breezed to victory. Unless my memory is faulty I got fifteen of the eighteen votes. Ingrid Bergman picked up two citations, Barbara Stanwyck one. At the time I wasn't too elated. I was told of the vote when our armies were in flight before the Germans in the Battle of the Bulge. A personal victory seemed absurdly petty. Later I was to exult. At last I had licked the screen, a screen which had six times betrayed me. Did I get an Academy Oscar? No! The people who vote in that free-for-all know on which side their *crêpes Suzette* are buttered. I wasn't under contract to any of the major studios, hence was thought an outlaw.

News of my salty antics in *Lifeboat* seeped through the blockade. I hadn't been home long when Ernst Lubitsch asked me to impersonate Catherine of Russia in *A Royal Scandal*. It was to be a satiric treatment of the promiscuous Empress, pointing up her flirtations, her adulteries, the havoc wrought on her retainers. Since nothing like a good play was in the offing, since Windows was still consuming my cash at an alarming rate, I accepted. I learned one thing from *Lifeboat*. In spite of Hitchcock, weeks had been wasted before the first camera turned. From Lubitsch I wrenched the stipulation that my salary would start the day I set foot in Hollywood. They might fiddle while Tallulah burned, but it would be expensive fiddling.

The Royal Scandal was completed in fifteen weeks. I was given $125,000 for my sultry services. That's a nice round sum, $125,000. But I couldn't keep much of it. Once the Collector of Internal Revenue got through paring it I was lucky to have enough left to pay my artesian and swimming pool bills.

Lubitsch, on the completion of the picture, said my Catherine was the greatest comedy performance he had ever seen on the screen. Otto Preminger, who directed the picture, can so testify under oath. If any of the critics agreed, they muted their convictions. *A Royal Scandal* got "mixed notices," trade term for conflicting estimates. Mixed notices is a very elastic term. I thought I was pretty good as the Slav Delilah, but *A Royal Scandal* led to no dancing in the streets, no critical hat-tossing.

Now that I was the mistress or the victim of eighteen acres, I was able to indulge in yet another excess, pets. Elsewhere in this omnibus I have lamented my lack of an alternate profession, a trade I might pursue were all the amusement roads mined. My conclusion was hasty. I could qualify as keeper in a zoo, for I've been pet-drunk so long as I can remember. For thirty years I've been over-Pekinesed. Those little flat-faced, bow-legged, soft-coated dogs enchant me. Napoleon was my first Peke. He appeared with me in *Her Cardboard Lover* in London, could pick up a cue as quickly as any ingénue. Because he thrived on malted milk tablets he frequently broke into print. Napoleon was succeeded by Maximilian, he by Sally, Ann and Brockie. Brockie was my first pet once I presided at Windows. While off on a transcontinental jaunt in *Foolish Notion* he was either stolen or met with foul play.

As I write this my kennel and/or living room shelters a French poodle, Daisy; Doloras, a Maltese poodle, and Donnie, a *puli*. Donnie is named after Donald Cook, with whom I wrestled in *Private Lives*. The *puli* is a Hungarian sheep dog, first brought to this country by Henry Wallace when he was Secretary of Agriculture. Are you up in your Hungarian? The plural is *pulik*.

I had a wire-haired terrier in London, still another in New York. I bought Magnolia, an English sheep dog, when she was five weeks old. She looked like a baby panda. Hitchcock, a Sealingham, was given to me by Alfred Hitchcock when he was directing *Lifeboat*. I was devoted to Bonnie, a mongrel, rescued from a dog pound.

I've owned but two monkeys. King Kong found shelter under my roof when I was in thrall to Paramount. The man said he was housebroken, a whopper if ever I heard one. When I fled the Pacific to resume life in New York hotels, King Kong, a doubtful asset under any circumstances, promised to be a frightening liability. It's not easy to find a proper home for a wayward monkey. I gave King Kong to Lionel Barrymore. They got along famously. Irene Fenwick told me in the ten years of their marriage she had never heard Lionel laugh before noon until King Kong was given the run of his chambers.

About to tour in *The Little Foxes* I bought a golden-haired marmoset, Senegas, named for my first hairdresser. The woman who sold Senegas to me swore he had impeccable manners, that he could sing and whistle like a bird. He could sing and whistle, I'll grant you, but his indoor conduct was reprehensible. Marmosets have claws instead of nails as do the other monkeys. Senegas had a capricious appetite. He had a preference for the upholstery in hotel furniture, could commit nuisances in the most unlikely places. He added a thousand dollars to my bill at the Ritz in Boston, bruised my budget in every hotel. You can't recarpet a hotel suite for peanuts. Marmosets are delicate, pick up colds and vapors easily. When Senegas died I was saddened, but my bank balance took a turn for the better.

I picked up Winston Churchill when in Reno getting a divorce

from John Emery. Idling until free, I went one night to a circus.
There I met the head lion tamer, Captain Noble Hamilton. After
the show he took me to see two lion cubs eight days old. The tawny
tots were adorable. They had lovely blue eyes, were as playful as
kittens. I bought one of the cubs for a hundred dollars. Since the lion
was the symbol of the British Empire, since I felt then, as now, that
Winston Churchill was the greatest man of our generation, I named
my new pet for England's Premier.

Winston Churchill was bottle-fed until he was four months old.
At first he was intimidated by my Pekinese. Later he began to
look upon the Peke as a breakfast item. Once freed of Emery I
flew back to Chicago with Dola Cavendish and menagerie. The
airline people were squeamish about Winston. They validated his
ticket only after I drugged him into tranquillity. When we arrived
at Chicago, Winston had emerged from his coma and was making
noises indicating that he could do with a piece of pilot, or the
hock of a hostess.

On my return to New York Winston took a truculent turn. He
began to fix me with a hungry eye. After he had nipped a couple
of reporters and sampled a hotel porter, I gave the ungrateful whelp
to the Bronx Zoo. There, at last reports, he was quite happy.

Before I get into my feathered phase, I must say a word about
Doloras, my Maltese poodle. She was given to me by the great jazz
pianist, Joe Bushkin and his wife Fran, and is named for the baby
dragon, cousin of the head dragon, Ollie, in "Kukla, Fran and
Ollie." Doloras is pure white. She weighs three pounds and sleeps
on my pillow. She requires a great deal of cleaning and ignores
me when I call her. Annoyed at her indifference I call out: "Daisy!
Daisy!"—that's my French poodle—and Doloras bounds to me. She's
jealous of any dog that approaches me. Doloras looks like an

animated mop, with her hair hanging over her eyes. She is delicate, playful and easily injured. She's my pride and joy.

For years I was a cat smuggler. On tour I was forever picking up woebegone strays, taking them to my quarters to nurse and coddle. I found Flora on a street in Sacramento. For the next two months I led a furtive life. In hotels I used the freight elevators. Assistant hotel managers get very snooty about cats, though indifferent to the conduct of bipeds. Flora rewarded me with a litter of kittens every three months when I got back to Windows.

I've been catless for three years. That's because I have birds. I've mentioned Gaylord. She's my budgereegah, sometimes called the zebra parrot and the lovebird. I first saw a budgereegah in Chicago when sweltering in *Private Lives*. That's the summer I lived on *vichyssoise*, daiquiris and watermelon, and was wracked with neuritis. Dave Garroway, a TV stylist, had a budgereegah. Once I had seen his I wasn't happy until I had one.

Gaylord may be of the parrot tribe but she has yet to open her trap in conversation. But she has other talents. She's deft at untying the shoelaces of male guests. Perched on my shoulder she has often caused me to renege in bridge through her heretic choice of cards. Once she escaped her cage in the rotunda of the Brown Palace hotel in Denver. The management had to summon a hook-and-ladder company. Guests sipping after-dinner brandy from outsize inhalers think they have been taken down with the DTs on finding Gaylord at the bottom of their glass. Gaylord is one of the reasons that we have so much screen-door trouble at Windows. Guests and inmates must enter and leave on the double, lest Gaylord take off for the azure, lest Daisy get in and start to go to work on my Louis Quatorze sofa. Gaylord has the run of the castle, whips through the air with the greatest of ease. She is partial to ear lobes.

273 .

She's given more than one visitor quite a turn with her acrobatics.

Visitors entering my home often retreat behind their own goal line when a challenging voice rings out: "Who Are You?"

The sentry is Cleo, my myna bird. "Who wants to talk to you?" is her favorite gambit. Another of Cleo's caprices is to blurt out: "Birds can't talk." She can spit out Lillian, the first name of my cook, but has yet to master Tallulah. Cleo is skilled in the derisive hoot, the ghoulish cackle. She has routed more than one visitor with her catcalls. She is mute only when her cage is blanketed.

I saw my first myna in St. Louis. A rival conversationalist impressed me. I caught up with my second myna when on a radio show with Fred Allen. Mynas are treasured by sponsors and advertising agencies because they can be taught to give commercials. In good voice a myna brings anywhere from twelve hundred to three thousand dollars. Hearing of my passion my doctor volunteered to get me one. A friend of his goes to India twice a year to bring back monkeys for experimental use in seeking a cure for polio. On his return from his next trip I had my myna. We've never had a quiet moment since. With Gaylord doing loops, my dogs in full bay, Cleo sounding off, pandemonium is the order of the day.

13.

Creed of a Random Voter

That banner line scorched the front page of a Tasmanian newspaper in early November, '48. In his enthusiasm the down-under editor laid it on a little thick. But it pleases me to believe I contributed something to the comeuppance of New York's governor. That would be Thomas E. Dewey, two-time loser. Remember Ethel Barrymore's devastating comment on Tom when he ran against Roosevelt in '44? She said he looked like the bridegroom on a wedding cake. This stab is commonly credited to Alice Longworth, but Ethel is the author.

In September I was playing in *Private Lives* in Philadelphia, a warm-up in the Coward comedy just before our opening in New York. I needed a warm-up in *Private Lives* like I needed a loudspeaker. I'd just finished a year's tour in it. I could recite the dialogue backwards. I was aroused from my reveries at the Ritz by a call from an official of the International Ladies' Garment Workers Union, A. F. of L. Since I'm an Equity actress I've been an A. F. of L. girl since 1919. Three weeks hence the I.L.G.W.U. was to sponsor a nationwide radio address by Harry Truman. For reasons too flattering to go into, David Dubinsky, head of the Union, wanted me to introduce the President over the air.

I agreed, provided the producer of my play, John C. Wilson, had no objections. Jack, a Republican, winced but assented. Jack's my favorite producer—charming, tactful, alert.

The great majority of the people of the theater had been enthusiastic supporters of Franklin Delano Roosevelt in his four campaigns. Extravagant, warm-hearted, they had given lavishly of their services in rallies, fund-raising campaigns, radio appeals. Aside from their conviction that Roosevelt was our ablest man in such critical times, they admired him for his eloquence, for his gifts as a phrase-maker, for his theatrics, for his ability to touch their hearts as well as their minds.

Grief-stricken on his death, they were indifferent to Harry Truman. He lacked Roosevelt's fire and assurance, his gusto and style. Along with the experts and the poll-takers they were almost unanimous in thinking his defeat inevitable.

I was positive Truman would win. In terms of electoral votes and trends and polls I cannot explain how I arrived at this conclusion. But reliable and sober witnesses will swear I was sure Truman would upset Tom. Having such convictions, I jumped at the chance to introduce the President to the largest audience ever to hear the voice of an actress.

The radio time purchased by the I.L.G.W.U. was from ten to ten-thirty on the night of October 21, 1948. I was to face the microphone at ten on the dot, speak for three minutes. This presented a problem. Usually ten o'clock found me wrestling with Donald Cook on a sofa. Jack Wilson behaved admirably in this crisis. He agreed to send the curtain up ten minutes early that evening. Thus my introduction could be given during the intermission. Mechanics littered my dressing room with their gadgets. I had to crawl through a wire entanglement to reach my dressing-room table.

I sweated over my introduction, rewrote it ten times. When I had finished this, in part, was the text:

There were Alabama Bankheads in one or another of the houses of Congress for sixty consecutive years. My father was Speaker of the House for four years, served with that body for twenty-five. My grand-father, John, sat in the Senate for thirteen years. My Uncle John spent twelve years of his life in the Upper House. They all died in harness. I would be outraging their memories, I would be faithless to Alabama, did I not vote for Harry Truman. Yes, I'm for Harry Truman, the human being. By the same token I'm against Thomas E. Dewey, the mechanical man.

Mr. Dewey is neat. Oh, so neat. And Mr. Dewey is tidy. Oh, so tidy. Just once I'd like to see him with his necktie knotted under his ear, his hair rumpled, a gravy stain on his vest, that synthetic smile wiped off his face. It seems a great pity to risk exposing Mr. Dewey to the smells and noises and ills of humanity. Far better to leave him in his cellophane wrapper, unsoiled by contact with the likes of you and me.

Mr. Dewey is trim and neat and tidy, but is he human? I have my doubts. I have no doubts about Harry Truman. He's been through the wringer. And by the wringer I mean that 80th Congress. That 80th Congress which ignored his passionate pleas for veterans' housing, for curbs on inflation, for legislation to aid and comfort the great mass of our population.

Mr. Truman has made errors, even as you and I. Mr. Dewey makes few errors. Why does Mr. Dewey make few errors? Because, to borrow a phrase from baseball, he plays his position on a dime. He ignores fielding chances unless the ball is hit right at him. He's a stationary shortstop. Not so Harry Truman. Like all winning players he tries for everything. He ranges far to his right. He ranges far to his left. (Careful, there, Tallulah.) He races back for Texas Leaguers. He races in for slow rollers. Truman is a team player. Dewey is playing for the averages. Harry Truman doesn't duck any issues.

What is Mr. Dewey for? Well, he has come out for one thing that, by his standards of caution, is revolutionary. Again and again he has said that he is for UNITY. Will all the candidates for DISUNITY please stand? Come, come, Mr. Dewey. Act like a grown-up. The next thing we know you'll be endorsing matrimony, the metal zipper and the dial telephone. If Mr. Dewey has any genius it lies in his ability to avoid expressing an opinion on any controversial subject. Mr. Dewey is the great neutral. Harry Truman is the great partisan—the partisan of our troubled millions.

In my lifetime I've enjoyed many thrills. I'm about to enjoy my greatest one. For now I have the distinguished honor to present to you the President of these United States.

Ridicule is a powerful weapon against so smug a candidate as Thomas Dewey. I concentrated on that device. It wasn't for me to discuss platforms, tariffs, sound money. I'd leave that to the politicos. No sooner had I written my talk than I bumped into protocol. An equerry of Mr. Dubinsky's asked for a copy. It had to be sent to Washington and cleared by the President's press secretary, the late Charles Ross. Shortly word came from Ross that parts of the speech seemed too violent, too scathing. "After all," said Ross, "the President will be sitting there in the White House, ready to pick up his cue on Miss Bankhead's last word. Can't you get her to tone down her language?"

Ross wanted to strike out the phrase about leaving Dewey in his cellophane wrapper. I was adamant. "If that line is cut," I told Dubinsky's man, "all bets are off. Get yourself another girl." I did concede two objections. "Just once I'd like to see him with his necktie knotted under his ear." "Did Miss Bankhead realize the significance of that figure? People might interpret it to mean she wants Dewey hanged." I waived, too, "He ranges far to his right. He ranges far to his left." Ross felt my "left" might link the President up with the Communists and fellow travelers. I was on the air at ten on the button.

The next day the tarter portions of my introduction were quoted on the first page of all the newspapers in New York, save the tabloids. These midget journals only use pictures on page one. From all over the nation friends sent me clippings. Had Dewey come out for bundling he wouldn't have been given more space. The London papers gave Harry and me front-page splurges. Transcripts of my talk were put on records, were played daily on dozens of stations right up until the midnight the Chicago *Tribune* announced Dewey was elected.

Don't think I introduced Harry Truman for publicity's sake. Publicity I didn't need. I have a terrific tug for the rejected. Since most of Truman's friends in the theater were mute or hiding under culverts until the shooting died down, since most Democratic leaders conceded catastrophe, I rejoiced in being an exception.

Ten days later, Truman was to talk at Madison Square Garden. I was asked to address the audience of 20,000 once the President had finished. I agreed, over the protest of friends. Most of them thought I was off my rocker. I couldn't get to the Garden until 10:50, just as the President was finishing his talk. "You're a dope, Tallulah," they said. "Rest on your laurels. Your second speech will be anticlimax. Once the President is finished the program goes off the air. The audience will walk out. You'll wind up on the platform talking to yourself." I waved these protests aside.

On my arrival at the Garden I crept into a chair at the rear of the stage. His address over, the President stood near the microphone to acknowledge the applause. Then he joined Mrs. Truman and Margaret, seated not far from me. On my way to the microphone, I stopped briefly to pay my respects. When the President offered me his hand I leaned over and touched it with my lips. The President didn't walk out on Tallulah. He stayed until I had given my three minutes to the crowd. Cued by Harry Truman, it stayed to listen.

The next morning the picture of Truman and me covered the

entire first page of the New York *Daily News,* tabloid newspaper with the largest circulation in America. The caption over this splurge read: "He's Her Man." The *News* was a violent foe of Truman, the hoodwinked champion of Dewey. Its box-office sense smothered its political prejudice.

On election night I anchored in my hotel to await confirmation of my intuition. Dewey and his camp-followers were to start celebrating around eleven o'clock at the Roosevelt Hotel. The champagne was iced, the paper cups and tin horns distributed. Once news hit the wires Truman had conceded, carnival would reign. The champagne stayed in the tubs until the ice melted. The horns went untooted. Dewey never showed up. Dozens of columnists, political oracles and poll conductors sat down to the largest feast of crow ever consumed at a sitting.

With convivial friends, most of whom thought I was deranged, I stayed in front of my radio the whole night long. Around daybreak the most fanatic of the Dewey commentators were hinting a monkey wrench had been found in the machinery. As luck would have it there was a matinee of *Private Lives* that afternoon so I had to curb my celebration. When Dewey tossed in the towel I sent a telegram to Harry Truman at the Muehlebach hotel in Kansas City: "The people have put you in your place." A friend glanced at it and said: "You can send the same telegram to Dewey."

President Truman sent me two tickets for the inauguration ceremony in January of '49. I sat in the official grandstand along with members of his cabinet and the diplomatic corps, Justices of the Supreme Court, high Army and Navy brass. We didn't get to our seats without incident. A police officer questioned my credentials. I gave him quite a going-over before he conceded. This skirmish led a few newspapers to say I had tried to crash the proceedings without tickets. I cooled them off in a hurry.

Listening to Chief Justice Vinson swear Truman in, I felt Daddy would have been proud of me. He would have been proud of me for my faith in Truman, for my refusal to concede an inch until the last vote was counted. I almost knocked myself out getting to Washington and back to New York in time for the performance of *Private Lives*. I was still imprisoned in the Coward romp—my only reward some $4,500 a week. Otherwise I could have stayed on for the Inauguration Ball, perhaps ripped off a mazurka with Vice-President Barkley.

I wasn't through with Harry Truman. Early in '51 his daughter Margaret appeared with me on "The Big Show." She bandied insults with all the pros, pattered with Fred Allen, won everyone's affection and esteem by her easy manner, her graciousness, her good humor. After the program Margaret and I went to our dressing rooms. I hadn't had time to get out of my high-heeled shoes, when an attendant rapped on my door. "The President wants to speak to Miss Bankhead on the telephone," he said. I thought it was Joseph McConnell, president of the National Broadcasting Company. "Tell him to call me later at the hotel," I said.

"But it's the President of the United States."

"You've come to the wrong dressing room," I said. "If it's the President, he wants to speak to Margaret Truman." So I called out, "Margaret, your father's on the phone."

"He doesn't want to speak to me," said Margaret. "I'm calling him at eleven tonight."

What if it was the President? Here I was shillyshallying while he held a receiver in his hand. "Come with me," I said to Margaret. "If it's a practical joker, I'll put you on and upset him."

It was the President. I pulled myself together.

"Mrs. Truman and I want to thank you for being so sweet to our baby tonight," he said. "I recall an evening I went to see you at the National Theatre in Washington—that was when your uncle and I were both in the Senate. Will and your Uncle John were in a box. At the final curtain when you looked up at them I saw the Speaker brush a tear from his eye. Well, that's what I did tonight when I heard our baby on your program."

"Mr. President, we're all very proud of Margaret," I said. "She's a first-rate gal, a credit to you and Mrs. Truman and to the country. I want you to know that she was on this show tonight strictly on her merits, not because she's the daughter of the President of the United States."

"What you have just said means a great deal to me," said the President. "I'm sure Margaret will be glad to hear it." "She's just heard it," I said. "She's standing right beside me." With that I put Margaret on the phone and retreated.

Conforming with my background, I'm a dyed-in-the-wool, bottled-in-bond Democrat. Backtrack through five generations of Bankheads and you will not find a renegade. When Al Smith ran for the Presidency in '28, eight Southern states, to their everlasting shame, bolted to Herbert Hoover. Not Alabama. Daddy campaigned for Al like a Trojan, was shattered when he read the returns. Alabama was one of the four Southern states to cast its vote for Thurmond in '48. Truman's name was not even on the ballot. This revolt of the Dixiecrats would have broken Daddy's heart. Had he and Uncle John been alive it wouldn't have happened.

I think the Republican party should be placed in drydock and have the barnacles scraped off its bottom. Robert Taft is less a liberal than his father, William Howard. Most of its high mucky-mucks are pure isolationists, whatever they may call themselves. The G.O.P. is a political dodo.

Brought up on a diet of election talk, I can get as excited as the next man in an election year. I stumped for Franklin Roosevelt in

'40 and '44, and I stumped for Franklin, Jr., for Congressman. I stood up on platforms and denounced Impellitteri when he ran against Judge Pecora for mayor of New York. I have scorn for those lofty folk in the theater who go around babbling the artist should be above politics. Is an actor any less a human being than a cowhand or a college professor? Does he think he can divorce himself from the rest of humanity? What dithering nonsense!

The Hanna Theatre in Cleveland, Ohio, is named for a family that has been black Republican for generations. Playing there in *The Little Foxes* in 1940 I was asked to sign my name in the theater's memory book, a volume which boasts the signatures of Modjeska and Eleanore Duse. Each of the pages is divided into three columns. In the first of these the immortals sign their names, in the second give their home address, in the last make such comment as can be crowded into six or seven words. Flattered at being listed with the theater's elite I flourished Tallulah Bankhead, listed Jasper, Alabama, as my home less subsequent signators think me a vagrant, under "Comments" wrote "Vote for Roosevelt." The press made quite a to-do over this vandalism, but there was nothing the custodians could do about it unless they wanted to scrap a page that bore the names of John Barrymore, Walter Huston and thirty others of the theater's aristocracy.

My political loyalties are not so hidebound that I can't detect merit in the opposition. Fiorello La Guardia was the best mayor New York ever had. It was my devotion to the great Republican liberal, George Norris of Nebraska, that led me into one of the riskiest adventures of my life.

When Norris was retired from the Senate by his noodleheaded constituents, Freedom House paid tribute to him at Carnegie Hall. Herbert Agar, who served with Ambassador Winant at the Court of St. James during the war, was to deliver an appreciation of

Norris. I was to speak briefly. Agar asked me to open the exercises by singing "The Star-Spangled Banner."

"Who, me?" I asked. "Freedom House must be getting low on singers." Many of the world's greatest have sung on the stage of Carnegie Hall. An outburst from me might well cost the place its license.

"All you need do is start it," said Agar. "The audience will join in. Sergeant Eugene List will be your accompanist." List was the enlisted man who played the piano for Roosevelt and Churchill and Stalin at Potsdam. List promised to lower the key of the anthem that my skull might not split on the first high note. I sat up half the night learning the lyrics. I had misgivings, but Agar soothed me. He made me feel it would be unpatriotic to snub the assignment.

When I barged into "Oh, say can you see, by the dawn's early light," the audience rose to its feet as one, but not a soul supported me, despite frantic beckons. My first words transfixed the congregation. Strong men on the platform blanched. Schemed as a community sing, the anthem turned into a Bankhead solo. Never was there a greater demonstration of the democratic processes. Never was the national anthem submitted to such abuse.

I get apoplectic about Communists. I have an unspeakable loathing for them, for the Communist party, for all the nasty fellow travelers who curry favor with the stooges of the Kremlin.

My phobia is so great more than once I've lashed at innocent people, liberals and rationalists who have no more sympathy for the Reds than I, but who point out to me that capitalism is not lily white. I don't confine my political hatred to Communists. I think Senator McCarthy of Wisconsin is a disgrace to the nation. He has held us up to more ridicule, more contempt at home and abroad, than the reddest Red in the land. His blanket smears of everyone with whom he disagrees disqualify him for the office he holds.

Trying to flush one subversive he slanders everyone who has so much as chatted with his victim. I'm of the tribe that would rather see a hundred guilty men go free than one innocent lynched. Caught up in a tirade against the Reds I occasionally get overwrought. One of my cooler-headed friends once charged I thought the late Nicholas Murray Butler was a Communist. My last act before retiring was to look under the bed lest delegates from the Cominform were lurking there. That's what he said. I'm not that big a nitwit. I even have respect for Communists who admit they're Communists, but I have nothing but contempt for the furtive Communists, especially those members of my profession who protest their loyalty in public, while secretly bowing to Uncle Joe. I'll go along with Voltaire in his "I disapprove of what you say, but I will defend to the death your right to say it." I also hold that he should face up to our convictions—not slink behind false fronts. I have respect for Budd Schulberg. He was a Communist, admitted as much, but repented when fed up with the party treacheries and practices.

For all my concern with politics, for the fevers I run during a campaign, I didn't cast my first vote until 1950. There are a number of reasons for this omission. Not all hold water. My eight years in London will stand up. On my return I rarely had an established residence, what with flitting to Hollywood and back. More than one national election found me on tour. Most often I failed to vote because of my inability to find anyone who could do it for me. When Roosevelt was a candidate for a fourth term, I resorted to low animal cunning. I knew that in votes in Senate or House, attendance was unnecessary could the member find a fellow of opposed view with whom to pair. I talked as many lazy Republicans as I could find into pairing with me. I was paired with a hairdresser, a costumer, two stage hands, a box-office man, a headwaiter and four taxi drivers. It wasn't quite cricket. What is, in an election year?

Though my contributions to Presidential campaigns have been chiefly vocal, I've had rewards. The one I treasure most came from Brooks Atkinson. In his preface to Maurice Zolotow's *No People Like Show People* he said:

All the performers whom Mr. Zolotow has memorialized in this book are public idols. They are admired, worshipped and envied. They earn fantastic sums of money. Since each of them is the master of at least one aspect of life, the public is inclined to expect them to be masters of all aspects of our national life. In some cases, the public follows their political guidance. The man who makes you laugh is occasionally the man who also urges you to vote for the candidate he admires. During the 1948 campaign, all America paused one evening to hear Tallulah Bankhead introduce the President of the United States over the radio.

In view of the nature of our national politics, I see nothing bizarre about that. By and large, I feel competent to do my own political thinking. But I would rather follow Miss Bankhead's political advice than that of a great many other people, including many who are professional politicians. Since I'm associated with the theatre in the guise of a newspaper reviewer, I regard it as especially fortunate that Miss Bankhead has put all her magnetism, passion and art behind the party that I'm inclined to support whenever it gives me half a chance. Life being what it is in the theatre, I should not want to quarrel with her about politics.

That salute from the gentle, quiet scholar whose great love is Thoreau, whose printed verdicts have a greater box-office impact than any other single influence in America, is praise indeed. Every fiber in me warmed. I felt a touch ennobled. Here was a magistrate who saw through my noise and fury and caterwauling, and seeing through it found something honest and sincere and worthy. I hope I never let him down.

286.

14.

Loose amid the Microphones

I first menaced a microphone, or vice versa, in the spring of 1927, while playing in *The Gold Diggers*. King's College Hospital was making a drive for funds for a new maternity ward and Lady Eileen Stanley asked me to make a plea over the air. Ever eager to tackle the unknown, I consented. As the hour approached, a thousand fears closed in on me. I wasn't cheered up when friends said, "Tallulah! Your plea will be heard by hundreds of thousands throughout the British Isles."

It was one thing to banter with a leading man across a living room, still another to address an audience scattered all the way from the cliffs of Dover to the Orkney Islands. As I faced the microphone it assumed the guise of a contraption that might let loose a death ray. I had a feeling such as I experience when an ether cone is slipped over my nose. There was a pounding in my ears a buzzing in my head. My hands grew frosty. A dank dew coated my brow. My first word sounded like the caw of a crow. Fearful those invisible thousands might not hear me, I shouted. I was reading from a prepared script and my hands shook so violently the words blurred.

The broadcast didn't last over five minutes. When it was over, I was as near a faint as I have ever been. I was elated when cash responses poured in. I felt akin to Florence Nightingale.

On a subsequent Armistice Day I renewed traffic with the wireless. I was in Cornwall, recuperating from some indiscretion. I had taken a wireless along that I might listen to the Prince of Wales' address. It was to be preceded by two minutes of silence throughout the realm. I had stayed up until daylight reading my first mystery book, Wilkie Collins' *Moonstone*. I had warned Edie to waken me at a quarter of eleven. When she shook me, crying, "Die Donner, Die Donner. Wake up! Wake up! Wake up for the two minutes of silence," I was so addled I replied, "Goddam it, Edie, I'm not saying anything."

On my return to New York, almost every name player in the theater was succumbing to radio offers. My friends hinted I was a jughead not to cash in on this easy money. But I struck a snooty attitude. I demanded approval of scripts.

I relented when my budget came down with beriberi. My first appearance was on the program of Rudy Vallee, Maine's challenge to Caruso. Part of the crooner's program was devoted to a scene from *The Affairs of Anatole*, Schnitzler's frisky comedy, in which I felt I would be at home. Rehearsals went smoothly. Perhaps I'd been too apprehensive about this mechanical monster. I was shortly to be disillusioned. Since we'd rehearsed in privacy, I thought we would broadcast in privacy.

A few minutes before the fatal hour I learned we would have a studio audience of three thousand. I had an immediate attack of buck fever. My spine jellied. I leaned on a character actor for support. A fine piece of treachery! Again I survived, pocketed the plunder and vamoosed. I vowed never again to risk such an ambush.

In all my years in the theater I've never had an agent. I've handled my own business, done my own haggling over salary and other indignities of imprisonment. I never felt it necessary to pay anyone ten per cent of my wages. The agent could only repeat my terms. I can shout as loud as any proxy. But radio was another kettle of fish. A broadcasting company calls upon the leading agencies when seeking to cast their carnivals. Since agents are under oath to die for, and only for, their clients, it was not strange they suggested only such actresses as were linked to them percentage-wise.

Faced with this, I signed up with the William Morris Agency. By our pact it was to act for me in all my activities save the stage. I've never had cause to regret that choice. Were it not for their Helen Strauss, this catalogue might never have been compiled. The Morris Agency engages in a minimum of hanky-panky, never treats its charges as if they were delinquent children. They carry on with dignity and intelligence. I've profited vastly from their counsel.

Rudy Vallee was years behind me when I agreed to appear as a guest star on the Eddie Cantor show. Mr. Cantor is one of the braver and more enduring of our entertainers. I had hysterics when I read my part at rehearsal. The script was a stinker. I'd see them all fry in hell before I'd go through with it. Into this crisis came couriers from the Morris office, olive branches in their teeth.

The Morris people insisted the script writers be summoned from their gin games, and their product sandblasted, retreaded and provided with words and plot to minimize the affront. The scuffle smothered and order restored, I went on the air, seething inwardly, outwardly ecstatic. In those days there were no tape recordings. Programs beamed to the Pacific Coast had to be done twice, because of the difference in time. The duplication wasn't up to the original. I thought up a new set of grievances between chats but on the whole I was content. My bit permitted me lines I could deliver with gusto and insinuation. So I took the thousand dollars and went away from there.

A telegram from Anita Loos, the imp who coined Lorelei Lee in *Gentlemen Prefer Blondes*, cheered me up. "The day you go on the radio permanently should be declared a national holiday," read her message. That telegram did me more good than the swag.

Thereafter I succumbed to radio offers only when poverty-stricken. The need for moolah led me to make a frontal attack in the spring of '41, just as I was about to entrain for Reno. Thanks to my long engagement in *The Little Foxes*, in New York and on tour, I was solvent. But time would lie heavy on my hands on the Truckee. I would need money for experimental work in the casinos. I told the Morris office to book me for as many radio engagements as could be crowded into a week, at the best fees attainable.

This reversal delighted my agents. Over a six-day span, I got tangled up with Orson Welles, with "Duffy's Tavern," with a program dedicated to the miracles of a shoe polish, in a tribute to Abraham Lincoln, in a slice of an S. N. Behrman comedy, in a melodrama in which I brought a brigand to justice. I didn't quibble about material. I was rehearsing or playing from dawn to midnight. In the six days I totted up something like $7,500. My fees ranged widely. For one show I got as much as $2,500, for another only $850. Little of that money got out of Nevada, thanks to the contrary dice, the folly of drawing to bobtailed flushes.

My mike fright had eased off. In need of cash, I threw caution to the winds, for fancy sums bobbed up on the programs of Hildegarde, Kate Smith and other thrushes. Then I was baited into appearing in condensations of some of my earlier plays. Condensation hardly covers what was done to *The Green Hat, Camille* and *Dark Victory*. On the stage these ran a good two hours, exclusive of intermissions. It was child's play for the nabobs of radio to shrink them to eleven minutes. What went on in those eleven minutes is too gruesome to set down here. In view of the revolting nature of these corruptions, a reader may logically inquire, "Why did you do them?"

For money, darlings. My tenure in plays was too erratic, my expenditures too frightening, to permit dawdling. Were I to survive, I must work, come hell, high water or moldy script.

Over a period of five years, I made fifteen or twenty guest star appearances. Fred Allen and I did a burlesque of the "Mr. and Mrs." shows then cluttering the morning air. It was a hilarious script and Fred and I gave it the works. The travesty created such a furore, we twice repeated it.

Early in 1950 the Columbia Broadcasting Company raided NBC's personnel. It made off with many of NBC's top artists and lashed them to long-term contracts. NBC had another worry. TV, the brash infant, was making inroads on advertising revenue. NBC's executives didn't take these depredations lying down. In rebuttal they decided to group into a Sunday night show such an outlay of stars that no man, woman or child in the nation would be so foolish as to listen to anything else in the interval between 6:30 and 8:00 P.M., Eastern Standard Time. It was schemed to destroy competition. A lofty project, it was a little frightening, especially when I learned I had been tapped for Mistress of Ceremonies. I've never been too happy about that identification. It's been worn out through abuse. I prefer *conférencier*. That's what Balieff, the antic Russian with the violent accent, used to call himself when first he sought to explain *"Chauve Souris"* to bemused New Yorkers. But who knows the feminine of *conférencier?*

Even before the first rehearsal, I was harried. In the newspaper ads NBC listed such famed folk as Fred Allen, Jimmy Durante, Ethel Merman, José Ferrer, Paul Lukas, Mindy Carson and Frankie

Laine, ended with "All This—and Tallulah, Too." This shook me up, caused me to bristle. These notables had definite assignments in the show. I merely introduced them, or so I thought. The first rehearsal raised my temperature. Ethel Merman was to sing six songs in the first half of the show, Russell Nype another. I read a dark significance into this. Hadn't NBC backed Ethel's show, *Call Me Madam?* I was sure I was being sandbagged. I had three "Yassah, boss" in a takeoff on Jack Benny in the last half of the program. Who was I imitating? Rochester!

I walked through the rehearsal like a woman under water, numb with humiliation. The NBC executives, Bud Barry and Dee Engelbach, were a little numb, too. Listening to my dreary reading, they were dismayed. My reading was dreary because I wasn't trying, so dark was my despair. It wasn't that I refused to try. Did I try I was sure to break down and cry in front of a fifty-piece orchestra. If I did, I'd be branded the greatest exhibitionist of all time, a temperamental witch who waited until she had an audience to kick over the traces.

There was another reason for my fright. The flashy entertainers were famed for their work in revues, musical comedies and vaudeville. I was an outlaw, a dramatic actress. I felt the cards were stacked against me.

After rehearsal I went to see Dee Engelbach, director-producer of "The Big Show" and one of the ablest and most understanding men ever to weave coherence out of chaos. I told him I was sick with disappointment, that I wanted to get out. I could have stood anything, I said, but "All This and Tallulah, Too." Was I to be the sacrificial lamb, mute and disgraced, while the comedians and the singers had a field day? By the terms of my contract I had to carry on for four weeks, willy-nilly. After that, I would rather starve in a garret than submit to such shame, adrift among the quality with nothing to do, and less to say.

Bud Barry and Engelbach told me later my rehearsal unnerved them. I would have no difficulty in getting out of the show after four weeks. Unless I came out of my coma my option wouldn't be picked up. William Joyce, my representative from the Morris office, came over to console me, to reassure Barry and Engelbach. When they told Joyce of their disappointment with my rehearsal, that gentleman gallantly said: "You don't know Tallulah. She doesn't give out at rehearsals. Wait until she gets on the air." I'm not sure Joyce believed his own brave words.

At the dress rehearsal, I was little better. The other players on the program were conscious of my desperation. Jimmy Durante whispered, "Remember payday, baby!" He was my knight in armor, that Jimmy! NBC's bigwigs were ready to jump off a cliff. Me? I'd jump from my own cliff. In my leap, I'd need no collaborators.

At six o'clock on the Sunday night of November 4, 1950, with some thirty million of the curious listening in, I submitted to the knife.

Guess what happened! Your heroine emerged from the fracas hailed as Queen of the Kilocycles. Authorities cried out Tallulah had redeemed radio. In shepherding my charges through "The Big Show," said the critics, I had snatched radio out of the grave. The autopsy was delayed.

Even John Crosby, long convinced radio was dead though unburied, revised his verdict. In type that danced before my eyes, he wrote:

It was in practically every respect a perfectly wonderful show—witty, tuneful, surprisingly sophisticated and brilliantly put together.

293.

Warming up to his work, he continued:

The opening program of "The Big Show," presided over and more or less blanketed by that extraordinarily vibrant lady known as Tallu, was one of the fastest and funniest ninety minutes in my memory. It was housed in N.B.C.'s newly-acquired Center Theatre (3000 seats); it had a forty-four piece orchestra and a sixteen-voice choir presided over by Meredith Willson; it cost about a trillion dollars—and well, it was big.

Crosby and others commented that NBC had made a bold and shrewd gamble in this extravagant attempt to win back its Sunday night audience.

However, [this is Crosby again] N.B.C.'s biggest gamble may have been Tallulah Bankhead, an unpredictable volcano who has been known to sweep away whole villages when she erupts. As mistress of ceremonies, though, she was sharp as a knife and succeeded somehow in outshining even the most glittering names on that glittering roster. . . . Tallulah is more or less inherently iconoclastic, if that's not too mild a word, and consequently the passages between her and her guests were happily lacking in that overwhelming mutual esteem which marks the pleasantries between most emcees and guests. . . . Tallulah even sang "Give My Regards to Broadway" in a voice that almost had more timbre than Yellowstone National Park.

Don't think Crosby was an isolated champion of "The Big Show." Almost every radio critic in the nation hailed us for an uproarious evening. If ever a dame was dynamited from the depths of despondency to the peaks of elation overnight, it was me. Doomed one day, deified the next, I was the most surprised girl in the world. I guess Bud Barry and Dee Engelbach were surprised, too. So, too, was William Joyce, despite all his cemetery whistling.

Overnight I became the darling of NBC, the toast of its vice-presidents, its far-from-secret weapon with which it hoped to cow the opposition.

How do I account for my pre-show terror, my black pessimism?

294 ·

Congenital panic! The doubts that embrace me when challenged by a new gamble, when I intrude on a field with which I'm not familiar. All my fears were as of sand. Ethel Merman cut her six songs to four, without any prompting from me. The "Yassah, boss" with which I aped Rochester convulsed the studio audience as well as the millions who listened. My concern was the extension of an ancient ailment, the dread I was being slighted.

Save for its summer recess, "The Big Show" prospered. At one time or another most of the elite of the amusement world appeared in it. Such diverse personalities as Ethel Barrymore, Margaret Truman, Groucho Marx, Dr. Ralph Bunche, Joe Bushkin, Gary Cooper, George Sanders, Judy Holliday, Bob Hope, Eddie Cantor, Edith Piaf, opera stars Jan Peerce, Melchior, and Robert Merrill, Joan Davis, Gloria Swanson, Shirley Booth, Charles Boyer, Clifton Webb, Marlene Dietrich, Louis Armstrong (my beloved "Satchmo") have added to its sparkle, wit and impertinences.

I reveled in every performance because it was a tonic for my ego. When I bandy insults with Ethel Merman or Judy Holliday of a Sunday night more people hear me than have witnessed all my performances in my thirty-three years in the theater. I have other reasons for elation. Working in a play, appearing before a camera, demands constant application. "The Big Show" is so organized, that I'm a free agent from Monday through Friday of every week.

In October of 1950, poised on the brink of "The Big Show," and apprehensive about the whole business, I was cornered by a young man who said there were thousands of women in our democracy who would pay money to hear me lecture. The proposal numbed me. But the prospect of getting $1,500 per lecture gave me pause. What if "The Big Show" laid an egg? Worse yet, what if I laid an egg in "The Big Show"?

The young man showered me with assurances. I could talk about anything that came into my head. Lecture dates could be so arranged as not to conflict with rehearsals and appearances in "The Big Show." Everyone of note took to the platform. Authors, polar explorers, Elsa Maxwell, war correspondents, Salvador Dali, basket weavers, big game hunters, paroled prisoners and reformed murderers all had a fling at it. It seemed a soft touch. It demanded little from the speaker save her presence, the ability to stand upright for an hour and a half and keep talking.

When I protested I had never lectured in my life, that the thought of addressing an audience of strangers unnerved me, my friends went into hysterics.

"You've been lecturing every night of your life," they screamed. "You've lectured in hotel lobbies, in restaurants, on railroad platforms, in smoke-filled cellars, in Congressional committee rooms. Here's your chance to practice your natural calling! Get paid for it besides! It's like being paid to take your bath and brush your teeth."

After a lot of palaver, I gave in. Queasy as I was at the prospect, I was in no position to slough off five grand a week. Did I click in "The Big Show," the lecture tour prosper, I'd be making more than I ever have anywhere. To be sure the dual assignment would make great demands on my physique, on my vocal organs, on railroad and plane timetables. But I wasn't called Tallulah the Indestructible for nothing.

It was on December 5, a month to the day after my debut in "The Big Show," that I faced my first audience from the stage of McFarlin Auditorium on the campus of Southern Methodist University, Dallas, Texas. Fearful that my account of that address might be overly modest, I quote Clifford M. Sage, of the Dallas *Times Herald:*

296.

Neither snow, nor ice, nor cold of night could stay them from their appointed rendezvous with Tallulah. Outside it was 20 above zero but La Bankhead promptly thawed them out—all 2800 of them—and later sent them skidding merrily home over icy roads.

It was 90 minutes of what Tallulah laughingly labeled a lecture. In actuality, during that crowded, amusingly digressive hour-and-a-half, the throaty star who fell from Alabama on London, Broadway and Hollywood, in the order named, danced The Charleston (first introduced by her in London); sang (?) "You Go to My Head," which she recently recorded, and "Give My Regards to Broadway" (à la George M. Cohan); mimicked Katherine Hepburn, mugged, clowned, emoted, recited, chain-smoked (half a package); and, oh, yes, talked and talked and talked.

Wearing a fetching, clinging black velvet creation ("I've been dieting a week to bring you this figure, dahlings"), Tallulah stalked on to the stage with an informal gait, blowing kisses to the applauding multitude. Making for the microphone, she purred, "Thank you, dahlings." The chilled customers roared, forgot their chilblains and the show was on.

Obviously, on her best behavior, (only one "damn" and one "hell" to a cigarette) Tallulah worried the rear seams of her frock, and with disarming candor confessed to jitters. "I don't know who is taking the greater chance, I, attempting this lecture medium, or you, coming to hear me." She hastily added, "But it's foolish to call this a lecture because, let's face it, it just isn't." Then peering up at the second balcony, "Can you hear me up there, dahlings?" They could and were loving it. She looked out at the ground floor auditors and told them: "I have a wonderful friend here, Margo Jones, but she let me down this time—she promised she'd find a Confederate flag for me but she didn't." After that, the audience forgot the elements without and within. Tallulah had them.

Those Texas gals and I really had a rowdy hour and a half. I confessed to them that my bracelet was phony, that I was wearing stage make-up, that my beauty wasn't what it had been twenty years earlier. Once I paused to take a sip of water from a glass, in a confidential whisper said, "I'll bet you think this is gin." They roared, then roared again when I added, "I wish it was." It was a strictly *ad lib* shindig, since I spoke without notes. Once I paused to ask, "Am I boring you?" On getting a resounding vote of confidence, I added: "If I am, you can always walk out—and I can faint." Mr. Sage paid me a gallant compliment in his last sentence. "There is no doubt that Mr. Charles Laughton, tonight's 'lecturer' at McFarlin Auditorium, has what vaudevillians call 'a tough act to follow'!"

The next morning, I flew through a snowstorm to address the flower of Cook County, Illinois, from the dais in a Chicago synagogue. The next night found me on the stage of the Playhouse in Wilmington, Delaware. In four days I had traveled three thousand miles, used up thousands of words and a lot of anecdotes. Saturday morning I raced to New York to rehearse "The Big Show." I had bitten off more than I could chew. Tales have been told in Alaskan saloons, in plantation cabins, on peaks in the Rockies about my vitality, my iron constitution. I gloried in them. But I had to cry quits. I was exhausted. Stewing with anxiety about plane schedules, weather reports, and the strokes of the clock, got me down. I was on a treadmill that never stopped. I didn't need the money *that* badly. Besides, "The Big Show" was booming.

Seeking new worlds to conquer, NBC plotted a coup that "The Big Show" might start its second season on a high note. After a lot of cable palaver it was decided our first performance would originate in London, our second in Paris, on successive Sunday nights in September. Tape recordings would be made of both shows. Thus both could be broadcast in America on our return, plus commercials. A commercial never pollutes a British Broadcasting Company program. Regardless of the miracles any soap or shellac may work, they're taboo on the wireless.

This overseas safari gave me pause. It had been twenty-one years since I appeared on a London stage. How would the London I had loved, the London in which I won my spurs, the London in which I had romped and reveled in the 20's, receive me? The trip was at once a challenge and an anxiety.

For a month prior to our departure I foreswore all nonsense. I went on the wagon. I dieted rigidly, lest I dismay old admirers with excessive tonnage. I spent all the daylight hours on my lawn that my tan, symbol of health, might enchant old friends and new acquaintances. I stopped at nothing in my determination to foil the calendar. I plucked my jewels, which I hadn't worn in years, from the vault, went on a clothes-buying spree that all but flattened me. I even bought a hat.

Only a very brave or a very foolish woman would chance such a business. When last I strode a London stage I was twenty-eight, the target for such soothing adjectives as "lovely," "radiant," "glamorous," "ebullient." Now I was fourteen plays, eight pictures and one husband older. Why risk disillusionment? Why submit my London note to re-examination? I might not be the only one who would be disillusioned. I didn't have to go. Did I demur NBC would be content to get under way in Radio City.

But it was a dare I couldn't resist. Rash and impetuous I accepted the challenge, even though a glance in the mirror stirred doubts.

It was an expensive undertaking. I was accompanied to London by a swarm of NBC executives, by Meredith Willson and Dee Engelbach, the two gentlemen who make "The Big Show" tick. That both the English and the French might see and hear one of the wittiest men in our theater, Fred Allen was drafted to the colors, and Portland Hoffa (Mrs. Fred Allen). That our show might not be too heavily weighted with American stars, we recruited some of the top names of the British stage and music halls—Beatrice Lillie, Jack Buchanan, George Sanders, Vera Lynn, and Michael Howard and Robb Wilson, two of England's top comedians.

Remember my first night in London in '23? Jobless, suspect by the customs men, bewildered by my own audacity, I had registered at the Ritz, a defiant gesture. Carefully inspecting available omens I decided that it would be fitting did I register at the Ritz again. The dramatic parallel! I would have come full circle.

The evening after my arrival I held court for the gentlemen of the press. London hadn't changed and, I hoped, I hadn't. A report on that reception?

She walked regally down the wide, soft carpet which spans the entire breadth of the staid and old-fashioned Ritz foyer. Photographers pounced on her, sat her in a chair and banged off flash-bulbs from all angles. Then she strode into the Marie Antoinette Room and like the sea parting before the Israelites, the mass of journalists made a passage for her.

In keeping with the occasion and the dimensions of my legend, the rout was awash with champagne. To increase the velocity of the legend I took off my slipper, filled it with wine and tossed off the contents, to the great delight of the photographers. The Ritz does not condone such rowdy goings-on as press parties. To conform with its code, this was no reception for the press, merely a private party given by Miss Bankhead.

For all the white paper shortage which has reduced the great English newspapers to a shadow of their former size, my arrival and subsequent activities won columns of space.

Tallulah Bankhead has done a shattering thing. She has swept us out of the past to date us. At the mention of her name middle-aged men square their shoulders and pat what remains of their hair. Middle-aged women eye each other and wonder whether to own up to their period.

That comment brought a lump to my throat.

"How many of Tallulah Bankhead's hysterical fans of the '20s, I wonder, are now grandmothers?" speculated my old friend, Hannen Swaffer, then added, "To me she was always a lamb trying to be a tigress."

How did London react to "The Big Show"?

The jury couldn't reach a verdict. It was both cheered and jeered. Some Britons found it hilarious, some baffling, some downright dull. The comedy of insult, over-all pattern of "The Big Show," is dedicated to the conviction that even the most spectacular entertainer has feet of clay. My guests make scornful allusions to my age, my thirst, my romantic bents and frustrations. In turn I deflate my opponents in scathing fashion. This kind of calculated rudeness is rarely heard in either English or American radio programs. Usually the contestants drip sweetness and light, try to outdo each other in logrolling. "The Big Show" drips venom—ersatz venom. To the uninitiated, our conversations seem perilously close to a free-for-all.

In our Sunday night show at London's Palladium, I started the proceedings by saying:

"After twenty years I return to the scene of my triumphs—of course most of them are married now." Bantering with George Sanders—who surprised even the English by breaking out in song—I boasted: "Whenever I'm in Hollywood I turn down dozens of offers." "Any for pictures?" he asked. Introducing Jack Buchanan I volunteered, "I'm in very good shape." "Yes, that's the word around London," said Jack. I avenged myself on my old friend, Bea Lillie. When Bea asked me if I had seen her on television in New York I admitted as much. "I just loved the close-ups. Your face looked life four yards of corduroy."

What really annoyed most English critics was my recital of Gene Fowler's poem, "The Jervis Bay." Fowler wrote it as a tribute to the gallant crew of a wartime freighter. The ship had dropped out of convoy that it might distract a German raider, thus permit other British ships to escape. The English do not care for emotional reminders of their courage in extremity. Such sentimentalities are bad form. One English critic called my rendition of "The Jervis Bay" "a most regrettable breach of taste"; another said it was "as out of place as boogie-woogie on the organ of the Canterbury Cathedral." For this unwitting blunder I apologize to a people for whom I have nothing but respect and affection.

The critical reception of "The Big Show" ranged widely. The anonymous reviewer in the austere *Times* wrote that it was "an amusing mixture of audacity and ingenuousness. It exploits for all it is worth, of course, Miss Bankhead's legendary reputation of a woman as wicked as she is fascinating and her undoubted ability to make a pretended acrimonious wit appear the real thing."

The Communist *Daily Worker* wasn't buying any of that tosh. "Very small beer, indeed," it said. "The audience at the Palladium tore down the house," said one paper; another said "the show had the perfect timing and zest of a Commando raid."

How did I look?

She was bareheaded, her tawny hair swept back across her forehead, she wore a loose-fitting three-quarter length coat of light suede in an unusual shade of crushed tomato red. Her shoes and bag were brown. She wore light pigskin gloves, a gold choker and one heavy bracelet of gold on her wrist. She was tanned and used a dull red lipstick to match her coat. She had the same husky voice that thrilled the young men over twenty years ago.

See? Once again my alarms were baseless. They were either baseless or that reporter was suffering from astigmatism.

15.

Affidavit of the Accused

I've been called many things, but never an intellectual. It's just as well. Once a flattering term, the rabble-rousers and reactionaries now use the word as an epithet. Too many of our countrymen rejoice in stupidity, look upon ignorance as a badge of honor. They condemn everything they don't understand. A little more of that talk and I'll be branded a subversive.

Did Dr. Gallup poll my friends and foes he'd find them in agreement on one item: I'm a romantic. A review of my past, a survey of my present, can lead to no other conclusion. My formal education was sketchy. A greedy, if sporadic, reader in my youth, even in my maturity, there has been little form to my literary taste. You're more likely to catch me reading Walter Winchell than Walter Pater, "Red" Smith than Bertrand Russell. I devour the daily newspapers, the column writers, *The New Yorker* and the prose of critics and commentators for whom I have respect and affection. An example? Sportswriter John Lardner! In one of my hospital sieges I read Walter de la Mare's *Memoirs of a Midget*, twice in three days. As a rule I read what's exciting and amusing rather than what's profound. I'm a sucker for a detective story, a mystery novel, almost anything by Graham Greene, Somerset Maugham or James Thurber. I read in waves.

I race through everything I read as one possessed since I'm always prodded by time or my conception of time. It's characteristic of me that thus haunted, I waste hour on hour in nonsense, in idle chatter, in marathon sessions before my TV screen.

I'm not the girl to engage in cool detachment when confronted with a crisis. I'm inclined to confuse an issue with my prejudices for or against its champions. I'm a setup for a tale of woe. My heart goes out to people of talent and brains who never achieve their professional due because of flaws of conduct. In London I was shocked to learn the pubs closed at eleven, whereas the toffs and the likes of me could keep right on drinking in bottle clubs.

Although I knew there were Communists in the Federal Theatre Project, I raced to Washington to plead with the Appropriations Committee to extend its life because it was the only source of employment for hundreds of the stage's needy. I even converted Uncle John after he barked: "What have those actor folk ever done for the farmers?" When our appearance before the Committee was delayed, I blackjacked Sol Bloom, its head. "If you don't get us in at once, I'll tell Daddy on you." The threat worked though our mission failed. Actors, forever giving of their time and their talent to all sorts of charities, crusades, fund-raising campaigns, political rallies and what-nots, are looked upon as feeble-minded clowns, when they seek relief from distress.

I'm given to explosive rages. Three or four times a day I'm irritated to the point I want to commit murder. Shrinking from the penalty, I fall back on my tongue. I'm something of a hellion when I lash out. In these spasms I may get obnoxious. Later I suffer pangs of repentance, save when convinced my opponents have deliberately tried to upend me. Then I go all out—an eye for an eye and a tooth for a tooth.

Great as is my admiration for Lillian Hellman as a playwright,

I could never again rejoice in her company. Professing to be liberal in her views, she was outraged when Heywood Broun was converted to Catholicism, expressed her indignation in violent terms. That's where I differ from Miss Hellman. I would have thought none the less of Heywood Broun had he become a fire-worshiper.

Some of my judgments may be confused, even sour. I'll accept full responsibility for them, right or wrong. They haven't been willed to me. I haven't picked them up at any intellectual notion counter. I'm never a neutral, save when the challenge confronting me lies beyond my understanding. I'd be suspicious of Thomas E. Dewey if he was Chairman of the Democratic National Committee. I'll root for any politician, actor, second baseman or bankrobber who combines talent and personality. I'd rather hole up with a juicy rogue than a sour-faced missionary.

Katharine Hepburn is one of the most stimulating women I know. She's unfeminine in that she scorns gossip, backbiting, and logrolling. She has an intelligent curiosity about everything. She spits out her opinions no matter how unpopular they may be. She makes no professional or social concessions. She's a gal I'd like to have on my side in a jam. In this same classification, high in the list of those for whom I have great respect, was the late Arthur Hopkins. Hopkins made many fortunes in the theater, more than once was wiped out. But he never wavered from his code. He had contempt for yes-men, sycophants, parasites, free-loaders, hangers-on. He made professional blunders. But once he had appraised a play or an actor, he backed his judgment to the hilt. He was immune to the suggestions of friends and the carping of foes. He had professional serenity beyond anyone I've ever met in the theater, with the possible exception of Estelle Winwood. George Kelly, also, had this quality in high degree. Both Hopkins and Kelly gave their professional best to any task they undertook. If the result was rewarding they were pleased. Did the undertaking fail, they were not crushed. They engaged in no breast-beating, no recriminations. Though they may have had scorn for the popular verdict they shunned self-pity. They never struck the pose of martyrs. People like Hopkins and Kelly are rarities. Producers, actors, directors and authors are all victims of excessive advice. Anyone who has ever sat in on a midnight séance in New Haven or Wilmington following a tryout performance of a play is aware of the ludicrous lengths to which this can go.

They listen to everyone. Too often they are impressed by the last man they talk to. In their attempts to please all the kibitzers, they only succeed in pleasing no one. In the end they succumb to professional vertigo. It's only through a miracle of miscalculation that together they put over a hit. Thornton Wilder knew *The Skin of Our Teeth* would be a riddle to many, but he never thought of lowering his standards to win their support. Wilder, Hopkins, Robert Edmond Jones, Kelly—none of these made any concessions to their inferiors, to popular taste, to the *status quo*. Once they made up their minds, they were inflexible. High in this category of the resolute is my old friend Glen Anders.

Even the experts play around with personality as if it were a yo-yo. I'm not sure I can define it, but I can identify it when I see it on stage, screen, or diamond, in the prize ring or on the tennis court. Cochet was twice the tennis player that Jean Borotra was, but Borotra was the crowd-drawer. Cochet was an automaton on the courts, a colorless precisionist. He made the most difficult volley seem simple. The Bounding Basque made every return seem difficult. He was the showman, the exhibitionist. He'd rather be spectacular than right.

Personality has something to do with inner fire, competitive spirit, defiance of the norm, solo effort, showmanship, in the ability to transform a liability into an asset. There were many better singers than Mary Garden or Geraldine Farrar, but their color, their professional tricks and antics, set them apart from the run of divas, fascinated idolaters unable to distinguish an oboe from an ocarina. In the argot of the theater, people possessed of personality are loosely called characters. In Paris they're types. They've even been called screwballs.

Personality? Even the hostiles concede I have it. There are any number of actresses with as much technical skill, but few can cause such a page-one commotion. You won't find Lynn Fontanne or Katharine Cornell embroiled in name-calling, in Stork Club fracases, in feuds with Thomas Dewey or Henry Luce. They're immune to such temptations. I charge into them, my hair on fire. I attract disorder. I provoke controversy. Off-key conduct, dress or thirst may contribute to personality. The cut of my mane, my rowdy laugh, my preference for slacks, my refusal to let a slur go unchallenged, my husky voice—all these add up to a peculiar, if not always praiseworthy, prestige.

My throaty voice? It once almost provoked a murder. With a lot of other American players I had gone to Albert Hall for some charitable hi-jinks. It was the year the great American melodrama *Broadway* came to London. Successively all the invaders were introduced to the proper Englishman presiding. Following me, Olive Blakeney, one of the night club girls in *Broadway*, and her husband, Bernard Nedell, were presented. Like me Olive had a husky voice. Greeting Nedell, the host said amiably: "Are all American women hoarse?"

He regained consciousness in an ambulance on the way to the hospital. Nedell had made a faulty translation of the query and in patriotic fashion had flattened the chairman with a left hook.

In the theater lying is looked upon as an occupational disease. Actresses lie about their age, their salaries, their arteries, their offers, as part of professional routine. Since I blurt out the truth, or what I think is the truth, on all occasions, I'm looked upon as an insolent lunatic. A half-dozen actresses of my acquaintance say they never read reviews of their plays or performances. They lie in their teeth. What rubbish! Actors live for applause, printed or vocal. Without it we'd perish. My sisters could no more ignore the reviews than they could shrink from a raise in salary. An actor friend of mine once hailed a colleague in his dressing room. "Read a great notice for you today." "Where?" said the eager player. "In Krafft-Ebing," said his malicious comrade.

People seething with personality attract and repel in like measure. They're the targets for hero-worship and stone-throwing. They never inspire indifference. Librettist Howard Dietz once remarked, "A day away from Tallulah is like a month in the country." Ever since he's enjoyed the reputation of a great wit.

Publicity seekers find heckling headliners an easy way to get into the newspapers. When I hauled a onetime maid and secretary into the dock because she had swindled me out of thousands of dollars through raising my checks, feature writers, magazine editors and counsel for the accused had a field day. The case was given almost as much space in the press in December of '51 as the Cease-Fire negotiations in Korea. Had I been the defendant the hue and cry would have been understandable. I was a witness for the State.

The Cato who represented the accused woman felt his hour had struck. In his opening address to the jury he said that he would prove that his client had resorted to forgery that she might pay off the bills I incurred in my passion for narcotics, gigolos and other outlaw activities. He had broken out, I suspect, in a headline rash. A stranger reading the reports of the trial might have come to the conclusion I was a dope addict and a sexual deviant, at long last brought to bay. Even *Time*, which professes to capsule the news of the week, distorted the case. Under the heading: "Trial by Stage Whisper," one of its distortioners wrote: "Theater-goers who watched fully expected Miss Bankhead to pull out a small, pearl-handled revolver from her handbag and shoot both defendant and her counsel." Warming up to his libel the *Time*-monger hinted broadly I had bullied the court, run the trial, concluded by saying that if our judicial system survived me it might well last for another thousand years.

The *Time* report was pure vilification. It was an enlargement of the vicious innuendo of defense counsel in his opening address. It was a demonstration of the lengths to which a national magazine will go in its thirst for sensation. Had Jane Doe brought a similar suit against the defendant, it wouldn't have got a line in any New York newspaper. Because I was a witness, even the *New York Times* assigned a by-line writer to the trial.

On sentencing the accused woman, Judge Harold A. Stevens said, in part:

This case has been rendered unusual by reason of what the Court is constrained to term charges of a sensational nature which received wide publicity, but which the jury by its verdict has labeled as false and unfounded. . . . There is no question but that the verdict is supported by the evidence.

Then the jurist addressed defendant's counsel:

You were directed by me to show cause why you should not be cited for contempt. Your actions during the course of the trial were reprehensible and unworthy of any member of the bar. Your constant insertion during the trial of matters which you knew or should have known were extraneous to the issue, indicating either a lack of knowledge of the law or a complete and willful disregard of your obligation as an officer of the Court. Had the Court disposed of the matter at that time it would have committed you to jail. Frankly, such punishment would have been merited.

I went into the trial aware that I had no chance of recovering the money stolen from me. The only reward would be my satisfaction in knowing that by my action I would not cowardly capitulate to blackmail. But I was to have other rewards. The dozens of newspaper editorials applauding my courage, the hundreds of letters cheering my stand, warmed my heart.

The commotion attending the trial stresses one of the penalties of being a legendary figure. A legend prospers even when its owner relaxes and waxes nunlike. Eventually it may engulf the gal for whom it was tailored. She becomes its slave rather than its mistress. Although I wince at many of the absurd items that have added to the Tallulah fable—my fictional fiancés, my sham night club rioting, my bogus witticisms, my ersatz adulteries—I have not sought to curb my detractors in the courts, even though in the first flush of resentment I have often threatened to.

What stays my hand? The knowledge that I am the co-author of the canards. Who first hinted that I was devoted to the delights of cocaine, to errant sexual practices? I'm the victim of my own inventions. I sowed the wind, now I reap the whirlwind. A legend grows or collapses. It cannot remain stationary. As well try to cap a geyser. There is one antidote. If its owner will keep her mouth shut it may simmer down. The monster created by Mrs. Shelley's Frankenstein is kin to the Bankhead legend. Attempts to extricate myself from the maelstrom get me no place. The more I thrash about, the more I protest, the greater grows the myth. All right, semi-myth! But, as I've too often repeated, I'm not easily intimidated, even by a legend. I may not survive it. Failing that we'll both be buried in the same grave.

We're well out of that, don't you think? I'm not at my best when I start to moralize or philosophize. Logic is elusive, especially to one who so rarely uses it.

A friend of mine whom I've permitted to mull over this manual says its authenticity will be challenged because it is practically free of dahlings and divines, two words that commonly flood my conversation. I'll confess dahlings has become my professional trademark, just as that roaring lion is supposed to symbolize Metro pictures. It's my contention few people write as they talk. It's a good thing they don't. Book sales would shrivel overnight.

Those dahlings and divines date back to Piccadilly. Rarely was I able to catch the name of the dowagers and drinkers I met at parties, in dressing rooms, or in Bond Street. It simplified matters to have a blanket identification for all of them. Darling has implications of affection, or, at least, friendliness. It cannot disturb the recipient. Did I try to pin the correct caption on every clown I encounter I'd make embarrassing blunders. They're all darlings to me. So it is with divine. I found it a serviceable adjective to indicate all shades and degrees of my approval.

Don't think I'm such a dunderhead as not to know the meaning of divine. Let's face it! It is a sloppy device of speech. But what of those addlepates who describe everything they like as terrific. Terrific really means terrible, appalling!

Since I'm tattling on Tallulah I admit that on occasion I swear like a trooper, employ Anglo-Saxon expletives—there's a Nice Nelly evasion—not commonly voiced in mixed company. I'm not proud of my profanity. Deft use of words from the dictionary can be more devastating. My first curses were a manifestation of my desire to be daring and heretic. A habit thus developed is not easily shaken. But I gave up cigarettes for three months. I've gone on the wagon for long and tiresome stretches. Why can't I stop swearing?

It's one of the things I'm lax about. My friends scarcely notice it, although timid strangers get quite a turn. I'm likely to wax profane when angry, when exasperated by bungling, when confronted by a cove I loathe or suspect. When I find my vocabulary can't match my indignation I resort to blistering oaths, an occasional four-letter volley. I'm impressed by friends who never curse. I'm not really conscious of swearing. I shudder when an interviewer quotes me verbatim. Cued by me, some of them enlarge on my original text. That's why I like being interviewed by *New York Times* men and the boys from the *Herald Tribune*. You won't find any "goddams" and "sons-of-so-and-so," in Mr. Sulzberger's columns, or Mrs. Ogden Reid's.

My love life? I've rejoiced in considerable dalliance, and have no regrets. I'm a single-standard girl. I found no surprises in the Kinsey Report. The good doctor's clinical notes were old hat to me. I've said there have only been two men in my life with whom I was deeply in love. One of these was Napier—Lord Alington. The name of the other I withhold in the interests of good taste. I've had many momentary love affairs. A lot of these impromptu romances have been climaxed in a fashion not generally condoned. I go into them impulsively. I scorn any notion of their permanence. I forget the fever associated with them when a new interest presents itself. I always feel lost without a male escort, whatever my errand. I hope you won't think me impudent when I say I have no difficulty finding one.

It's been said of me that I get along best with men of indecision, that strong, resolute males cannot long put up with my insistence on dominating the stage, the breakfast nook or the hotel suite. These analysts have a point. I can't discipline myself to coddling my opponent. I've gone through many an emotional wringer. Few of these spasms were the fruit of romantic frustrations. I can enjoy the ecstasy of collaboration as well as the next authoress, but I don't go around mooning over the prospect of a repetition once my confederate has gone about his business. Does that clear everything up? I didn't think so. What do you want? *Forever Amber?*

I doubt I'll ever marry. It's too late for me to adjust myself to the compromises necessary for such a union. I'd be frantic did I have to face the same man over the table every morning. Besides, I always eat breakfast in bed. Aggressive males get up and thresh about and snort under the shower. For a good half of my professional life I didn't know where my next magnum was coming from. I've always been a free agent, aware that whatever my lot, whatever my problem, I was the author. On me the guilt! A husband might have problems of his own. A lot of confusion might ensue when his trials intruded on mine. I've lived for too long, stage center, to submit to second billing. No man worth his salt, no man of spirit and spine, no man for whom I could have any respect, could rejoice in the identification of Tallulah's husband. It's tough enough to be bogged down in a legend. It would be even tougher to marry one.

Besides, I can't cook. I'll settle for that couplet from Kipling: "Down to Gehenna or up to the Throne, he travels the fastest who travels alone." I'm too opinionated, too consuming and demanding a person, to abide by domestic house rules. Those within my sphere of influence are likely to suffer if long exposed. The brave will revolt, the timid crumble. Where would that leave me? That's why I shun permanent attachments, that's why my romantic life is a paradox. The men for whom I have the greatest respect could not long condone my excesses. Those who could would only gain my scorn.

At one time or another I've been branded a harridan, a hussy, a rebel, a calculated trouble-maker. Frustrated in any design, no matter how daft, I fume and riot until I've untangled myself. I'll submit to wheedling, but never to bulldozing. The man doesn't live who can bludgeon me into a contract, a circumstance or a settlement at odds with my creed. Such attempts stiffen my spine. I'd have agreed to tour in *The Skin of Our Teeth*, even prowl through one-night stands, had producer Myerberg not been so prone to ultimatums. But when he said that did I not report for rehearsal between a matinee and evening performance he would have me barred from the theater and hauled up before Equity on charges, he cooked his goose. He also cooked the goose of the Wilder comedy.

Though I'm not one to dish out advice, I would say to anyone who hopes to prosper in the theater to stick to his standards, whatever they be. Raise them! Never lower them. Success is too hard won to be siphoned off in compromises. Often the temptation to compromise is great. Often such a course seems to be directed by necessity. The only time I ever made a salary concession I lived to rue it. In my eagerness to play Sadie Thompson in London I practically agreed to do it for nothing. With what result? I was sideswiped by Somerset Maugham. My humiliation would have been eased had I been sacked at a salary of two hundred pounds a week, instead of being sacked while working for a pitiful forty.

I've read somewhere that a friend is the one who walks in when all the rest walk out. That's accenting friendship too sharply. I'm not a girl for long and demanding friendships. I prefer the casual alliances. My profession is too haphazard to permit of staunch and enduring relationships. You may play with ten agreeable, even exhilarating, people for a year, then through mischance not see them again for five. They're in another hit in New York while you're prowling one-night stands in California and Utah, or vice versa, if your dice are cold.

Estelle Winwood has been my constant, my closest, friend these last thirty years. I was first attracted to Estelle because she was unlike me in all respects. She never raised her voice. She never drank. She shunned publicity and notoriety—there is a difference. She was inconspicuous in dress and conduct. She has collaborated on most of the important decisions in my life.

It was Estelle who urged I go to England, when my prospects

314·

looked so black. It was Estelle who endorsed my marriage, when I was caught in indecision. It was Estelle who told me I'd be as mad as a hatter, did I not play Sabina in *The Skin of Our Teeth*. Estelle has seen me through professional and personal crises, through petty uproars and major riots. I have never gone to her without being rewarded or solaced. She has a detachment I envy. She's without jealousy, is indifferent to reputation or medals.

Though not a notorious wit, she has a keen sense of observation, a gift for paradox. Once I persuaded her to attend a Stork Club party with me. It was given for Burris Jenkins, the sports cartoonist, and the place was awash with champagne and celebrities. Estelle was perched on the edge of her chair in birdlike fashion, a touch bewildered by the ruckus raging about her. Catching her eye, a squaw at an adjoining table said, "I prefer beer to champagne, don't you?"

Estelle turned her great eyes on the lady and said in a hushed whisper, "You must be very rich."

Estelle scored a great success in John van Druten's *The Distaff Side,* as did Dame Sibyl Thorndyke. On the insistence of the management, they went to a women's club luncheon in New Jersey. Actresses commonly avoid these adventures as they would defusing an A-bomb. But the management hoped to whet the appetite of potential customers. Estelle and Dame Sibyl were flanking the chairwoman on the dais, after concluding their short addresses. A paid-up member leaned across Estelle and said to her leader: "Why, they're quite charming, aren't they?"

Estelle's eyebrows shot up as she turned to the errant ogress: "Look here! We're no more 'they' than you."

Estelle was a star when first I met her at the Algonquin. She'd made a great hit in her native England in the Liverpool Repertory Company, was much sought after in New York. When I'd get too deeply in arrears to Frank Case, she'd offer me a cot in her suite at the Great Northern. She was indifferent to my tantrums. When I would rage about my misfortune, she'd say in her quiet fashion, as if addressing a naughty child, "Tallulah, darling, don't get upset. You'll only spoil your good looks. You're hurting no one but yourself." She was and is a genuine friend because she gives much, asks nothing. For all her apparent unworldliness, her indif- ference to flashy fame, she's vitally interested in everything about her, though outwardly she gives no sign. Always serene and un- ruffled, she's the best-adjusted person I know.

"Tallulah, you're a great actress, but Estelle is a great artist." That was George Cukor's verdict.

I have no formal convictions about religion or life in the here- after. I rarely go to church. I feel I'm closer to my Maker in the hush of my bedroom than in any group ritual. When I seek solace I don't want to be spotlighted. I want solitude.

I have never pondered long on salvation, nor mooned over the seeming conflicts of religion and science. The miracle of spring, the spectacular display in the heavens on a cold winter's night, for me is proof of an over-all plan, as it is proof there must be an author of that plan. Those millions of stars don't romp about haphazardly. A director put them in their places, set their routines.

None of us can go through life swindling, lying and outraging our fellows and escape retribution. My philosophy is best expressed by a vagrant line from some book or play: "We're all paid off in the end, and the fools first." I approach religion as I grapple with life, emotionally. When I sin I can't plead ignorance. I'm familiar with all the commandments. When I violate them, I repent in varying degrees depending on the nature of my offense. Thoreau summed up my pessimism: "We all lead lives of quiet desperation." Relaxed, I lean to the bibulous Omar:

316.

Ah, my Belovéd, fill the Cup that clears
To-day of past Regrets and future Fears—
To-morrow?—Why, To-morrow I may be
Myself with Yesterday's Sev'n Thousand Years.

I was but thirteen when Aunt Louise's son, William, died. Aunt Marie recently sent me the letter I addressed to Aunt Louise on Bill's death. I was then at the Convent of the Holy Cross in Washington.

Aunt Louise, dear, you must not grieve, for William is so happy. There is only one defect in his happiness, and that is for you. He does not want you to weep like that. He does not have to study law or work hard for a living, and I know he has added so much to heaven with those beautiful brown eyes and his dimples. God loved him so much that He could not wait for him any longer. He did not belong here. His home was in Heaven.

Aunt Louise, you must try to forget about your sorrow and think only of William's happiness. Life is merely a bad dream to show us the beauty of Heaven. God put us here to form our characters, and we all have a crown in Heaven and every good word or deed we do, God puts a little jewel in our crown, and when it is full of jewels, and all bright and glorious, God takes us to Heaven, and there he places the crown on our heads, and as a fairy tale would end, we live happy ever afterwards. Dear William did so many good deeds that his crown was all bright and glorious at eighteen. Maybe to you and me he made his crown too soon, but dear, sweet Aunt Louise, try to be content until your crown of jewels is finished.

With a heart full of love, I am

Your "little daughter"

Tallulah Bankhead.

I was fourteen when Daddy was elected to the Congress. Unaware his nomination insured victory, I rattled off Hail Marys all election day. I felt my prayers contributed to his election. Save for my opening night plea, "Dear God, don't let me make a fool of myself," I get down on my knees only when anguished by a calamity or threat of a calamity. I sobbed my prayers when the British were evacuating Dunkirk, when our soldiers were in retreat in the Battle of the Bulge, when the *Repulse* and the *Prince of Wales* were sunk in the South Pacific, when the British clashed with Rommel's Afrika Corps at El Alamein. I was agonized by the deaths of gay and gallant young men, sacrificing their lives that you and I, never to hear a shot fired in anger throughout the whole war, might suffer no more inconvenience than gas rationing.

I have never prayed for myself, except the time I went to St. Patrick's to seek help in getting a role in *Heartbreak House*. My faith flares brightest at Christmas. For as long as I can remember I have hung up my stocking. Since one or more confederates are aware of this, it is always filled with nuts and oranges and trinkets on Christmas morning. As a child I was tremendously impressed by the Roman Catholic Mass, the pageantry, the chanting, the Latin hymns, the pouring of the wine and the lighting of the candles. Yet at Sacred Heart I was bewildered by the teaching that all sinners must pass through Purgatory before reaching Heaven. Devoted to the mother I'd never known, I thought it outrageous that so young and beautiful a spirit should thus be punished.

Though I fear many things—my shadow, opening night audiences, the dark—I have no fear of death. Angry or frustrated I sometimes cry out, "I wish I was dead." Moonshine! I accept the inevitability of death but have no desire to hasten it. My speculations on life after death are sketchy. I have a suspicion we go through dozens of reincarnations. Though I believe in survival I can no more phrase my notion of it than I can explain the mechanism of my watch. If I only believed the things I understand I'd live in a state of panic. That, I suppose, is faith. Many of my friends are agnostics. They neither affirm nor deny. Failing proof, they reserve decision. I feel that proof beats upon us constantly, that our fault lies in our inability to recognize it.

We're all victims of our prejudices, our fears and superstitions. I have a violent antipathy for rare meat. My steaks and roasts must be cooked to a frazzle. At a party back in the thirties my host, Nathan Gibson Clark—famous hat maker—was boasting of his cook and the canapés he prepared. Shortly Clark approached me. "Close your eyes, Tallulah, and try this." An obliging guest, within my limitations, I shut my eyes and swallowed the tidbit. It was delicious. "What was it?" I asked Clark. He showed me its mate on the salver. It was spiced raw meat, fashioned in the shape of a pickle. I fled the room to become violently ill.

My philosophy of life? All our follies, our brutalities, the outrages perpetrated on humanity, have a common root: Ignorance. Most of the men and women who have contributed to our civilization or our culture have been vilified in their day. Most of our countrymen thought the Wright brothers belonged in an institution. Henry Ford was looked upon as a harmless eccentric. Lincoln's Gettysburg Speech was dismissed with a paragraph in most of the New York papers. They were filled with the two-hour rant of Edward Everett. Jeanne d'Arc was burned at the stake. Columbus was thought balmy. We're prone to denounce things we don't understand. As we denounce the rebellious, the nonconformists, so we reward mediocrity so long as it mirrors herd standards.

Though we owe our national birth to revolution, we are singularly suspicious of other revolutions. Yet revolution goes on all about us. Someone is always in revolt against the accepted order. If I have read my history aright, it is the heretics, the nonconformists, the iconoclasts who have enriched our lives, added both to our knowledge, our progress and our happiness.

16.

Motion to Adjourn

Granted an opportunity, no actor can resist a bid to purge himself publicly. The itch to parade his chills and fevers, crow over his triumphs and alibi his defeats is inherent in every one of us. The compulsion is congenital, otherwise he wouldn't have been actor in the first place. Acting is a form of confession. Is he familiar with elementary economics, the actor must know that even by coolie standards he's doomed, at best, to a lifetime of insecurity, at worst, to slow starvation. Me? I'm an exception. After thirty-three years in the theater I'm almost even. Shortly I hope to have my Cadillacs paid for. With any luck I'll square accounts with the Revenue Bureau next season. I've just received reminders of a few loose and annoying arrears.

Consider the conduct of an actor, if he is so fortunate as to get a part in a play. He practices four weeks for wages his maid would scorn that he may get up on a platform before an audience of bronchial strangers to parrot lines written by another. He toasts the heroine with cold tea poured from a vintage bottle, makes love to her in front of papier-mâché trees or in a canvas-walled living room. When off-stage, his abode is a windowless cell, no larger than an outsized phone booth.

Comes the opening night in New York and he's gripped with

stark terror. He may give his impersonation with skill and eloquence only to be unemployed by eleven-thirty the following Saturday night because the critics have branded the play an offense to the community. To participate in this humiliation he may have had to dye his hair and shuck fifteen pounds.

Aware of these probable indignities—not one play in ten runs for as long as eight weeks in New York— why does he continue to be an actor?

To put the most charitable construction upon our mass lunacy, it's because we thrive on applause, even random applause. We're harmless megalomaniacs, fanatic in our devotion to a profession which rarely rewards us with a livelihood. Since we court public display we're the foes of privacy. The glass house is our favorite residence. Once an actor has been cheered by an audience, he is automatically disqualified for any of the sounder professions. Mercurial, actors often pop off about retirement, once they've been fortunate enough to acquire a bank balance. They just talk about it. Few of them do. They'll be trapped in tryouts in New Haven or Wilmington at eighty if a role is offered them. Sir Harry Lauder, crawling with money, made at least six farewell tours of America. Occasionally an actress, ambushed by marriage, chucks the theater for domestic bliss, but the desire to again enter, stage right, will gnaw at her to her grave.

Earlier in this odyssey I beat my breast and swore I'd never act on a stage again unless so crushed by professional disasters I had no alternative did I hope to survive. Don't bet on that. It's one of the most baffling paradoxes that while actors can't afford to pursue their elected trade, no more can they afford to retreat from it. They're imprisoned.

As they can't forgo practice in their haphazard profession, so actors lack the will power to flout an offer to air their lives in type.

This weakness has the merit of consistency. In putting their follies and frustrations, their loves and their lapses, between covers they may find an audience, conceivably purr to applause. The odds against them are no greater than they encounter in the theater. Genial exhibitionists, they know the bitter turns up more often than the sweet, but that doesn't deter them. Rather does it spur them on.

Over the years I've occasionally been baited with dares to let down my hair, bare my soul, shrive myself for profit. These invitations were flattering. They caused me to coo inwardly. But hurdles of my own invention stayed me. I've long associated memoirs with the wheelchair. Seventy! That was the age to loose my saga. But I was in my prime, at the box office and elsewhere. Time enough to meditate over my past, when I had no future, when the present seemed "flat, stale and unprofitable."

My friends pooh-poohed this quibble. Given the chance, if I didn't compose my recollections and reflections I ran the risk of being cited as an eccentric, argued these partisans. I should leap at the bid like a trout at a fly. Wasn't my friend Ethel Barrymore on the brink of her history? I couldn't plead lack of time. I had a roof over my head and my radio activities gave me five days a week for dillydallying and dawdling, two devices for which I have exceptional talent.

For a good eighteen months this avowal never got beyond the conversational stage. It was great fun sitting around talking about writing a book. At two in the morning in convivial company I fancied myself a fusion of the Brontë sisters, Willa Cather, Dorothy Parker and Madame de Staël. Two hours later my confidence would mount to the extent I'd be convinced I'd start work in the morning. I'd get this new adventure behind me in a couple of months through constant application. Constant application? Sane and sober, the words mocked me. I couldn't get up in the morning.

In late summer of '51, idling on my acres preliminary to my return to England, I started talking into a recording machine, one of those contraptions which operates a two-sided record, each face geared to absorb a half-hour monologue. The disc can be started and stopped on whim. Once a platter is completed, its content can be played back to its startled author. This device fascinated me. I could address it at length without fear of interruption or reprisal.

I poured a lot of words into that whirligig. Once I was so careless as to impose two successive recitations on each face of the record, one on top of another. Mary Resnick, who undertook to unscramble the resulting bedlam, had to be put to bed in a dark room with ice packs on her temples. More than once I set the disc to spinning, talked into it for a half hour, only to find later I had failed to release the voice intake. For thirty minutes I had been talking to myself. Conversations broke into this narrative which had nothing to do with this chronicle. An irrelevant dialogue with Edie Van Cleve took up one side of a record because I had neglected to turn off the voice inlet while we debated the advisability of bathing Doloras, my Maltese. Transcribing the records, Miss Resnick blanched when one of them erupted a long discourse on the life and times of Evelyn Nesbitt, for love of whom Harry Thaw ventilated Stanford White. "What are you going to call the Evelyn Nesbitt book?" Miss Resnick wanted to know.

Once my first sentence was waxed, I knew I'd see my life through, though the graves yawned and the heavens burst. I may temporize and back and fill on the edge of a new experience but once I've plunged in, I'll wrestle it to a decision, win, lose or draw.

I muted such alarms as nibbled at me. Was I presumptuous in thinking onyone could be interested in my story? Would I be wiser to ape the shoemaker and stick to my last? How much could I tell without outraging the living or smirching the dead?

323 .

All these speculations would be idle were it not for the great professional skill of Dr. Abraham Rubenstone of Philadelphia. He it was who saved my life when I was stricken in *Clash by Night*.

I've told as much of the truth as I dare, without winning the frown of the Postmaster General. In the interests of good taste I've not blueprinted all my delinquencies. I've ducked the truth only when it would injure an innocent. Beyond hope of reward and applause, I had another reason for pouring my past on paper. I wanted to get my record straight, sieve the tommyrot from the truth.

In retrospect some of my juvenile conduct seems touched with lunacy. My adult conduct? Let's not have any last-minute heckling. Could I live my youth over again I doubt I'd alter it by an iota. I'm not a girl who wastes time looking over her shoulder. Remember what happened to Lot's wife? Do I start to stew about yesterday, I may succeed in fouling up tomorrow. A fig for regret.

I've done a lot of goofy things in my time, but I've profited from most of them. Could I whip up an adage I'd sing a psalm to experience. But I distrust adages. "Consistency, thou art a jewel" is soothing until Ralph Waldo Emerson rebuts with "Consistency is the hobgoblin of little minds." My sins have left no scars on my conscience. Long since I've repented and atoned for such escapades as may have wounded others.

I'm more likely to get upset over a trifle than a calamity. I was fit to be tied when George Frazier wrote in *Life* that I "lumbered" across a room. "Lumbered" was an unfortunate verb. I have slithered across rooms, weaved across rooms, bounced across rooms, even cartwheeled across rooms, but no man alive can produce a room across which I have lumbered. Even as weighed down as Atlas I employ a fascinating glide. I steamed with indignation when artist Rex Whistler stood me up for dinner in London, but I thawed when, two hours late, he handed me two tulip bouquets.

His delay was caused by the failure of the paint to dry. He had touched up the yellow tulips with black dots, the white ones with black stripes.

Anyone who talks as much and as long as I do is sure to come up with some howlers. More than one companion has quailed under the impact of "I never eat on an empty stomach," "I've had six juleps and I'm not even sober" and "We're reminiscing about the future." Then there's the night I blurted my way into a boner at the Stork Club. I had a tentative appointment with Herbert Agar, following a Freedom House rally. We were to have a drink together could he get away in time. When Mr. Agar did not show up at the agreed hour, about to depart I turned to the major-domo and said:

"Should Mr. Agar come in, tell him I've gone home to bed and he may join me there." Many an eyebrow shot up at this addled instruction.

The gossips and the gadabouts made a great to-do about Bette Davis' characterization of a truculent actress in *All About Eve*. These busybodies said Miss Davis had patterned her performance after me, had deliberately copied my haircut, my gestures, my bark and my bite. For comedy reasons this charge was fanned into a feud on my radio show. I was supposed to be seething with rage over the alleged larceny. In superficial aspects Miss Davis may have suggested a boiling Bankhead, but her over-all performance was her own. I had seen Miss Davis play Regina Giddens on the screen, thus knew I had nothing to worry about.

Speaking of imitations reminds me of Will Rogers' comment after seeing Fred Stone imitate him in his rope-twirling routine. Asked what he thought of Stone's tribute, Will replied: "One of us is lousy." I could never imitate Laurette Taylor. Her superb art came from an inner something I could not snare. Florence Desmond, an Englishwoman with an acid sense of caricature, gives a really devastating impersonation of me, but it lasts but five minutes.

What's ahead of me? Who knows? Engaged last April in banter with playwright John van Druten on "The Big Show," I had occasion to remark that radio was the mother of television.

"And who is television's father?" asked van Druten.

"Television has no father," was my reply.

This slur on the paternity of TV was a touch hasty. Right this minute I'm deep in palaver with the National Broadcasting Company which may lead to my television christening by the time this work is in your hands. For years I scorned radio, than capitulated and rejoiced. For two years I've cried to anyone who would listen that my face would never flower on a TV screen. Who am I to throw myself in front of the wheels of progress? Television is another taunt, another challenge. Despite my protests I can resist a challenge just so long.

By my own standards I've lived to the hilt. I've soared in the clouds and touched bottom. Much as I like to idle, I know I must carry on or perish. I have a tiger by the tail. Better than anyone, Edna St. Vincent Millay has expressed my plight, my philosophy:

> My candle burns at both ends;
> It will not last the night;
> But ah, my foes, and oh, my friends,
> It gives a lovely light.

POSTSCRIPT

Tallulah, like Eudora, Flannery, and Coretta, is a notable Southern woman easily identifiable by only her first name. She lived sixteen years after this autobiography was published, but even into the twenty-first century she remains "the one, the only, Tallulah." Released in the heyday of her celebrated NBC radio program The Big Show, *her book crowned a sparkling, audacious life. Through the 1950s and 1960s she remained rambunctiously active and fiercely opinionated. She died in 1968 and is buried not in her Alabama homeland but in St. Paul's Churchyard, Rock Hall, Maryland.*

As Tallulah's career wound down, she rarely performed again on the dramatic stage, although she occasionally took parts on television. She guest-starred with Lucille Ball and Desi Arnaz, with the Smothers Brothers, and in the Batman *spoof. In 1965 she appeared in her final movie, a British film titled* Frantic *(*Die, Die, My Darling! *in U.S. release).*

Tallulah: My Autobiography, *published originally by Harper's in 1952, was a* New York Times *bestseller for twenty-six weeks. It is the first book selected for the University Press of Mississippi's Southern Icons, a series that includes new editions of choice biographies, each featuring a world-class Southerner. The inimitable Tallulah Bankhead's rousing life gives the series an exhilarating launch.*

Like Miss Bankhead, Kathryn Tucker Windham, who wrote the following reminiscence, is an Alabama icon. She is a beloved, acclaimed Alabama journalist, oral storyteller, and author of several books. Recalling the 1930s, she reflects on meeting the remarkable Miss Bankhead two times in Montgomery, Alabama, where Windham was then a student and where the actress was visiting relatives. With astonished eyes and ears the young reporter saw the phenomenal Tallulah in Southern perspective. On both occasions Miss Bankhead was no less indelible at home that she was on the stage.

Indeed, she was, always and ever, "on stage."

Most memories fade after sixty-six years, but it would be nigh impossible to forget Tallulah.

I was still in my teens in the late spring of 1937, a sophomore at Huntingdon College in Montgomery, when I first met the actress. Back then my friend Frances Lanier and I wrote what we both considered a very clever and sophisticated column called "The Newshounds" for the *Huntress*, the student paper.

We interviewed Pulitzer Prize winner Grover C. Hall, Sr., of the *Montgomery Advertiser*, the singer/actor Nelson Eddy, some cooks with a small carnival, the metropolitan opera singer Lawrence Tibbett, Alabama governor Bibb Graves, and other notable figures, and we collaborated on colorful columns about each character. When we heard that Tallulah Bankhead was coming to Montgomery to star in a touring production of *Reflected Glory*, we began at once planning to add her name to our list of interesting-people-interviewed-by-The-Newshounds. Tallulah was more than interesting: she was Tallulah.

Getting access to Miss Bankhead was more difficult that we had anticipated. Our usual sources of helpfulness declared they had no information about where she was staying. Even the promoter of the play declined to help us set up an interview, saying he did not wish to run the risk of upsetting the unpredictable star. He did placate us somewhat by giving us two free tickets to the play. Our seats were in the balcony.

The usually resourceful Newshounds were growing discouraged when help came from an unexpected source. The faculty advisor of the *Huntress* happened to be a friend of Tallulah's aunt, Mrs. Marie Bankhead Owen, who graciously arranged an interview for us.

On the appointed day, we clad ourselves in our best garments, including hats and gloves (no Huntington girl ever left the campus without wearing a hat and gloves) and set out in a Dime Taxi. The transportation was cheap, but it was also unpredictable; the drivers usually had at least four passengers, and all four might be taken to different destinations in no rational order. What would normally be a ten- or fifteen-minute ride often stretched into half an hour or longer. Since we feared that tardiness would jeopardize our appointment with Miss Bankhead, we allowed plenty of time for the taxi ride.

"We're going to interview Tallulah Bankhead," we told the driver, hoping this information would encourage him to speed us to our

McDonough Street destination. He became almost as excited as we were. Not only was he (he had red curly hair) an ardent admirer of Tallulah, he claimed kin to her. He spent the trip explaining how his family and Bankheads were related by marriage, as complicated and tenuous a kinship as I ever heard.

As we got out of the taxi, he requested, "Be sure to tell Cousin Tallulah hello for me!" We promised that we would, but we didn't.

A check of our watches showed we were ten minutes early, so we paced up and down the sidewalk, reassuring ourselves that we had enough probing questions to ask and deciding which question to ask first. As it turned out, we need not have been concerned with questions: our appointment with Tallulah turned out to be not so much an interview as a listening session.

Checking our watches again, we climbed the front steps and rang the door bell exactly on time. A cordial woman greeted us and invited us into the living room.

"Tallulah will be out in a few minutes. Perhaps you would like to look at some of her photographs while you wait," she said.

Scattered about on tables were a dozen or more photographs of the actress in various roles she had taken during her career, photographs made both in New York and London. We, being young and having led sheltered lives, were more than a little shocked at some of the inscriptions on the photos. "Love from that hussy Tallulah," made us blush. *Hussy!* We never said the word—or even heard it said. We did know what it meant.

We had hardly regained our composure when Mrs. Marie Bankhead Owen, director of the Alabama Department of Archives and History and often referred to as The Tiger lady, entered the room. She was a formidable personage. Before the proper introductions were completed, the hussy herself made her entrance. We stared. We knew it was rude to stare, but we did. TALLULAH!!

"Don't mind me," she boomed in her deep, gravelly voice. "Aunt Marie is the important member of the family." she shook hands with us vigorously, not bothering to listen to our names.

Our hostess suggested that we sit down. We did. Tallulah chose to settle gracefully into a chair in the center of the room. She crossed her legs and draped her arms over the arms of the chair, took a long puff from her cigarette and asked, "Are those really college students? I can't imagine anyone being in college. I never finished the eighth grade, did I, Aunt Marie?"

Her questions to Aunt Marie unleashed her memories of a parade of schools and convents she had attended. Then declaring that they all ran together in her mind, she was in the process of changing subjects when one Newshound seized the opportunity to slither a question in.

"Was *Reflected Glory* written especially for you?" the college student asked. It turned out to be the only question we managed to put to her. She answered quickly, "Oh, no! No indeed!" She tossed her head, laughed her throaty laugh, and was off on a fast-paced monologue, a montage of memories that included Leslie Howard (*Lezlie* to her), her English cigarettes, the theatre, London, her voice, even her maid Edie. I wish I could remember what she said about each topic, but it was very long ago.

I do remember her final comment when she rose to signal the end of the interview.

"About *Reflected Glory*—the difference between the leading lady in that play and me is that she is a good girl."

We Newshounds needed to return to our cloistered Methodist college.

Miss Bankhead's behavior had not improved when I had my second encounter with her a year and a half later, in November of 1938. I was editor of the college newspaper then, and I suppose that position qualified me to be included in a group of real reporters from the local newspapers and radio stations assigned to interview the world-famous Alabama actress. There, of course, was no television coverage back then.

Interest at that 1938 press conference centered on John Emery who had recently become Tallulah's husband. We all wanted to see and question that daring man.

As I prepared to write this current (2003) piece, cudgeling my memory and quizzing the few survivors of that era, I was blessedly fortunate to find in the archives at Huntingdon College a copy of my original account of that experience. I had written, using the plural pronoun:

> The neck-draping hair, the vivid red nails, the crimson lips, the
> throaty guffaw, the swinging stride and the semi-bass voice were the

same. So far as one could ascertain, no radical changes had taken place. We made those observations as we stroked the silky hair of a Pekingese named Ann and waited impatiently the arrival of John Emery, he who is often referred to as Tallulah Bankhead's husband.

This last period of our wait was made entertaining by the famous actress herself. The long waits, we were told, were necessary for Mr. and Mrs. Emery to attire themselves properly to be received by the press at the "crack of dawn." It was 12:30 p.m. One of them failed to accomplish that goal. Or perhaps 'Lulah, which she hates to be called, didn't realize how inadequate her sheer, purple monk's gown dress would be in the revealing light of the living room.

But she was delightful striding about flipping ashes first in the fire and then in ashtrays and draping herself in easy chairs while she "reminisced" and put on her act for the third estate.

"Do you know what my name means? It disgusts me for people to think I just made it up. I'd never think of a name like that. It means terrible!" Throaty laugh.

"What ever became of the old blind man who sold us candy at school, Aunt Marie?"

"Did you ever get hold of that bookie? I love gambling of any sort—poker, bridge, races. Of course I keep up with the race horses, but I often choose a horse because of his name. My hunches are surprisingly lucky."

Then followed a long discussion of races and S. T., her new Orleans Catholic-reared Negro maid, who doesn't object to her saying damn and worse.

"John!"

Frankly we were startled.

"I can't imagine what could be keeping him. He must be primping, although I cannot imagine why."

Neither could we when we caught our first glimpse of him. A man with a profile so similar to that of another John of theatrical fame [John Barrymore] needs to add nothing to what nature so wondrously gave him.

Just as we were about to get acquainted, a photographer demanded the presence of this man descended from six generations of actors. He unwillingly went into the yard to pose with Tallulah, who was complaining that the panchromatic film would make her lips look white, but he dashed back into the house to give us our interview from the feminine angle.

After being assured that he could understand our southern drawl (he said he considered himself quite a linguist after associating with the Bankheads), we proceeded.

We became very friendly when we discovered that we both had hands that are always damp and actually drip in times of stress. This common suffering gave us courage to pry into the Bankhead-Emery romance.

"I was scared of her." He was obviously enjoying this, for his eyes twinkled. "At the very mention of her name I wanted to hide." He leapt across the room and cowered behind a chair to demonstrate.

"The first time I saw her she was backstage after a play I was in. She was calling, 'Tim! Tim!' in her throaty voice." He laughed, which was considered a definite sign of a sense of humor. "She found Tim, and I heard her say, 'Tim, you were horrible! Wheres the man who played Tommy?' I hid behind the door of my dressing room, for I was that man.

"I heard her coming. She flung open the door, threw her arms around my neck and said, 'Darling, you were wonderful!'"

Perhaps at the time of this initial encounter Mr. Emery did not know that Tallulah called everybody darling, punctuating the word with a toss of her luxuriant hair. In any event, that's how the romance began.

He added a brief account, casting mischievous glances at Tallulah to make sure she was eavesdropping, of how their relationship flourished and of how, at a houseparty in Connecticut, she misinterpreted one of his remarks and screamed triumphantly to the assemblage, "John has proposed!"

Obviously he was no longer afraid of Tallulah.

The interview ended. Tallulah bade farewell to the bevy of reporters, showering them with darlings before falling into John Emery's waiting arms. It was a dramatic final scene, so perfectly Tallulah.

How could anyone forget her?

—*Kathryn Tucker Windham*

Index

INDEX

INDEX

INDEX

INDEX

51977747R00203

Made in the USA
Lexington, KY
11 May 2016